Human Development

Human Development

A Christian Perspective

Joseph Bohac, Ph.D.   Stan DeKoven, Ph.D.

Copyright ©1993 Joseph J. Bohac, Ph.D.

ISBN 978-1-61529-090-1

Copyright ©1993 Joseph J. Bohac

Copyright ©2013 Second Edition with Stan E. DeKoven, Ph. D.

Contents

Contents i

Acknowledgements v

Foreword by Dr. Richard Walters vii

Introduction xi
    What is Human Development? xi
    The Research Methods xii
    The History of the Study of Human Development xii
    Author's Note xiv
    Review of Introduction xv

1 **What is man?**   **1**
    Descriptions 6
    Personal Reflections 12
    Review of Chapter 1 14
    Glossary for Chapter 1 15

2 **In the Beginning**   **21**
    The Three Stages of Prenatal Development 22
    Personal Reflections 26
    Review of Chapter 2 28
    Glossary for Chapter 2 29

3 **Stage Theories of Human Development**   **35**
    Sigmund Freud (1856-1939) 37
    Psychocognitive Stages 39
    Moral Development 40
    Psychosocial Stages Erik Erikson (1902 - 1994) 43
    Human Development 50
    Personal Reflections 51
    Review for Chapter 3 53
    Glossary for Chapter 3 57

4	**Ages 0-2**	**63**
	Birth	63
	Temperament	65
	Physical Development	68
	Psychosexual Development	69
	The Anal Stage	70
	Psychosocial Theory	71
	Phases of Attachment	72
	Moral Development (Spiritual)	73
	Psychological Development	74
	Personal Reflections	76
	Review for Chapter 4	78
	Glossary for Chapter 4	80
5	**Ages 2-3**	**85**
	Physical Development	85
	Freud's Anal Stage	86
	Psychosocial Development	90
	Disturbance in Family Relations	91
	Personality Style	92
	Infantile amnesia	93
	Minimizing Negativity	94
	Prelinguistic speech	96
	Personal Reflections	96
	Review for Chapter 5	99
	Glossary for Chapter 5	101
6	**Ages 3-5**	**105**
	Physical Growth	105
	Psychosexual Development	107
	The Girl's Oedipus Complex	108
	Psychosocial Development	109
	The General Stage: Initiative vs Guilt	109
	Identification	110
	Gender Identity	110
	Cognitive Development	111
	Emotional Development	112
	Social Development	113
	The Ever Widening Environment	114
	Personal Reflections	115
	Review of Chapter 6	117
	Glossary for Chapter 6	119

7 Ages 6-12 — 125

- Physical development — 125
- Cognitive Development — 127
- Moral Development — 128
- Kohlberg's Theory: Moral Reasoning — 129
- Levels and Stages of Moral Development — 130
- Psychosexual Development — 131
- Psychosocial Development — 132
- Introduction of the Gospel — 135
- Intellectual Developmental — 135
- Implications for Education — 135
- Personal Reflections — 136
- The Road to Healing — 139
- Review of Chapter 7 — 140
- Glossary for Chapter 7 — 142

8 Ages 12-18 — 145

- Psychosexual Development — 147
- Psychosocial Development — 149
- Health Problems — 150
- Nutrition — 150
- Drug Abuse — 151
- Sexually Transmitted Diseases — 152
- Death in Adolescence — 152
- Cognition — 156
- Personal Reflections — 156
- A Time For Healing — 159
- Review of Chapter 8 — 160
- Glossary for Chapter 8 — 163

9 Ages 19-35 — 167

- Gender Differences and Identity — 172
- Marriage and Family — 173
- Summary — 177
- Personal Reflections — 178
- A Time for Healing — 179
- Review of Chapter 9 — 181
- Glossary for Chapter 9 — 183

10 Ages 35-65 — 187

- Erikson's psychosocial development — 189
- What makes middle-aged couples split up or stay together? — 193
- Personal Reflections — 193
- A Time for Healing — 197
- Review of Chapter 10 — 198

Glossary for Chapter 10 200

11 Over 65 — 203
Physical Changes in Old Age 206
Death and Dying: A Many sided Occurrence 207
Some other problems older people must face. 212
Personal Reflections 214
Review of Chapter 11 217
Glossary for Chapter 11 219

12 Review, Conclusions, and Implications for further study — 223

Appendix A: Prenatal Development — 225

Appendix B: Time Table for Development — 227

Appendix C: Who's Who in the Study of Human Development — 229
Closing Note 237

Bibliography — 239

Glossary — 243

Acknowledgements

For both Doc Bohac and me, much of our understanding of human development comes from being acutely interested in people. We were/are observers, and we have studied much in this dynamic field. That being said, we are not really academics...more practitioners, and we have written this book to be read by students who may not do much additional study in the field of Human Development than this work. Thus, though we believe it is scholarly, it is not written for the advanced scholar, but the average person who is also fascinated with God's special creation...mankind.

This is the second edition of the book originally crafted by my dear friend, mentor and now member of the great cloud of witnesses, Dr. Joseph J. Bohac. Doc was a pastor, counselor, teacher and friend...who was strongly influenced by his family, blessed by a wonderful wife Marie, and children who were challenges and the joy of his life. I am sure he would acknowledge all of them if he could today. As for me, well, my influences, besides Doc and my general academic pursuits, include a mom and dad who were a case study in contrasts, sister and brother who are survivors of life in the DeKoven home, and my wife Karen, now dancing no doubt with Dr. Bohac in heaven, and my daughters who I observed, up close and personal, as they have grown into beautiful, strong women, and have provided grandchildren to help reinforce my observations...I am so proud of them all.

So, on behalf of Dr. Bohac, and me, we acknowledge that it is God who gifts, and it is God who gives opportunity, and we are grateful for the privilege to share insights that will hopefully help many to become better servers of God and man.

Dr Stan DeKoven
December 2012

Foreword by Dr. Richard Walters

Second only to the study of God is the study of human behavior. The search for who we are as humans and how we are unique has been a fascination of mankind since the beginning of time.

The Psalmist David stated so well the question at hand, "What is man that you take thought of him, and the son of man that you care for him? Yet you have made him a little lower than God, And You crown him with glory and majesty! You make him to rule over the works of your hands; you have put all things under his feet," (Psalm 8:4-6).

What is man? How can we understand this wonderful, glorious creation of God who has such an infinite aptitude for greatness and folly, courage and cowardice, love and hate, good and evil.

Much of this question has been researched and debated in universities and churches for centuries. Many outstanding books have been written on man and his/her development, yet none as clearly Christian and thoroughly scientific as this work by Dr. Joseph Bohac and Dr. Stan DeKoven.

Human Development: A Christian Perspective is an outstanding accomplishment written by scholars, counselors and pastors with the maturity and wisdom of sages. For both the novice in the field of human behavior and the advanced student, this work will stand as an authoritative look at how we grow and change as human beings. For the Church of Jesus Christ to be more effective in winning and transforming the souls of men to the living Christ, we need a thorough understanding of God's crowning glory: mankind. This book provides us with just such an understanding and the wisdom to minister as God intended.

Richard Walters, Ph.D.
Dean, Counseling Program
Vision International University

"Such as we are made of, such we are."   —Shakespeare

Introduction

It would not seem necessary to have yet another textbook on the subject of the nature of human development. Almost every introductory text in the field of psychology will devote at least a few chapters on the subject. Most of the general public has certain assumptions about the nature of development, and teachers, clinicians, therapists and other professionals fall into one of several theoretical schools.

Unfortunately, most of the "quality" research in this field has been done by investigators who are not necessarily Christian oriented. Some of the professors with whom this author studied, were either of the older Freudian, the NeoFreudian, the Eriksonian, or one of the Humanistic disciplines of thought.

What is Human Development?

Human development is the study of the quantitative and qualitative changes in the development of the human being. Quantitative changes are changes in the number or amount of something, such as height, weight, or size of vocabulary. Qualitative changes have to do with changes in kind, structure, or organization, such as changes in a person's intellect, personality, moral understandings, etc.

The scientific study of human development includes all people regardless of race, color or cultural background. The study of human development is primarily interested in patterns that govern the development of the species Homo sapiens.

Jesus said that we would know the truth and that the truth would set us free. The study of human development is an effort to learn the truth that can be used in dealing with the problems humans experience in the process of growing. There are two ways of studying the development of humans. Basic research is that kind of research that is undertaken in the spirit of intellectual curiosity with no immediate practical goal in mind. Applied research addresses an immediate problem. Both of these kinds of research complement each other.

Introduction

Many of the theories that are explored in this study may not completely fit into the Christian frame of reference. Many of the theories have been, in part at least, rejected at one time or another by other theorists, Christian and non-Christian alike. What then is a theory?

A theory is a set of interrelated statements about a phenomenon. The four main theories of human development are: psychoanalytic, mechanistic, organismic and humanistic.

1. **Psychoanalytic perspective** — There are underlying, unconscious forces that motivate behavior.

2. **Mechanistic position** — Human beings are reactors rather that initiators, and change is viewed as quantitative. It includes observable behavior. This theory is held by those who are called "behaviorists."

3. **Organismic position** — People are active contributors to their own development. Development occurs in a series of qualitatively different stages. The main proponents of this theory are Piaget and Kohlberg among others.

4. **Humanistic perspective** — The individual has the ability to foster his or her own development and to do this in a positive way through human characteristics of choice, creativity, and self-realization (Maslow, Buhler, Charlotte, Rogers).

The Research Methods

Understanding research methodology is important in understanding how theories are developed. There are five non-experimental methods for studying people: case study, naturalistic observation, the clinical method, interviews, and correlational studies. Each approach has its weaknesses.

The two major techniques of data collection are the longitudinal and the cross-sectional design. Further discussion on these methods and their importance to our study can be found in Chapter Three.

The study of people must reflect certain ethical considerations. In a carefully designed study, the researcher considers its effect on the participants, as well as its potential benefits to the field of human behavior.

The History of the Study of Human Development

Although it is probably true that man has always been interested in the changes that can be observed in the development of the human being, it is also true that what might be considered as the beginnings of scientific investigation of the subject began with men like Locke and Rousseau (John

Locke, 1632-1704; Jean Jacques Rousseau, 1712-1778). Before Locke and Rousseau, people looked on children as little adults. The Preformation theory posited that there was a fully formed human in the ovum or in the sperm. (Aries, 1960)

Whether Darwin was responsible for the beginning of more serious consideration of the study of human development or not is debatable. It is true that in the middle of the 1800's there began to appear more and more literature related to the subject. Most of the earlier studies concentrated on the early years of development. It wasn't until the 20th century that theorists began including the entire life span of man in their research. Since the very last of the 19th century and the early 20th century the literature in the field of human development had expanded to staggering proportions. Theorists began to think of man as the many faceted being that he is.

The concepts that one develops with regards to human development depend largely on whether the individual sees man as being simply mind and body, or whether man is seen as being a tripartite being: body, soul, and spirit. The Christian sees man as tripartite according to the Bible verse in I Thessalonians 5:23

> "Now may the God of peace Himself sanctify you entirely; and may your spirit and soul and body be preserved complete, without blame at the coming of our Lord Jesus Christ.(NSV)"

This concept of man will be developed further in the first chapter of this book dealing with the whole man.

In addition to man being three parts made in the image of God, he is also a social being. A careful study of human development will bring the student face to face with the truth that social relationships play an important part in man's development. Counseling in today's society deals with the problems of interpersonal relationships more than any other problem.

Two areas of human development that have been greatly neglected are 1) moral (or spiritual) development, and 2) prenatal development. Chapter 2 of this text will concentrate on the importance of prenatal development in the whole area of human development. Freud, as well as others, placed considerable importance on the experiences of early childhood but almost no attention was given to the prenatal period of development. This author, along with countless others in and out of the professional arena, agree that what happens to the fetus from the earliest moments of conception will have an important impact on the development of the individual throughout his life.

Chapter 1 of this manuscript will be devoted to the question, "What is man?" The emphasis will be primarily on the concept of the "Whole Man" and what the Bible teaches about man's physical, emotional and spiritual makeup. It would be literally impossible to cover in great detail any one of the various areas of the nature of man. The subject of the anatomy and physiology alone could take volumes of texts. This course will only

Introduction

consider the elementary aspects of man's physical, spiritual, emotional and social makeup.

Some space will be devoted to examining man as a tripartite being: body, soul and spirit, and to reemphasize the concept that man is more than the sum total of his parts. He is also a social being and is greatly influenced in his development by the society around him beginning with the immediate family and then extending to the impact of peers during school years and especially the great mystery of the most interpersonal relationships of all: marriage and family.

Chapter 2 will review the latest findings in the prenatal development of the human being. The appearance of the strong antiabortion movement has resulted in the publication of volumes of literature in the forms of booklets, films, and even entire books aimed at convincing the general public of the fact that life begins at conception, when the male sperm enters the female ovum.

Chapter 3 will focus on the stage theory of Human Development. Such theorists as Freud, Kohlberg, Fowler, and Piaget will be considered for their contributions to developmental theory. The bulk of this study focuses on the Eight Stages of Psychosocial Development, the theory developed by Erik Erikson.

Chapter 4 will deal will the first stage of development after birth. This is Erikson's Oral Sensory Stage which covers ages 0-2. Information about every area of development may not be readily available for each of the stages, but an effort will be made to cover the substance of what has been written and what would be of value to those interested in pursuing studies in the field of Christian Counseling.

Chapters 5-11 will consider the rest of the eight stages of development with recommendations for further study.

Chapter 12 presents a summary of the subject of human development with some further implications for the Christian Counselor. Some suggestions will also be made regarding further study and research needed in the entire field of human development.

Author's Note

We have endeavored to write this text in a somewhat scientifically objective style. We have not included many personal experiences or observations in the regular text for that reason. Though there are lessons to be learned from the personal experiences of those who have spent many years in the field of human relation, we want the research to speak first and primarily. We have decided, therefore, to add at the end of each chapter a section entitled, "Personal Reflections" in which we endeavor to relate some case studies or personal experiences that will illustrate the points of the chapter. The reader is free to agree or disagree with the conclusions made in these personal examples. All of the names that will be used in the various case studies have been changed to protect the individuals (especially the authors!).

Review of Introduction

The main points in the introduction are:

- Human development is the study of the quantitative and qualitative changes in the development of the human being from conception until death.

- Quantitative changes are those changes in the number and amount of something, such as height, weight, etc.

- Qualitative changes are those changes such as intellect, personality, moral understanding, etc.

- A theory is a set of interrelated statements about a phenomenon. This book has discussed four main theoretical disciplines. They are:

  1. Psychoanalytical
  2. Mechanistic
  3. Organismic
  4. Humanistic

- The Psychoanalytic theory states that there are underlying, unconscious forces that motivate behavior.

- The Mechanistic position is that humans are reactors rather than initiators and change is viewed as quantitative.

- The Organismic theory says that people are active contributors to their own development and that development is qualitative.

- The Humanistic theory says that individuals have the ability to foster their own development and to do this in a positive way through human characteristics of choice, creativity, and self-realization.

- There are different types of research methodologies used in the study of human development. They include:

  1. Case Study
  2. Naturalistic Observation
  3. The Clinical Method
  4. Interviews

Introduction

    5. Correlation Studies

- Each of the research methods discussed has its own weaknesses.

- Two major techniques for data collection are longitudinal and cross-sectional design.

- The history of the study of human development began at about the time of John Locke (1632-1704) and Jean Jacques Rousseau (1712-1788).

- Before Locke and Rousseau, the predominant theory held that children were simply little adults.

- The preformation theory held that there was a fully formed human in either the ovum or the male sperm.

- This study was based on the concept of man as a tripartite being: body, soul, and spirit.

- In addition to the three parts of man taught in the Bible, man must also be considered a social being.

- It is the interaction of the body, soul, and spirit and the environment that determines the course of man's development.

- The areas of human development that have been neglected are:

    1. Moral development

    2. Prenatal development

"...For you are dust, and to dust you shall return."
—Genesis 3:19b

Chapter 1

What is man?

There are many significant scriptures that discuss and describe man and his (meaning his and her) unique relationship with the universe. They include:

> "But one has testified somewhere, saying, "What is man, that You remember him? Or the son of man, that You are concerned about him?" —Hebrews 2:6 (NAS)

> "You have made Him for a little while lower than the angels; You have crowned Him with glory and honor, and have appointed Him over the works of Your hands;" —Hebrews 2:7 (NAS)

> "You have put all things in subjection under His feet. For in subjecting all things to him, He left nothing that is not subject to him. But now we do not yet see all things subjected to him." —Hebrews 2:8 (NAS)

> "What is man that You take thought of him, And the son of man that You care for him?" —Psalms 8:4 (NAS)

> "Yet You have made him a little lower than God, And You crown him with glory and majesty!" —Psalms 8:5 (NAS)

> " You make him to rule over the works of Your hands; You have put all things under his feet." —Psalms 8:6 (NAS)

Man has always been consumed with the questions posed in the Scriptures noted above. "What is Man?" King David asked,

> "But who am I and who are my people that we should be able to offer as generously as this? For all things come from You, and from Your hand we have given You."
> — I Chronicles 29:14

What is man?

The earliest hint of what man was to be like is found in the first chapter of the first book of the Bible.

> "Then God said, "Let Us make man in Our image, according to Our likeness ; and let them rule over the fish of the sea and over the birds of the sky and over the cattle and over all the earth, and over every creeping thing that creeps on the earth."
> —Genesis 1:26 (NAS)

> "God created man in His own image, in the image of God He created him; male and female He created them."
> —Genesis 1:27 (NAS)

In reviewing these scriptures, the first and most important consideration about the divine plan for the creation of man was that he was to be created in the image and likeness of God. God is thought of as a triune being: Father, Son and Holy Spirit. Man must, in like manner, be thought of as a triune being: spirit, soul and body. Again, as Paul stated;

> "Now may the God of peace Himself sanctify you entirely; and may your **spirit and soul and body** be preserved complete, without blame at the coming of our Lord Jesus Christ."
> —1 Thessalonians 5:23 (NAS)

In the book of Hebrews, chapter 4 verse 12, we find another reference to the fact that man is made up of many parts.

> "For the word of God is living and active and sharper than any two-edged sword, and piercing as far as the division of soul and spirit, of both joints and marrow, and able to judge the thoughts and intentions of the heart."
> —Hebrews 4:12 (NAS)

This verse indicates that the soul and spirit are capable of being divided. In the previous verse the third component of man's make-up is mentioned as the **body**.

Illustration 1 presents a schematic of how man is made up of many parts that are so interlocked that they can be studied only in a way that they relate to one another.

The Greek words used in New Testament Scripture are:

Soma = Body
Psyche = Soul
Pneuma = Spirit

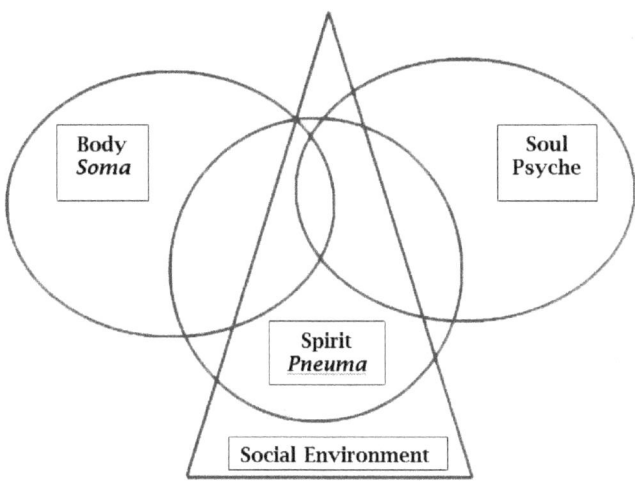

1 Thessalonians 5:23   3 John 2   Hebrews 4:12

Illustration 1

Whatever happens in one part effects the other part. Man is more than a sum total of all his parts. His environment plays an important role in his total development.

The term psychosomatic has reference to a physical illness that originates in the mind. The Spirit is generally considered as that part of man that came from God as he breathed into the nostrils of His creation as recorded in Genesis.

> "Then the LORD God formed man of dust from the ground, and breathed into his nostrils the breath of life; and man became a living being."   —Genesis 2:7 (NAS)

As Bible scholars will affirm, the Hebrew word for breath in the above verse was ***naphach***, meaning breath, puff, etc., Another important Hebrew word that is often used in Theology is ***ruwach*** found in the first Chapter of Genesis:

> "The earth was formless and void, and darkness was over the surface of the deep, and the **Spirit** of God was moving over the surface of the waters."   —Genesis 1:2 (NAS)

Here the word *ruwach* has about the same meaning as *naphach*: breath, wind, etc. Theologians believe therefore that the breath that God breathed into the man was actually the Spirit of God that transformed Adam from a model of clay into a living breathing soul. The Spirit of man can therefore, be thought of as that part that was given by God and distinguishes man from the other forms of animal life on earth.

What is man?

> "Then the dust will return to the earth as it was, and the **spirit will return to God who gave it**."
> —Ecclesiastes 12:7 (NAS)

The spirit of man is that part of man that communicates with God. In the Gospel of John, Jesus tells us that man can only worship, communicate with the Father in the spirit.

> "God is spirit, and those who worship Him must worship in spirit and truth."
> —John 4:24 (NAS)

The Greek word **Psuche** is almost always interpreted as soul.

> "So also it is written, "The first man, Adam, became a living soul." The last Adam became a life-giving spirit."
> —1 Corinthians 15:45 (NAS)

> "Now may the God of peace Himself sanctify you entirely; and may your spirit and soul and body be preserved complete, without blame at the coming of our Lord Jesus Christ."
> —1 Thessalonians 5:23 (NAS)

The soul of man is that which is comprised of the **mind** (intellect), the **emotions** (feelings), and the **will** (volition).

> "Now these were more noble-minded than those in Thessalonica, for they received the word with great eagerness, examining the Scriptures daily to see whether these things were so."
> —Acts 17:11 (NAS)

The Bible lists many positive emotions. The following verses mention only a few.

> "But the fruit of the Spirit is **love, joy, peace, patience, kindness, goodness, faithfulness, gentleness, self-control; against such things there is no law.**"
> —Galatians 5:22-23 (NAS)

The Word of God also lists many negative emotions such as found in the following verses:

> "But if you have **bitter jealousy** and **selfish ambition** in your heart, do not be arrogant and so lie against the truth."
> —James 3:14 (NAS)

> "Let all **bitterness** and **wrath** and **anger** and **clamor** and **slander** be put away from you, along with all malice."
> —Ephesians 4:31 (NAS)

> "But now you also, put them all aside : **anger, wrath, malice, slander**, and **abusive speech** from your mouth."
> —Colossians 3:8 (NAS)

> "For we also once were foolish ourselves, disobedient, deceived, enslaved to various lusts and pleasures, spending our life in **malice and envy, hateful, hating one another**."
> —Titus 3:3 (NAS)

> "Therefore, putting aside all **malice** and all **deceit** and **hypocrisy** and envy and all slander," —1 Peter 2:1 (NAS)

Man is capable of both positive and negative emotions. All through the Bible there are examples of the consequences of the improper expression of these negative emotions. Cain slew his brother Abel because of the anger that controlled his life. David was obviously led astray by the lust in his own heart.

The will, or volition is also a part of the soul God created. Man has the ability to choose; he was created by God with free will.

> "I call heaven and earth to witness against you today, that I have set before you life and death, the blessing and the curse. So choose life in order that you may live, you and your descendants," —Deuteronomy 30:19 (NAS)

> "If it is disagreeable in your sight to serve the LORD, choose for yourselves today whom you will serve: whether the gods which your fathers served which were beyond the River, or the gods of the Amorites in whose land you are living; but as for me and my house, we will serve the LORD."
> —Joshua 24:15 (NAS)

> "How much better it is to get wisdom than gold! And to get understanding is to be chosen above silver."
> —Proverbs 16:16 (NAS)

A good deal more will be said about the soul in the following chapters, because so much of man's problems in this life are the direct result of negative emotions. Christians are aware that negative emotions are the result of sin. Many of the human development theorists that will be considered in this book may not have recognized or acknowledged the sin factor in man, but a careful reading of most of their works will convince the student that most of these theorists were directly or indirectly influenced by the teaching of Christianity.

Another part of the human species that is truly marvelous to behold is the human body. Although the physical body of all of God's creatures is "fearfully and wonderfully" made, for the purposes of this study, attention

What is man?

will be focused on the human creature. In order to truly understand the nature of the human body, one must study both anatomy and physiology. However, because this text is intended as an overview of the totality of human development, only a simplistic over view will be presented here. The author is fully aware that to some students, the information presented will be of a highly elementary nature.

Descriptions

The body is composed of millions of specialized cells, the product of 23 chromosomes from a male and a female, making 46 in all. Even the slightest variation results in some form of abnormality, the most common of which may be Down's syndrome that is thought to be caused by one extra chromosome (No. 21) resulting in 47 total instead of the normal 46.

Down's syndrome is characterized by certain facial and body features such as a short nose, flabby skin, hypotonic muscles and a thick tongue. The slightly oriental shaped eyes gave rise to the term mongolism because of the resemblance to members of the Mongolian race.

In addition to the physical abnormalities, Down's syndrome also is characterized by mental retardation. Down's syndrome children seldom live more than 35-40 years.

There are 206 bones in the human body that serve as a skeletal frame and protective covering for the skin, muscles, organs and other components of the body. One fourth of the 206 bones are in the feet. The skeleton comprises less that 20 percent of the total body weight.

The skeletal system serves to protect many of the body's vital organs such as the heart, lungs, spleen, liver, kidneys, etc. It also serves as a frame to which the muscle tissue is attached. Forty percent of men's bodies are muscle; women's bodies are thirty percent muscle.

The human body has a certain amount of fat cells in and either under or over the muscles. The muscles for the most part connect to the skeleton and serve to provide movement for the entire body.

The outer layer of the body is covered by epidermal tissue (skin). The average body has 14 to 18 square feet of skin and would weigh about six pounds if collected in one mass. The skin contains millions of sweat glands that serve as the body's cooling system.

There are about 45 miles of nerves in the human body. Nerves serve to send messages to the brain: messages of pleasure and pain. The question of why God created the body with the ability to sense pain has plagued Christians and people in general for as long as time itself. Dr. Paul Brand, author of a monumental book entitled, *Fearfully and Wonderfully Made*, presents the answer to that age old question, when he relates that, as a result of his many years treating leprosy in Africa, he gained a deep respect for the function of pain in the body. Leprosy is a devastating disease that often results in the loss of many of the body extremities, such as fingers and toes. The cause of the loss of these body parts is not some form of heinous disease that attacks the skin and muscles.

Leprosy actually results in the destruction of the nerve endings in various parts of the body. With no feeling in the feet, for example, an individual would not feel the pain of a blister of a severe laceration to the foot. Not knowing that he had been injured would result in the individual ignoring the injury which in turn would result in an infection setting in that in turn could result in the eventual loss of part or all of the foot.

Anyone interested in pursuing further information on the function of pain, should read Dr. Brand's book as well as Philip Yancy's book entitled, *Where is God When It Hurts?*

Pain can be viewed as "God's Gift" to man for the protection of the body against infection and injury. Knowing this does not help when one is suffering intense acute pain, but it may help to know that without pain man could not survive. Paul Brand says that," pain is unpleasant, enough so to force us to withdraw our fingers from a stove." It is that characteristic of pain that saves us from destruction.

Pain can be physical or psychological. It can be acute or chronic. An individual who expects to pursue a career in counseling should become well acquainted with the traditional clinical theories of pain and the treatment of pain. One excellent source of reference is Bond, M. R. *Pain: Its Nature, Analysis and Treatment.* New York: Longman. 1979.

Acute pain refers to pain of a limited duration, while chronic pain is pain that lasts for several months or more. The term **pain threshold** refers to the point at which an individual first perceives the sensation of pain. It appears that different people have different pain thresholds, or a different level of tolerance at which they accept the sensation of pain.

Theories of pain have changed over the years. Earlier theories thought of pain as a "specific sensation with intensity proportional to the extent of tissue damage." (*Baker's Encyclopedia of Psychology*, David G. Benner, editor, Malzack & Wall) posit however, that a more plausible theory is the "Gate-control" theory that "emphasizes that pain perception and response are complex phenomena resulting from the interaction of cognitive-evaluative, motivational-affective as well as sensory-discriminative components. Even more recent research places more emphasis on gating mechanisms in the brain. The entire field of research into pain, its anatomical and physiological bases is ongoing and new and innovative therapies continue to appear in the proactive treatment of pain, acute and chronic.

The pain with which counselors deal most often is psychological pain. However, as will be discussed later, pure physical pain can result in psychological pain, and the counselor must not ignore the original source of the pain the client is experiencing.

On the other hand, severe psychological pain can be the source of physical pain as in psychosomatic illnesses such as ulcers, migraine headaches, and so on. It has been posited by many researchers that anywhere from 75-90% of all sickness treated by physicians is of a psychosomatic nature. More will be said about psychosomatic illness in a later part of this chapter.

It must be obvious to the reader that more of this chapter has been given to the discussion of the nervous system than to the other systems of the human body. There can be no doubt that when all else is said, the greater part of human concern is with pain of one kind or another. There are several other important systems that need to be mentioned before passing on to the actual discussion of human development.

Thus far the text has presented an all too incomplete discussion of the **skeletal-muscular** system and the **nervous system**. The rest of the chapter will present a brief review of the other systems of the human body. It is important for the individual who plans on working as a care giver, whether in the medical field or as a counselor, to become as aware of the various systems and to the various ways they interact with each other. It is also necessary to see the way the entire physical plant interacts with the soul and the spirit. The other systems are equally important to the study of human development.

The digestive system begins with the mouth and ends with the anus. This system functions to take in food and process it in order to provide the fuel that the body needs to keep running and to grow. The digestive system includes the mouth, with the teeth, tongue and salivary glands that all aide in the first step in the process of digestion; the esophagus, which carries the food to the stomach where the food is further digested. Food then passes in to the small intestines which are 20 to 23 feet in length. Here the goodness from the food is absorbed into the blood stream and taken to the liver where some of it is stored. The rest of the food continues into the large intestines that are five feet long, where water from the food passes into the blood. Any of the food that was not digested collects in the rectum before leaving the body through the anus.

The urinary system has the important task of regulating the body's liquid intake, and plays a major role in cleansing the body of waste products. The body produces three kinds of waste: solid waste left over from the digestive process; gases, such as carbon dioxide; and liquid waste, including water which is expelled as sweat or urine.

About two-thirds of the body is water. It is imperative that this level be maintained. A loss of 20 percent of the body's water would result in a painful and certain death. The longest time that the human body can go without water is about a week and a half (with the exception of a few Bible characters such as Moses and Elijah). The longest time on record is eleven days in the history of modern medicine. The body takes in about 2.5 quarts of water a day through food and drink. It loses about 2 quarts per day through urination. The other 0.5 quarts is lost through breathing and perspiration.

The urinary system includes: the pituitary gland which controls the levels of water in the body; the thyroid gland, which directs energy levels; the adrenal gland which controls feelings of shock or excitement. The kidneys filter water and urea (a waste which forms in the liver and is poisonous to the body) from the blood and expels the mixture as urine through the ureter into the bladder. When the bladder is full, urine is pushed from the body through the tube called the urethra.

It is the pituitary gland that furnishes growth hormones that regulate individual differences in height.

The respiratory system takes in oxygen when a person breathes. Oxygen is needed in every part of the body. We exhale carbon dioxide, a waste product of the body. The respiratory system also gets rid of some of the moisture in the body. Cells use oxygen to break down food into energy.

When an individual breathes, he takes in air, through the nose and mouth that travels down the windpipe to the lungs. The windpipe divides into two bronchi, one going to each lung. The lungs are made up of air sacs called alveoli, totaling more that 300 million in number, each of which is surrounded by small blood vessels. The oxygen from the air seeps through the walls of the alveoli and is carried by the red blood cells to the various parts of the body. The blood exchanges the oxygen for a gas (carbon dioxide) and returns it to the lungs by the system of veins. The poisonous gas is discharged from the body by the next exhale.

Air is breathed in and expelled about 15 times per minute. Breathing is an automatic (or involuntary) function of the brain directing the muscle called the diaphragm to arch upward forcing air out of the lungs. When the diaphragm relaxes, air is drawn into the lungs without a person having to think about the process, thus, it is called an involuntary function. The diaphragm can move as much as 2 inches when breathing is deep.

Closely related to the respiratory system is the heart and circulatory system. This system is made up of the heart and a system of arteries and veins. It was suggested that if the arteries and veins of the average adult were tied end to end, they would form a rope that would reach around the world. The aorta is the main artery of the body. It carries fresh oxygenated blood from the heart. Its branches, comprised of arteries and arteriole, get smaller and smaller until they become known as capillaries. The capillaries have thin walls through which passes oxygen and food substances to the cells of the body and waste products to return. Finally, the blood flows back to the heart through a system of veins, the largest of which is the vena cava, the large vein that enters the heart. The heart beats about 37 million times in a year, or 70 times a minute. The heart rests between beats. The total resting time of the heart in a lifetime of a 70 year old person would be 40 years. The heart pumps about 13 tons or 3000 gallons of blood every day.

The average adult has about 1 gallon of blood, smaller people less, larger people more. The blood contains a total of 25 million red blood cells in the average man. Red blood cells only live for 4 months, but they travel about 930 miles around the body. Another part of the blood is made up of white blood cells. White cells are much like an army that will attack and kill germs that may infect a wound. The slightly yellow matter that can be seen in an infected wound (called pus) is an accumula-tion of dead soldiers who gave their all in the fight against infection.

The final system that will be reviewed here is that of the reproductive system. This is that system by which babies are produced, making it possible to carry on the human race.

> "God blessed them, saying, "Be fruitful and multiply, and fill the waters in the seas, and let birds multiply on the earth."
> —Genesis 1:22 (NAS)

> "God blessed them; and God said to them, "Be fruitful and multiply, and fill the earth, and subdue it; and rule over the fish of the sea and over the birds of the sky and over every living thing that moves on the earth." —Genesis 1:28 (NAS)

Reproduction is accomplished by the sperm cell from a male uniting with an egg (ovum) cell in a female.

The process of ovulation and the development of the new life in the process of reproduction will be the subject of Chapter 2 and will be discussed more at length at that time. For the purposes of completing this review of the various parts of man, a simple short listing of the parts of the reproductive system will be made.

The male reproductive organs include the penis or external male reproductive organ used for copulation and for urination; the testes (testi, singular) in which sperm cells are produced; the scrotum, a sack of skin which contain the testes; sperm, the male reproductive cell (A total of about 400 million sperm are contained in one ejaculation by a male); semen, a mixture of sperm and special fluids produced by the male in the seminal vesicles and the prostate gland; the sperm duct through which the sperm in its seminal fluid travel to the penis in the process of ejaculation.

The female reproductive organs include: the ovaries where the egg cells are stored. Woman are born with all of the egg cells they will ever need, but men continually produce sperm cells from the age of 13. The other reproductive parts are the fallopian tubes, which carry the mature egg cell to the uterus; the uterus or womb in which the fertilized egg will take up residence until birth; the cervix, opening at the bottom of the womb; and finally, the vagina which is the canal leading from the cervix to the exterior of the body.

At the beginning of this discussion, the reader was warned that it would be elementary at best. The writer makes no apologies for this in view of the fact that a complete study of human anatomy would be impractical for this volume. It would be inexcusable to end this portion of the book, however, without a short discussion of the brain which, in fact, should have been included in the section about the nervous system.

The brain with the nerves and senses comprise the great control and communication system of the body. The human brain in an adult weighs about 3 pounds. Eighty percent of the brain's weight is water. There are a total of about 12 billion nerve cells in the brain. Once growing is complete, thousands of cells are lost every day and not replaced. The brain is like a super computer capable of storing and processing millions of bits of information at a truly remarkable speed. The brain itself is insensitive to pain. It is thought that a headache comes from the nerves and muscles surrounding the brain rather than from the brain itself.

The brain is the central processing plant of the human being. This is where thinking takes place as well as feelings of emotion. The brain helps man to experience his world through the senses of sight, sound, taste and feel. The brain is also the place where the soul and spirit of man operate.

The brain is considered an electro-chemical organ. The electrical activity of the brain can be analyzed through the use of a test called the electroencephalogram. The electrical patterns of the brain can be altered by various chemical substances. This is where the term mind altering drugs came into use. It may be interesting to point out that many people use mind altering drugs without being aware of the fact that they would be considered as such. Aspirin, caffeine, nicotine, and sugar are only a few that may not fit into the same level of danger as morphine, cannabis, or crack cocaine, but they are never the less chemicals that do, indeed, alter the brains electrical fields, if only slightly.

There are times when the use of a mind altering drug may be of some help, especially in the treatment of certain mental disturbances.

This chapter has taken a look at man as a spiritual, psychological, and physical being. The one further point that needs to be made is that man is also a social being.

In the chapters that follow, a developmental look at man will reveal that two factors play the all important role in the development of his person and personality. They are heredity and environment. It is not a question of one or the other but a matter of both nature and nurture contributing to the final product.

A reference to the theory called psychosomatic illness was made earlier. This theory simply stated says that what happens in the emotions can cause physical illness, such as ulcers, heart problems, etc. At this point the writer wishes to point out that one's environment, especially one's interpersonal relationships, plays an important role in the development of the person or personality. B. F. Skinner, the father of behavioral psychology, tried desperately to demonstrate that if a person's environment could be completely controlled, he would not develop personality or behavioral problems later in life. His research (though faulty at best) was a total failure in the opinion of most modern psychologists.

What is man?

Personal Reflections

John

John and his wife Alva were the pastors of a church near us for a number of years. They had three children, and we became good friends. John was called to a larger church several hundred miles north of us, and we ceased to communicate with them.

One day Alva called me to relate an almost unbelievable story. John had announced to her that he no longer loved her and planned to get a divorce. He had plans of marrying another minister's wife from a neighboring state. He had moved out of their home and was living in another city. As a result of this irrational behavior, John lost his church, his family, his position as a leader in the denominational district, and his ministerial credentials. He received no help from his superiors who simply told him that he was possessed of the devil and was surely going to hell.

Some months later, John called me and wanted to come to my office for a visit. When he arrived, I could see that he was a broken man. He asked for my help, and I agreed to do what I could. After talking for a while, we agreed to meet again in a couple of weeks, but I wanted him to feel as though we were already working on a solution to his problems. I asked that he visit an allergist for a medical evaluation.

He did not return to my office or even call. At first I thought that I should have done more or said more when he had come to my office.

To my great relief and joy, a few months later John wrote me a long letter in which he said that he had taking my advice and discovered that he was extremely allergic to certain food additives. He could only remember some of what he had done and felt like the entire incident had been a very bad dream. He concluded the letter by saying that he and Alva were back together, and they were again pastoring a church in the Northwest.

It is my opinion that the food additives caused an imbalance in the chemistry in the brain. This in turn created what might resemble an electrical storm in much the same way that certain hallucinogenic drugs can create a totally false reality in the drug abuser.

This story serves to illustrate how a physical problem can manifest itself in the mind and emotions.

Allen

Some weeks after the beginning of the school term, I, as a counselor in a junior high school, enrolled Allen, a new student. His first class was Art, and I sent him off with directions on how to get to the room and with a warning to enter as quietly as possible because class had already begun.

At the end of the first period, Mr. Sinclair came bursting into my office. His face was slightly flushed, and as I remember, his words were something like, "What are you trying to do to me? That little monster almost destroyed my class!" As calmly as I could I asked what had happened. This was the story.

As Allen entered the room with his class schedule in hand, he jumped up on the last table in the back of the room and proceeded to jump from one table to the next until he reached the table in front of the teacher's desk. He smiled and politely handed the teacher his schedule slip. For the rest of the period Mr. Sinclair spent most of his time trying to keep Allen in or at least near his assigned seat.

I, of course, had to call the mother to come in for a consultation about her son's behavior. I could tell from her response to my call that she was expecting it.

Allen's mother told me, with tears in her eyes, that Allan had been sus-pended from a number of schools because of his incorrigible behavior.

I had only recently read some interesting articles on a relative new field of psychiatry called Ortho-molecular psychiatry. This Ortho-molecular psychiatry treated some seriously ill individuals with certain vitamins and minerals. There were also some various drugs having outstanding results with hyperactive children.

I referred her to a neurologist for an electroencephalogram. The results of the test indicated that Allen had one area of the brain that had, as the doctor described it, an electrical storm. He prescribed a common medication and suggested the mother wait and see what happened.

As there were no more complaints, I actually had forgotten about Allan until the first report card period. Allan and his mother stopped by my office after school that day, and his mother thanked me, with tears of joy in her eyes, as she showed me Allan's report card. He had all A's and all E's for excellence in citizenship. He had become a model student who came home each evening and immediately sat down to do his homework. What had been seen as pure mischievous behavior was indeed something beyond the boy's control. The storm in his brain was distorting his reality and literally causing him to behave in a completely bizarre manner.

What happened in the mind (brain) influenced what happened in the physical being. There are endless stories of this nature that could be told, but permit me to simply say that I feel strongly that man is a tripartite being created by God. Each area of man's being intricately interacts with each of the other areas. In a later chapter we shall discuss how the fourth area, interpersonal relations, also plays an important part in the development of man.

What is man?

Review of Chapter 1

- The New Testament uses three Greek words to describe the tripartite nature of man. They are:

    - Soma = Body
    - Psyche = Soul
    - Pneuma = Spirit

- The spirit is that part of man that came from God as He breathed into the nostrils of His creation (Genesis 2:7).

- The spirit is that part of man that communicates with God (John 4:24).

- The soul of man is that which is comprised of the mind (intellect), emotions (feelings), and wil

- The body is the physical part of man consisting of:

    - 46 chromosomes,
    - 23 from each parent
    - 206 bones forming a skeletal frame
    - Epidermal cells (skin)
    - 45 miles of nerve cells
    - Muscles
    - A digestive system
    - A urinary system
    - A respiratory system
    - A circulatory system
    - A reproductive system
    - A lymphatic systeml (volition).

- The brain is an electro-chemical organ that can be affected by various chemical substances.

Glossary for Chapter 1

Glossary of Terms

Arteries — Any blood vessels which carry blood away from the heart to the rest of the body.

Bacteria — Microscopic one-celled organisms found everywhere - even in our bodies. Most are harmless, some are essential, such as those in the intestines, a few cause disease.

Bile — Greenish liquid produced by the liver and stored in the gall bladder. It helps to digest fat in the small intestine.

Blood Vessel — Any of the many tubes arteries, veins and capillaries that carry blood around the body.

Bronchus — One of the branches of the windpipe, leading to the lungs.

Capillaries — The smallest type of blood vessel.

Cardiac — Referring to the heart.

Cartilage — Soft, elastic tissue, often called gristle.

Cells — The basic living units of the body, sometimes called the "building blocks" of life. Every part of the body is made up of cells - one trillion of them in an average man.

Central Nervous System — The brain and spinal cord.

Chromosome — One of the 46 structures found in the nucleus of every human cell. Chromosomes carry the genes which determine inherited characteristics, such as sex, hair color, and height (among others).

Colon — Lower part of the large intestine.

Coronary — Referring to the blood vessels that supply the heart. Coronary arteries over the surface of the heart provide oxygen to its cells.

DNA (Deoxyribonucleic Acid) — Complicated chemical that makes up genes and chromosomes.

Diaphragm — Flat muscle which separates the chest from the abdomen.

Enzymes — Chemical substances that speed up chemical reactions within the body and control processes such as digestion.

Epiglottis — Small flap at the back of the tongue which blocks the windpipe when you swallow and so prevents food "going down the wrong way."

Esophagus — Gullet or food pipe leading from the throat to the stomach.

Follicle — Small pocket in the skin from which a single hair grows.

Gall Bladder — Small sac, about 3-4 inches long, which stores bile.

Genes — Combinations of DNA which make up the chromosomes in each cell.

Glands Organs — in the body, such as the salivary glands, the kidneys, and liver, which produce or work on chemical substances.

Hormones — Sometimes called the body's chemical messengers, produced in certain glands and released into the blood. They control many body processes, such as growth, the amount of sugar in the blood.

What is man?

Immune System — The body's own defenses against infection.

Intestines — The long tube, beginning at the stomach and ending at the anus, in which food is digested.

Keratin — The hard substance found in hair, nails, and skin.

Kidneys — Two organs that filter waste from the blood and produce urine, which collects in the bladder. They are located on either side of the spine.

Larynx — The voice box, located at the top of the trachea and containing the vocal chords.

Ligaments — Tough elastic bands of tissue which hold bone together at a joint.

Liver — The body's largest gland; it stores iron and some glucose. Processes amino acids and produces bile.

Lymph — Clear liquid which contains white blood cells. It flows through a set of vessels (tubes) called the lymphatic system.

Marrow — Soft, jelly-like substance found in the center of bones. Blood cells are made in some bone marrow.

Organ — Group of tissues which work together such as the heart or the liver.

Pancreas — Gland which produces the hormone insulin which controls the level of glucose in the blood.

Plasma — Liquid part of the blood.

Proteins — Bodybuilding chemicals, made of amino acids.

Pulse — The rhythmic throbbing which can be felt in the arteries as the heart beats.

Pus — The whitish-yellow liquid produced in certain infections made up mostly of dead white blood cells.

Saliva — Liquid released by three pairs of glands in the mouth. It starts the process of digestion.

Sebaceous Gland — Oil-producing gland in the skin.

Sinuses — Four sets of cavities in the skull, where air that is breathed is warmed.

Spinal Cord — The thick cord of nerves which begins at the base of the brain and extends to the bottom of the back.

Spleen — An organ that is part of the lymphatic system and helps to fight infection.

Tendons — Very strong bands of tissue which connect muscles to bones.

Thymus — Gland in the neck which helps the immune system.

Thyroid — Gland in the neck that produces a hormone, thyroxin, which controls growth rate and the speed of chemical processes.

Tissues — Groups of similar cells which form various parts of the body, such as nerve or muscle.

Trachea — Windpipe, leading from the larynx to the lungs.

Tumor — Swelling caused by abnormal growth of cells. It may be benign or cancerous.

Ulcer — Open sore on the skin, or on a membrane inside the body.

Ureters — Tubes which carry urine from the kidneys to the bladder.

Urethra — Tube which carries urine from the bladder to the outside of the body.

Veins — Blood vessels which carry used blood back to the heart.

Viruses — Microorganisms that cause disease if they invade the body.

Vitamins — Group of about 15 substances found in foods. They are needed for good health.

Vocal Cords — Two ligaments stretched across the larynx. They vibrate as air passes over them enabling speech.

"In my beginning is my end." —T.S. Eliot

Chapter 2

In the Beginning

Almost none of the early theorists in the field of human development even mentioned the significance of prenatal development. The first recorded theories about the development of a new being were the work of the two great pioneers in the field of human behavior: John Locke and Jean Rousseau. From about the fifth century to as late as the latter part of the eighteenth century there existed a theory of human development during pregnancy that has become known as "preformationism."

During this period, people tended to think of children as fully formed little adults. It is thought by some that the high rate of death among infants made it easier for adults to deal with the death of small children if they were thought of as little adults.

In the early stages of the science of embryology, it was postulated that within the male sperm there existed a fully formed human who only needed to find a mature female egg in which to grow and develop until birth. There was some division of thinking among the embryologist of that day, in that some held to the notion that the fully formed adult resided in the sperm while others argued that it was the egg (ovum) that carried the little adult.

During the last half of the eighteenth century, the idea of pre-formationism began to wane, largely due to the work of a medical student named Caspar Friedrich Wolff. Wolff made two suggestions. He said that the infant is not pre-formed at conception but is assembled out of small structures. He also concluded that the mother and father both contributed to the offspring. The use of microscopic examinations of the embryo indicated that the fetus developed by stages. However, even with this major change in thinking about the development of the human being in the womb, there appeared very little research or even serious speculation about the importance of the actual development process. Most of the early human development researchers concentrated on the development that took place after birth.

In the Beginning

John Locke (1632-1704) and Jean Jacques Rousseau (1712-1778) were, as mentioned earlier, the pioneers in the field. Although more will be said in another chapter (3) about these early pioneers, it is important to note here that both Locke and Rousseau based their theories on either pure observation or simple deductive reasoning. None of their work was based on scientific research.

The various developmental theories, based on the stage theories formulated by some of the outstanding researchers, will be discussed in Chapter 3. This chapter will be devoted and dedicated to that most glorious and amazing period in an individual's life: his journey from the union of sperm and egg to the birth of a new human child.

The writer must apologize to the author of the greatest text encountered in the production of this book. *In the Beginning: Development from Conception to Age: Two. second edition.* Rosenblith, Judy F. published by Sage Publication: Newbury Park. 1992. The title of this chapter had been seriously considered, before the book by Rosenblith came across the author's desk. It just seemed to be the right title for a chapter that deals with the true beginning of life. A number of quotes will be included throughout this chapter. Rosenblith's entire book is must reading for anyone contemplating a career working with children up to the age of two years.

The Three Stages of Prenatal Development

Stage One: Fertilization. The process of fertilization takes place when one of the 300-400 million sperm cells (also called spermatozoa) is introduced in the female vagina. This process is called copulation or artificial insemination. The sperm finds its way by swimming, with the help of the seminal fluid that was released during ejaculation by the male, through the female reproductive channel. The sperm swims until one of the sperm finally enters the mature ovum that has been released into the female fallopian tube. The sperm looks very much like a pollywog and swims in the same fashion. The sperm's 23 chromosomes unite with the ovum's 23 chromosomes resulting in a new cell of 46 chromosomes. These 46 chromosomes will determine physical, mental, and emotional characteristics of the new individual. Most of the physical and psychological development can be described as an interaction between growth (size and weight) and differentiation (increase in complexity and organization. (Baker: p. 865).

The new zygote/embryo begins to divide rapidly (a process called cleavage) within the first 12-40 hours. About half of the male's sperm are Y chromosomes and the other half are X chromosomes. If a Y chromosome fertilizes the egg, the off-spring is genetically male. If an X chromosome reaches the egg first the result will be a female. Fathers are the sole determiner of the sex of their progeny.

The Three Stages of Prenatal Development

The process of development is fascinating. The most popular theory of development of the zygote is according to the cephalocaudal principle that holds that development proceeds in a head-to-toe direction, i.e., that upper parts of the body develop first before the lower parts. Other authors describe the stages of development in slightly different terms, but in general the various descriptions agree. Two charts that describe the entire first nine months were developed by two different researchers in different works some eight years apart: Grunlan in 1984 and Rosenblith in 1992. The terminology is slightly different, but the stages are fairly well defined. There are clearly three stages in the development of the fetus. They are referred to as trimesters. As the term suggests, each trimester is about three months in length.

Different names have been given to each of the three stages. Stage 1 is the Fertilization Stage. Stage 2 the Organogenesis Stage and Stage 3 the Fetal stage. Each of the three stages presents particular dangers. Only a few of the more common dangers will be mentioned here.

During Stage 1, there is a slight possibility that fertilization and the zygote implant may happen in one of the fallopian tubes or somewhere else in the pelvic cavity. A small gap between the ovaries and fallopian tubes in humans makes such misses possible. This type of pregnancy is called an entopic (outside the uterus) pregnancy. An entopic pregnancy usually terminates in the first 2-3 months, either by severe bleeding when the placenta becomes detached, by rupture of the tube, or both. This type of miscarriage is usually accompanied by abdominal pains and vomiting. Death of the mother can occur in as few as six hours from the loss of blood if not treated.

The embryonic stage: starting at 2 weeks after fertilization, is often a critical period, because certain kinds of growth must occur during this time if development is to proceed in a normal fashion. Specifically, it is the physical development that is happening at this time. If it doesn't happen now, it never will.

At 8 weeks the embryo is referred to as a fetus and shows a definite resemblance to a human being.

During the second trimester (12 weeks) and the third trimester (24 weeks), problems can occur because of such factors as drug, tobacco and/or alcohol use by the mother. This can happen even if the use is in moderation. Injury to the fetus from the outside may also occur due to an accident, maternal malnutrition, and/or many other factors.

A smoking mother sends nicotine, carbon monoxide, carbonic acid and wood alcohol right down the line to her baby. Smoking two packs of cigarettes a day reduces the baby's weight by 10%, which can seriously reduce the infant's chances of survival.

More and more OB-GYN physicians are warning their patients to avoid substances such as tobacco, alcohol and drugs, even though in years past they were thought to be non-threatening to the health and welfare of the fetus. Even such luxuries as chocolate and salt are among the forbidden foods for the expectant mother.

The possible damage that can occur because of the use of prescription drugs during the embryonic stage was dramatically demonstrated in 1961. Thousands of babies, most of them from Germany and England, were born without arms and legs, a condition called phocomelia ("seal limbs"). The mothers had taken the drug thalidomide to prevent morning sickness, which many women experience during the first trimester.

It is during the second trimester when some of the more tragic birth defects may have their beginnings. Spina bifida (incomplete closure of the spine), cleft lip and cleft palate are only three of the many physical defects that may have their beginning during this period.

Other developmental problems can occur during the early stage of pregnancy, although some problems can come later in the developmental stages. Over exposure to radiation, infectious disease, (especially sexual transmitted diseases called venereal diseases such as gonorrhea, syphilis, etc.), serious anxiety, and chromosomal aberrations are a few of the more common causes of problems in the fetus.

Obstetricians tend to avoid the use of the X-Ray during the early stages of pregnancy, although ultra-sound is used to determine any potential dangers such as attachment of the fetus to near the bottom of the womb.

Serious anxiety, as well as other serious emotional dysfunctions, can have a pronounced effect on the fetus. Some researchers suggest that parents should practice talking calmly and reassuringly to the fetus, and that they should by all means avoid loud and harsh arguments during and hopefully after the pregnancy. The fetus's sense of hearing and feeling develop very early within the womb.

The stage of fetal development determines that degree of influence of environmental agents. During Stage One, certain noxious agents are usually fatal. If only a few cells are damaged, competition takes place.

Stage Two is the time of highest risk for the development of malformations. Remember, this is the critical stage of physical development.

During Stage Three it is usually the brain that is affected. One of the most common causes is oxygen deprivation to the fetus. This can occur in too many ways to discuss at this juncture.

Another fetal development area has to do with imbalance of hormones and enzymes. Monitoring this is usually done through blood and urine samples from the mother, and takes place through certain prenatal testing techniques. Some of these tests, however, present their own problems and dangers.

Prenatal Testing

There are three prenatal testing techniques that are in common use. Probably the most frequently used test is the **Amniocentesis**. This is done around the 16th week of pregnancy, and occasionally later in the pregnancy in the case of mothers who are a little older with their first pregnancy. This test presents some risks, including miscarriage, infection, bleeding, possible injury to the unborn child and accidental puncturing of the placenta.

Amniocentesis is performed by inserting a long, small needle into the womb and drawing out some of the amnio fluids which are then tested for genetic abnormalities and possible hormonal and enzyme imbalances.

Another test is the **Chorionic Villus Sampling (CVS)**. The risks are similar to those in the Amniocentesis test.

A third test is the **Fetoscopy** which is performed with the use of fiber optics which are inserted into the uterus. This allows the physician to actually see what is happening to the fetus. Again, because of its intrusive nature, this test presents some real dangers to the fetus and to the mother.

It should be noted that the use of prenatal testing may have been greatly overused. Rosenblith (1992. p. 85) noted that "Genetic and chromosomal disorders account for a number of problems that affect infants. Although most abnormal conspectuses do not survive to be born, or die shortly after birth, about .5% of newborns have chromosomal abnormalities and 3-5% have some genetic defect. This small proportion of infants accounts for a large proportion of hospitalizations of infants and children and for staggering sums of hospital costs."

In cases where there is a clear history of chromosomal abnormalities in the history of the family, prenatal counseling and even prenatal testing may be justified.

In some of the far Eastern countries, as well as elsewhere, the use of prenatal testing has been done to determine the sex of the fetus. Female babies are still not desired, and usually if the fetus is determined to be female, it is aborted. It is difficult for even the abortionists to agree with this as an acceptable reason for abortion.

Before proceeding with the process of development and birth, these parenthetic comments regarding **twins and other multiple births** may clear up some questions. The birth of twins and even triplets is not uncommon, but in recent years, with the introduction of certain **fertility** drugs, there are more and more occasions of multiple births involving four or five infants. This was an event that happened so seldom in years past that such births made front page news.

Occasionally, two ova will leave the ovary of the female. In such a case if both of the eggs are fertilized, the resulting birth will be that of fraternal (**dizyogotic**) twins. There could be two boys, two girls or one boy and one girl. They will not necessarily have similar physical characteristics, because they were both made up of two completely different sets of chromosomes.

When a single ovum divides in two after fertilization, the result will be identical (**monozygotic**) twins. These twins will usually be carbon copies of each other. It is true, however, that one may be larger than the other,

In the Beginning

and with the possibility of differing environments and nutrition, there is a possibility of other physical differences that may be evidenced over time.

For more information on multiple births the reader is referred to Rosenblith's book, *In the Beginning: From Conception to Age Two*. Scriptures are not silent on the importance of understanding that the life of an individual starts, at least physically, nine months before the actual birth. Jeremiah made it clear that he was known of the Lord even before conception, and certainly during his sojourn in the womb.

> "Now the word of the Lord came to me saying, "Before I formed you in the womb I knew you, And before you were born I consecrated you; I have appointed you a prophet to the nations."
> —Jeremiah 1:4-5 (NAS)

In the book of Luke there is a very interesting passage where John the Baptist proclaims that the Lord Jesus would be full of the Holy Spirit from the womb.

> "For he will be great in the sight of the Lord ; and he will drink no wine or liquor, and he will be filled with the Holy Spirit while yet in his mother's womb."   —Luke 1:15 (NAS)

When Mary was expecting the baby Jesus, she took a trip to see her cousin Elizabeth, who was also with child. As she approached the house of her sister, she called out to her. Here is what happened.

> "When Elizabeth heard Mary's greeting, the baby leaped in her womb; and Elizabeth was filled with the Holy Spirit."
> —Luke 1:41 (NAS)

Another verse that indicates that God has His hand on the infant even in the womb is found in the Psalms.

> "My frame was not hidden from You, when I was made in secret, and skillfully wrought in the depths of the earth; Your eyes have seen my unformed substance; and in Your book were all written the days that were ordained for me, when as yet there was not one of them."   —Psalms 139:15-16 (NAS)

There are other scriptures that the serious students of the Word can locate with the aid of a good concordance.

Personal Reflections

We have had the privilege of seeing both a natural birth and a birth by **Cesarean Section** (a surgical procedure in which the fetus is delivered through the abdominal wall of the mother). We must admit that natural birth is by far a more beautiful event, but in either case one can never cease to wonder at the miracle plan of God. There is no way that I could support abortion after holding a newborn infant in my arms, even though he may have been expressing loudly his displeasure with the entire birthing process. I am not one of the militant crusaders who spend their time blocking the entrances to abortion clinics, but I take every opportunity to make my voice heard on the subject.

I dislike getting into discussions about the situational ethics involved in the cases of rape, clear evidence of a malformed fetus, or the like. Each individual must answer those questions for him/herself. Then each must live with the answers and whatever grief and sorrow that results from decisions that were made.

As a Christian counselor, I have had to help many young women who, for one reason or another, decided to abort their child rather than give birth and place the child in a loving home if necessary.

The pain and grief that a mother suffers is many times so severe that the best of counseling cannot help to heal the scars that will forever plague the poor soul. However, some are so calloused that they either do not feel the pain or are able to rationalize the act to the point that the pain is not acknowledged.

There are literally millions of abortions each year, but there are also millions of good people who would give almost anything to have a baby to love and raise.

I cannot end this chapter without a word about the effects of abortion on the unborn. I have seen the movies, the pictures and heard the audio of the sounds of fetal screams during an abortion. I cannot accept in any way the concept that the embryo or the fetus is anything but a feeling being, and that the horrid methods used in abortion are no less than murder in the sight of God.

The material presented in this chapter is all factual and has been gleaned from many sources and through personal experience when I served in the operating room in the Navy Hospital Corp. I was a Qualified Assistant in Operating Room Technique (QAORT), which is the equivalent of a surgical nurse. However, as I warned in the first chapter, I reserved the right to express my own opinions at the end of the chapters under the heading of Personal Reflections. The reader may check the factual material for accuracy and may disagree with my opinions expressed in this part of the text. May God, Himself, guide you into all truth for the sake of unborn children everywhere.

In the Beginning

Review of Chapter 2

- Caspar Friedrich Wolff was largely responsible for a change in the concept of preformation through the use of the microscope.

- He suggested that the embryo developed in a series of stages.

- The work of Lock and Rousseau was based largely on the observation method of study.

- The three stages of prenatal development are:
  - Stage one: Fertilization
  - Stage two: Organogenesis
  - Stage three: Fetal Stage

- Many things can happen to cause damage to the fetus.

- Stage two is the time of the highest risk to the fetus.

- The use of prenatal testing has gained popularity, but all forms of prenatal testing are considered to have some risks.

- The different types of prenatal testing presented were:
  - Amniocentesis
  - Chorionic Villus Sampling
  - Fetoscopy

- Prenatal testing was first introduced to detect genetic and chromosomal defects.

- In some countries prenatal testing is used to determine the sex of the fetus. If the fetus is female it will be aborted.

- The text discussed the two types of twins:
  - Monozygotic
  - Dizygotic

- Monozygotic twins are the result of a single ovum dividing in two and producing identical twins.

- Dizygotic twins are the result of two separate ova being fertilized producing fraternal twins.

Glossary for Chapter 2

Glossary of Terms

Amniocentesis — An intrusive prenatal procedure where a sample of the amino fluid is extracted and analyzed to determine whether any of certain genetic defects are present

Anoxia — Lack of oxygen, which may cause brain damage.

Cephalocaudal Principle — A principle that development proceeds in a head-to-toe direction, i.e., the upper parts of the body develop before the lower parts.

Cesarean Section — Most commonly called a C Section. It is the surgical removal of a fetus from the uterus when the mother is not able to deliver normally or vaginally.

Chorionic Villus Sampling (CVS) — Prenatal diagnostic procedure in which tissue from villi (hairlike projections of the membrane surrounding the embryo) is analyzed for birth defects.

Chromosomal Aberrations — A defect in one or more of the chromosomes from either the mother or father that will result is some type of abnormality, i.e., Down's syndrome.

Chromosome — Segments of DNA that carry the genes, the transmitters of heredity; in the normal human being there are 46 chromosomes

Cleavage — The process of cell division that begins almost immediately after fertilization.

Critical Period — The period of development starting at 2 weeks because of certain critical growth necessary at that time.

DNA (Deoxyribonucleic Acid) — The substance that carries the program that tells each cell in the body what specific functions it will perform and how it will perform them.

Dizygotic — Fraternal twin that is the result of two eggs being fertilized.

Donor Eggs — Method of conception in which an ovum of a fertile woman is implanted in the uterus of a woman who cannot produce normal ova.

Ectopic Fertilization — An ovum in some area other that the fallopian tube.

Electronic Fetal Monitoring — Monitoring of fetal heartbeat by machine in labor and delivery, enabling delivery personnel to determine if the fetus is in distress

Embryo — The name given to the new life during the early stage of gestation.

Embryology — The science given to the study of nature and development of embryos.

Embryonic Stage — Second stage of gestation (2 to 8-12 weeks), characterized by rapid growth and development of major body systems and organs.

Environmental Influences — Non-genetic influences on development attributable to experiences with the outside world.

Estrogen — Female hormone; its decrease during the climacteric may result in hot flashes, thinning of the vaginal lining, and urinal dysfunction.

Fertility Drugs — Drugs that are given to women who are having a problem conceiving.

Fertilization — The penetration of a male sperm into a female egg resulting in the egg becoming fertile, and it begins the development process.

Fetal Alcohol Syndrome (FAS) — Mental, motor, and developmental abnormalities which may include stunted growth, facial and bodily malformation and disorders of the central nervous system. These effect the offspring of some women who drink heavily during pregnancy.

Fetal Stage — Final stage of gestation (8-12 weeks to birth), characterized by increased detail of body parts and greatly elongated body size.

Fetal Tobacco Syndrome — Growth retardation of offspring of some women who smoke heavily during pregnancy. Some believe that the same affect could be caused by the continuous breathing in of second-hand smoke in the workplace.

Fetoscopy — An intrusive procedure in which a small tube is inserted into the womb, and through which a fiber optical lens is passed to observe the inside of the womb.

Fetus — What the embryo is called after the first 8 weeks.

Gamete — Sex cell (sperm or ovum) gene basic functional unit of heredity, which determines an inherited characteristic.

Genetic Counseling — Clinical service that advises couples of their probable risk of having children with particular hereditary defects.

Genetics — Study of hereditary factors affecting development.

Germinal Stage — First 2 weeks of prenatal development, characterized by rapid cell division and increased complexity; the stage ends when the conceptus attaches itself to the wall of the uterus.

Heredity — Inborn influences on development, carried in the genes inherited from the parents.

In Vitro Fertilization — Fertilization of an ovum outside the mother's body.

Karyotype — Chart in which photomicrographs of a prospective parent's chromosomes are arranged to size and structure to reveal any chromosomal abnormalities.

Lanugo — Fuzzy prenatal body hair, which drops off within a few days after birth.

Malnutrition — Many mothers will not eat a well-balanced diet during pregnancy resulting in an undernourished fetus.

Maternal Blood Test — Prenatal diagnostic procedure to detect the presence of fetal abnormalities. This is used particularly when the fetus is at risk of defects in the central nervous system.

Monozygotic — Identical twins that result from one ovum dividing into two after fertilization.

Neonatal Period — First four weeks of life, a time of transition from intrauterine dependency to independent existence.

Neonate — A newborn baby.

Ovulation — Expulsion of ovum from ovary, which occurs

about every 28 days from puberty to menopause

Phocomelia — The malformation of a fetus caused by the use of the drug thalidomide during pregnancy. The word means "seal limbs".

Preformationism — A belief that lasted from about the fifth century until the second half of the eighteenth century, that a fully formed little adult existed in either the male sperm or the female ovum.

Prenatal — That time in the development of a human being from conception until birth, normally nine months.

Preterm Babies — Babies born before the thirty-seventh week of gestation, dated from the mother's last menstrual period; also called premature babies (preemies).

Proximodistal Law — Principle that development proceeds from within to without, i.e., that parts of the body near the center develop before the extremities.

Recessive Inheritance — Expression of a recessive (non-dominant) trait, which, according to Mendel, occurs only if the offspring receives the same recessive gene from each parent.

Sex Chromosomes — Pair of chromosomes that determine sex: XX in the normal female, XY in the normal male.

Sex-linked Inheritance — Pattern of inheritance in which certain characteristics carried on the sex chromosomes (usually the X chromosome) are transmitted differently to males and females.

Sexually Transmitted Disease (STDs) — Disease transmitted by sexual contact; also called venereal disease.

Spina Bifida — A birth defect characterized by an incomplete closure of the spine.

Spontaneous Abortion — Natural expulsion from the uterus of a conceptus that cannot survive outside the womb; also called miscarriage.

Teratogenic — Capable of causing birth defects.

Ultrasound — Prenatal medical procedure using high-frequency sound waves to detect fetus, judge gestational age, detect multiple pregnancies, detect abnormalities or death of the fetus, and determine whether the pregnancy is progressing normally.

Zygote — One-celled organism resulting from the union of sperm and ovum.

"Monday's child is fair of face,

Tuesday's child is full of grace,

Wednesday's child is full of woe,

Thursday's child has far to go,

Friday's child is loving and giving,

Saturday's child works hard for a living,

But the child born on the Sabbath day

Is happy and wise and good and gay."   —Anonymous

Chapter 3

Stage Theories of Human Development

Much of the literature that has been written on the topic of human development has been based on what is known as the stage theory. Before discussing the various stage theories that will be used during the rest of this text as a framework for understanding the process of human development, a word or two needs to be said about the broader beliefs involved in the study of the entire subject.

There are three major theoretical backgrounds concerning human development. These backgrounds involve the internal and external influences that affect the whole process. These influences are:

Heredity refers to the inborn biological endowments that people inherit from the genes of their parents. The reader will remember that the embryo/fetus receives a set of 23 chromosomes from each parent and from the 46 combined chromosomes will develop certain physical, intellectual and emotional characteristics that have been determined by the particular combination of genes from each parent. In the field of human development this is called **nature**.

Environmental Influences are the non-inherited influences that have an effect on development and which are attributable to the experiences that the individual has with the world outside the self. This type of influence is referred to as **nurture**.

The third approach to studying influences that affect human development is actually a combination of both of the other two. The question is not whether nature or nurture affects development, but which plays the greater part. Some researchers have spent many years of their lives trying to develop a program that would insure certain outcomes in human development. B. F. Skinner (1905-1991), for example, devoted many years in an effort to develop a pure environment in which an infant could be raised (known as the Skinnerian Box) without the negative influences of a harsh world. Needless to say, the experiment was a complete failure.

Early research into human development and human behavior that was conducted by such men as John Locke (1632-1704), Jean Jacques Rousseau (1712-1788), Charles Darwin (1809-1882), and the pioneer in the field of the development of intelligence, Jean Piaget (1896-1980), was for the most part based on pure and simple observation of a very small population. Rousseau based his theories of human development on a work of fiction he wrote entitled *Emile*.

Locke's, (an environmentalist) philosophy, though still considered by many as sound, was obviously based somewhat on a religious idealism. Crain (1985. p. 5) quotes Locke as saying, "It seems plain to me that the principle of all virtue and excellence lies in a power of denying ourselves the satisfaction of our own desires, where reason does not authorize them." His concepts included self-control, the use of rewards and punishments and the need to consider the **temperament** of children. Children have all found their way into modern-day concepts of child rearing. The whole idea of **behavior modification** stems from these early suppositions.

Locke's concept of ***tabla rasa*** (newborn children are like a blank slate) seems to be discounted in most of the ideas that he espoused in his writings, especially the concept that children are born with a particular type of temperament.

Rousseau, on the other hand, was considered a Romantic Naturalist. His ideas were expressed in his book about a young boy, Emile, whom he raised in a large home with what he considered a perfect environment for learning. Emile was exposed to all of the best in literature, music, science and other disciplines. He was not made to study at any prescribed course or program but was allowed to explore and investigate at his own pace and level of interest. It was only then that Rousseau, his main instructor, would step in and assist in the learning process.

A well-known educational system was developed by Maria Montessori (1870-1952) that persists, with some modifications, to this day and is known as the Montessori School. The major theory behind Rousseau and Montessori was that if children were permitted to learn at their own pace, in an educational and cultural environment, they would by natural initiative and drive, learn and grow in a most positive way.

In this chapter the various theories of development in the areas of personality, emotions, intelligence, morality, sexuality, socialization, and language will be presented in an abbreviated form. Later chapters will apply these theories to the various age groups discussed.

Theorists, with the exception of Piaget and a few others, would agree that the stage theory is simply a convenient way of studying human development. A more rigorous stage theory would include the following characteristics:

1) The stages will always be in an **invariant sequence**. People will progress through the stages at different rates, but they will always progress in order from the first stage to the second, etc. Some people may never progress through all of the stages, but will nevertheless progress at the invariant sequence.

2) The stages are divided into **qualitatively** different periods. There is a distinct quality of difference between the stages.

3) The stages refer to **general characteristics**, rather than more specific characteristics.

4) The stages represent hierarchic integration. The lower stages do not disappear once the individual has passed into a higher stage.

5) The stages unfold in the same way in all **cultures**. Piaget would say that children in India would develop intelligence in the same way that children in America would. Children in the ghetto would develop intellectually in the same sequence as other children. However, it was discovered some years ago that the reason black children in the ghettos did not seem to do as well on standardized intelligence tests as children from a more rural area was not because they were not as intelligent, but that they were culturally deprived of the environmentally richer surrounding of the other children.

For the most part, the bulk of this course will be studied against the pattern of Erik Erikson's eight stage theory of development. His theory covers the longest period of human life (from birth to old age). A more thorough look at his theory of the 8 stages of development will be presented last in this chapter.

Sigmund Freud (1856-1939)

Considered to be the father of modern psychology, Freud, in spite of the many flaws in his research, made a significant contribution to the study of human development and human behavior. Freud is considered by many to be a giant upon whose shoulders others have stood to see into the future of the science of human development.

Freud's **psychoanalytic** theory produced a stage theory of **psychosexual development**. His earlier work had to do with the term **hysteria** which was applied to physical ailments as well as losses of memory for which there was no physiological explanation. These early theories eventually led to the concept of psychosomatic illness, which many well-known authorities believe to be the cause of 70-80% of all illness. Brand (1980) suggests that the percentage of medical problems seen by physicians could be as much as 100% psychosomatic.

Freud's Stage Theory

Stage one was called the **Oral Stage** (Birth to 12-18 Months) which involves the lips, tongue and mouth. Freud (1920, p. 323) believed that if the infant could express itself it would acknowledge that the act of sucking at its mother's breast was the most important aspect of life. There can be no doubt that one of the very first reflexes that is noticed in an infant is the desire to suck.

Freud referred to the pleasure sucking reflex as autoerotic. Freud postulated that the autoerotic activities were not confined to the oral stage. That is what got him into trouble with some of his contemporaries such as Carl Jung (1875-1961) and Alfred Adler (1870-1937), both of whom developed theories of personality development that differed, but showed some of the early influence of Freud.

Stage two. Freud called his second stage of development the **Anal stage** (18 Months to 3 years) or as it is sometimes called the muscular anal stage. This is the time when the anal zone becomes the main focus of the child's sexual interest. According to Freud the child becomes increasingly aware of the pleasurable sensations that bowel movements bring to the mucous membranes of the anal region.

It seems reasonable to assume that one of the reasons Freud came to this conclusion is that it is at this age that children tend to play with and smear their feces, which in turn prompts parents to resort to rather rigorous potty training.

Some children resist this dramatic training effort and deliberately soil themselves. This rebellion can lead to wastefulness, disorderly, and messy traits, which sometime persist into adulthood as aspects of the "anal expulsive" character (Hall, 1954, p. 108; Brown, 1949).

Occasionally, a child will rebel by not wanting to release the feces because they have been programmed to think that it was nasty, smelly and dirty. The resultant personality disorder called "anal compulsive" refers to individuals who have an abnormal need to be clean and neat. They also tend to hold on to resentments over having to submit to authority.

Freud's stage three is the **Phallic or Oedipal Crisis** (3 to 6 Years). This stage is also referred to as the **Locomotor Genital**. It is at this stage that Freud introduced the oedipal complex in which a boy starts to take an interest in his penis. The stage is called oedipal because it is believed that the boy's main sexual attraction is his mother, although he is gener-ally interested in the sex organs of all females.

Girls experience a similar set of feelings, except toward the male sex, especially the father. Both boys and the girls at this age may go through times of disappointment with the parent of the same sex. Feelings of jealousy toward the parent of the opposite sex occur because of the attention given to the parent in which they have become sexually interested. It must be noted that the sexual feelings are not similar to the sexual feeling experienced by the adolescent or adult.

The Latency Stage, which lasts from about ages six to 11 years, is just what the name implies. Freud said that by this age the child has succeeded in suppressing the sexual and aggressive feelings and has them firmly stored in the unconscious.

Sigmund Freud's last stage was called **The Genital Stage** (or Puberty). Erikson noted that the latency "is only the lull before the storm of puberty" (Erikson, 1959, p. 88).

Freud felt that after puberty the individual's main concern was to free himself from his parents (1920).

Freud wrote little about adolescence. It was his daughter, Anna Freud, who carried on and made a significant contribution about this age group.

Freud may well be the one person most responsible for the modern day rash of pop psychology that tends to trace all psychological problems to the immoral acts of abuse suffered at the hands of parents which had been repressed into the unconscious.

Freud also introduced the concept of **fixation and regression** that suggests that each individual will go through the oral stage as well as every other stage of psychosexual development, and that we can become **fixated at any stage**. This means that no matter how far we may progress beyond a stage, we will continue to have a lasting preoccupation with the stage at which we had become fixated or stuck.

Psychocognitive Stages

Jean Piaget (1897-1980) is considered to be the most important theorist with regard to the development of intelligence. His main, early conclusion was that children were not less intelligent than adults; they simply thought in entirely different ways.

In order to find the answers to how children's thinking was different than adults, he stopped using a standardized test and developed an "open-ended" clinical interview format. He spent many hours observing children. He worked at the Rousseau Institute in Geneva where he established his research efforts in 1921. He interviewed primarily children from ages four to 12 years.

In 1925, his first daughter, Jacqueline, was born which led to an important series of studies on the cognitive behavior of infants. This study was continued with the help of his wife, on the next two children, Lucienne and Laurent. He later continued his studies with other children and adolescents. Many other researchers in the study of intelligence had problems with Piaget's methods. Piaget's crisis in his early life was due, in part, to his early religious training and philosophical beliefs that lacked a scientific foundation. His own research lacked most of the scientific principles he seemed to value.

The developmental stages in Piaget's theory are somewhat complex, and only a summary reference will be made at his point. The serious student of the development of intelligence and the processes of thinking should refer directly to his writings. (Piaget, J. *The Language and Thought of a Child.* New York: Consultant's Bureau, 1923). There are many other books by Piaget that can be found in any college library, although a second great work is *The Child's Conception of the World.* NJ.; Littlefield, Adams and Co. 1926.

Piaget's General Stages of Development

Period I. **Sensorimotor Intelligence** (birth to two years). Babies organize their physical action schemes, such as sucking, grasping, and hitting for dealing with the immediate world.

Period II. **Preoperational Thought** (two to seven years). Children learn to think - to use symbols and internal images - but their thinking is unsymmetrical and illogical. It is always different from that of adults.

Period III. **Concrete Operations** (seven to 11 years). Children develop the capacity to think symmetrically but only when they can refer to concrete objects and activities.

Period IV. **Formal Operations** (11 to Adulthood). Young people develop the capacity to think symmetrically on a purely abstract and hypothetical plane. More detailed illustrations of each of the stages will be used in the chapters that deal with the particular age group.

Although Piaget insisted that his stages unfolded in an invariant sequence (in the same order), he was not, as some believe, a matu-rationist. The maturationist believes that the sequence is tied to the genes and that the stages unfold on a regular timetable. Piaget, on the other hand, would insist that his stages were not genetically determined but were learned by the infant's interaction with his environment.

Moral Development

For the purposes of this text, two authors in the field of Moral De-velopment will be noted. There are many other researchers and authors that can be referred to by the interested student. The following two were considered among the best.

Kohlberg's Stages of Moral Development

As mentioned in the discussion of Piaget's theory, younger children think about things in an entirely different way than do older children. Younger children regard rules as fixed and absolute. "They believe that rules were handed down by adults or by God and that one cannot change them." (Crain, 1985. p. 118). Older children, on the other hand, are more relativistic. Rules are not sacred and absolute but are requirements by which adults get them to do things.

Lawrence Kohlberg (1927-1987) used a core sample of 72 boys from both middle and lower-class families in Chicago. They ranged in age from 10 to 16 years. He later added some younger children.

Using a story about a fictional character, Heinz, he tells the children the story of how Heinz steals some medicine from a druggist who refuses to help him. Heinz is poor and unable to pay for the drug that his dying wife desperately needs. From the answers given by the boys, Kohlberg constructed a six stage theory of moral development.

Level I — Preconventional Morality

Stage 1 — Obedience and Punishment Orientation

At this stage the children felt that Heinz should be punished because he broke the rules which must be unquestioningly obeyed. Heinz was wrong because "It's against the law," or "it's bad to steal." Some of the children, however, could reason that it was all right for Heinz to take the medicine, because he first asked and was refused.

Stage 2 — Individualism and Exchange

It is at this stage children feel that there is not only one right view that is handed down by the authorities. In this stage of thinking, everything is relative (shades of situational ethics). Both stages talk of punishment, but in the first stage it is tied to the wrongfulness of the act, while in stage II, punishment is simply a risk that one naturally wants to avoid.

Level II — Conventional Morality

Stage 3 — Good Interpersonal Relationships

At this stage children usually see morality as more than simple ideals. They believe that people should live up to the expectations of the family and community and behave "good." Crain (1985) says that this stage states that "Good behavior means having good motives and interpersonal feelings such as love, empathy, trust, and concern for others." These children would argue that Heinz was right in stealing the medicine, because the druggist was not acting in a truly compassionate manner.

Stage 4 — Maintaining Social Order

This level of morality has to do with what is best for society as a whole. The emphasis now is on obeying the law and respecting authority. This level of morality says, "What would happen if everyone did what they thought was right without any concern for the rights of others?"

Level III — Post-conventional Morality

Stage 5 — Social Contract and Individual Rights

This level of morality would say, "It is the husband's duty to save his wife. The fact that her life is in danger transcends every other standard you might use to judge his actions. Life is more important than property (Crain, 1985. p.123).

Stage 6 — Universal Principles

This stage suggests that we need to (a) protect certain individual rights and (b) settle disputes through democratic process. However, at this level there is some question about just what democratic process may entail.

Jack Wintz, editor, (1987) summarizes the discussion of stages of faith in the following manner. The student may wish to compare them with those offered by Kohlberg. (See also Benner, D. G. Ed. *Baker Encyclopedia of Psychology*. Grand Rapids: Baker Book House. 1985.)

Stage 1 — Imaginative Faith (until about the age of seven)

Stage 2 — Literal Faith (Early Years of School)

Stage 3 — Group Faith (Adolescent and Early Adulthood)

Stage 4 — Personal faith (Adults)

Stage 5 — Mystical Faith (Middle Adults)

Stage 6 — Sacrificial Faith (Older Adults)

Fowler (1981) suggested the following Six Stages of Faith:

Stage One — Intuitive-Projective

This early stage is a fantasy filled, imitative phase. The child can be powerful and permanently influenced by other models and their visible faith.

Stage Two — Mythic-Literal

This is the stage in which the individual begins to make personal the beliefs, observations, and stories that symbolize belonging to his or her community support system.

Stage Three — Synthetic-Conventional

At this level the individual reaches a coherent orientation in the midst of a more complex and diverse range of involvement. It synthesizes values and information; it provides a basis for identity and outlook. Also, it is a conformist stage in that it is acutely tuned to the expectations and judgments of others and does not yet have enough independence to construct and maintain an autonomous perspective.

Stage Four — Individualistic-Reflective

This stage is marked by a double development. The self, previously sustained in its identity and faith by a network of significant others, now claims an identity no longer built by the composite of one's role or meaning to others.

Stage Five — Conjunctive

This stage involves the integration of much of that which was suppressed or unrecognized in the interest of stage 4's self-certainty. Faith in this stage reunites symbolic power with conceptual meaning.

Stage Six — Universalizing

Here the issue is the making real and tangible the "imperatives of absolute love and justice" of which stage 5 has partial apprehensions. Stage 6 engages in spending and being spent for the transformation of present reality in the direction of transcendent actuality.

In any of these stages progress or retardation can be affected by the quality of the community of which one is a part.

Physical Development

The physical stages of development will be discussed in each of the following chapters. Because there has been so much written about the various stages of physical development it would be of little value to attempt to include even a few at this time. The last of the stage theories to be included in this chapter is that of Erik Erikson. The rest of the text will be written in reference to this theory. In addition, the remaining chapter will from time to time refer to the **Psycho-affective Stages** developed by Jersild but will not detail the stage theory of this equally important researcher in this chapter.

Psychosocial Stages Erik Erikson (1902 - 1994)

Erik H. Erikson's most important work is *Childhood and Society* (1950). His main contribution was to show that the stage theory of psychosocial development is the same across cultures. The fact that Erikson carried out his studies to include development from birth to old age makes his work of greater interest than perhaps any other single researcher.

Erikson believed that there were eight stages of development and that each stage had certain crucial developmental qualities and values that played a great part in the future personality of the individual. He agreed with all of the concepts mentioned earlier about the characteristics of a true stage theory. He believed that the stages unfold in an invariant sequence in any and all cultures. In each of the stages, Erikson believed that there were certain encounters between the individual's maturing ego and the social world.

Stage I — Oral Sensory Stage (Birth to 2 Years)

The encounters at this stage have to do with **Basic Trust vs Mistrust**. This is a period of total dependence and a need for initial bonding. The infant expects the world around him to meet all of his basic needs: feeding, changing, and especially the security of tactile comfort from the primary care takers. Without this tactile comfort an infant cannot survive. The prime virtue of this stage is **Hope**. The child either learns that he can trust his environment, or he may simply lose hope and develop a basic mistrust that can affect the rest of his life.

Stage II — Muscular Anal (Age 2-3 years)

This is the period that is often referred to as the "terrible two's" because of the emerging need of the child to explore his world and be free to experiment with his new freedom. Erikson called the encounter of this stage as **Autonomy vs Shame and Doubt**. If the child is successful in gaining a certain amount of autonomy and is successful in accomplishing certain tasks he will develop normally. However, if the child is continually thwarted in his efforts at autonomy he will experience shame and guilt that may well affect his efforts to accomplish goals in later life. This can be called a period of separation and individuation, because the child, although not wanting to be completely separated from the primary care taker, wants to be on his own to some extent. The independence that is so desired very often results in the dreaded "NO!" syndrome so hated by mothers. Erikson points out, however, the importance of the emergence of the child's own personality. The virtue of the period is **will**. The child is learning to exercise his own "free" will.

Stage III — Locomotor Genital (Age 3-5 Years)

Initiative vs Guilt are the concerns faced by the child at this stage of development. This is the time of self-motivation. He has a real desire to please others, especially his significant others. A child at this stage begins to make plans, set goals, and persevere in attaining them (Crain, 1985 p. 166). In Freudian terms this is the Phallic (Oedipal) Stage when the child's interest in the anal zone gives way to the primacy of the genital zone. The virtue of this stage is **purpose**.

Stage IV — Latency (Age 6-12 Years).

The prevailing encounters of this age group are that of **Industry vs Inferiority**. This is the stage at which the child tries very hard to accomplish tasks that have been set out for him. This time of life corresponds to the later elementary grades in school. The child is project oriented and has a great need to do well, because the doing verifies the being.

Hero worship is very common at this stage. In terms of social issues, it is important that children at this stage have the right kinds of heroes to admire.

This is also the stage when a child begins to develop a concrete view of God and a true sense of sin. Most teachers find this age group an absolute delight with which to work. The virtue of this age group is **Competence**. Continued failure can and does sow the seeds of feelings of inferiority and low self-image.

Stage V — Puberty and Adolescence (Age 12-18 Years)

These are usually turbulent years for the child as well as the mother and father (and often the other siblings in the family). The stage is characterized by conflicting emotions, hormonal imbalances and noticeable physical changes that may keep the child in a constant stage of confusion and often despair. The encounter that Erikson suggests for this age group is **Identity vs Role Confusion**.

The physical changes alone can cause concern as the boy notices things happening to parts of his body that set him off from some of his friends. Girls have as difficult a time dealing with the sudden growth of their breasts and menstruation, which can be a most frightening experience for some. Not all teens suffer in the same way. With proper guidance, much of the trauma can be eased.

Children at this stage begin finding their own values. The new values may not differ to any great extent from the values of the adults in their lives, but there seems to be a need for the adolescent to feel that the values he begins to hold are his or her own. He or she also needs to know that they fit into the value scheme of their peers.

This is also a time when the established norms are challenged and authority figures are often seen as the enemy.

A confusion of relationship with the father in this stage can result in severe role confusion and doubts and fears about sex identity. It is thought by some that the seeds of homosexuality are sown during this stage because of the lack of a good relationship with the father. The virtue of this stage is **Fidelity**.

Stage VI — Young Adulthood (Age 19-25 Years)

This is the stage when an individual must deal with the concepts of **Intimacy vs Isolation**. The virtue of this stage is **love**. The individual begins to think of such things as marriage and commitment and perhaps family. A new concept of love comes on the scene. The hormonal sensations that were thought to be love only a short while ago now begin to represent caring and concern for another person. This is often followed by a strong desire to spend the rest of one's life with that person. This can be a time of Hope vs Despair when the situation is such that the individual is not able to give himself or herself to intimacy.

Stage VII — Adulthood (Age 35-55 Years)

The adult in this stage has to deal with **Generativity vs Stagnation**. When life goals are set and progress is made toward those goals, there is a feeling of success and happiness. However, if the goals are set and not met for a number of years, the individual begins to develop a feeling of stagnation. "Is that all there is," becomes a nagging fear that often leads to serious problems in marriages, in work or career situations. The virtue of this stage is **Care**.

Stage VIII — Maturity (Ages Over 65)

The one age group that has been most neglected over the years is the elderly. This is not true in all cultures, but in most countries the elderly are a necessary problem that many wish would simply go away. It is only in the past few years that some serious attention has been given to such issues as elder abuse, death and dying and the scourge of old age, Alzheimer's disease.

Erikson says that the encounter of this stage is **Ego Integrity vs Despair** and that the virtue of old age is **Wisdom**.

This is the time of life when an individual must either find a valid reason for his or her existence or they will surely slip into that abyss called despair. There seems to be a need to feel that one is leaving something of value behind that will in some way be a continuance of one's self.

Soren Kierkegaard wrote about the sickness unto death in his book *Fear and Trembling*. He felt that the sickness unto death was a sickness of the spirit. When the spirit of man loses any reason to live, there is only one possible conclusion.

Erikson did not intend to suggest that man should live forever, but that man's life would be happier and perhaps a little longer if there was a valid reason to live that made life meaningful.

This present chapter has only touched on the significance of the ideas put forth by these theorists, but space and time will not permit a more extensive presentation in this book. However, in each of the chapters dealing with a particular stage of development, an application of each of the issues and virtues will be presented.

Before leaving this chapter and turning to the Personal Reflections, the author would be remiss if some of the other great and near-great researchers and writers in the field of human development were not at least noted.

Arnold Gesell (1880-1961) developed a theory that behavior unfolds according to Nature's inner plan or timetable. His was a classic example of maturation as an approach to human development. He also developed one of the first tests of infant intelligence and was one of the first researchers to make extensive use of film observations.

Gesell believed that a child is the product of his environment, but that a more fundamental fact is that the child's development is directed from within, by action of the genes. Crain (1985) noted that Gesell believed that "Maturation, then, refers to the process by which development is governed by intrinsic factors — principally the genes, which are chemical substances contained within the nucleus of each cell. The genes de-termine the sequence timing, and form of emerging action-patterns."

One further interesting point regarding Gesell's contribution to the science of human development is the concept he called **Reciprocal Interweaving**. He believed that humans are built on a bilateral basis; we have two hemispheres of the brain, two eyes, two hands, two legs, and so on. Some of the ideas that have appeared in recent years concerning the differences in personality, because of the dominance of one hemisphere of the brain over the other, most likely got their start with the work of Gesell.

Another important contribution was made by John Bowlby (1907- 1990) whose major contribution has to do with the theory of attachment. He posited that there were four basic levels of attachment. They are:

Phase 1 (birth to three months) Indiscriminate Responsiveness to humans.

Phase 2 (three to six months) Focusing on Familiar People.

Phase 3 (six months to three years) Active Proximity-seeking.

Phase 4 (three years to the end of childhood) Partnership Behavior.

Bowlby saw attachment as **Imprinting**, the same as is found in animals. The implications of his research is far reaching in relation to modern thought about bonding in the early months of life.

Another important contribution of Bowlby had to do with the effects of institutional care. Infants raised in an institution suffer from what Bowlby called "institutional deprivation" resulting in a failure to imprint or bond.

He noted that there was a period beyond which the process could not be reversed.

A reference was made to C.G. Jung (1875-1961) earlier in this chapter, but an additional reference needs to be made. Jung was one of the very few researchers who concerned himself with adult life. Although many Christians have some problems with the teachings of Jung, there are some positives that can help the student of human development understand some of the psychological phenomena that cannot be under-stood in any other way.

Jung introduced the concept of a "universal consciousness" wherein individuals of all periods of history and from every walk of life share in some form of quest for psychic wholeness.

One of Jung's major contributions was the idea that all human beings have some male and some female qualities to their personality. He referred to this as the **Anima and Animus**, or as the Chinese Taoists speak, the Yin and the Yang. Jung concluded that all humans are bisexual.

Although Jung broke with his early mentor, Freud, there remains much of the Freudian tradition in Jung's ideas. Most psychologists felt that his ideas were too mystical. For example, he believed in ESP and related phenomena (Jung 1961. P. 190). One of his best works, *Modern Man in Search of a Soul*, is still considered worthwhile reading.

Noam Chomsky (1928-) is worthy of mention, mainly because of his work in the study of language development. The reader is referred to his book, *Language and Mind*, published by Harcourt Brace Jovanovich in New York. There are also a number of other books and articles that would be of interest to those who wish to study the development of language.

There are many others who have made major contributions to the subject of human development such as A. R. Jersild who worked primarily in the field of education; A. Maslow whose work in the dynamics of human motivation is considered monumental; W. Damon (1962) who worked primarily in the area of social and personality development, and many others.

There is one more theorist, however, that needs some special attention because of the impact of his work on the entire field of personality development and the treatment of emotional problems. That man is Theodore Millon whose research led to the development of the DSM III: Axis II, the official source of reference for the diagnosis of *Disorders of Personality*. The reason his work is so important is that he has been able to connect certain personality traits (and disorders) to parental styles.

His eight personality styles are almost, if not completely, inclusive. A brief review is all that can be presented here, but it would be well worth the time for the student of human development, especially with regard to personality development, to seek out and study at length the work of this giant in the field of personality.

Millon's Personality Scale

Millon lists the following eight personality styles:

1. **Detached Passive** — This individual needs distance. His social style is indifference or asocial, and his self-image is complacent. This personality style is the result of a parental style of neglect. The neglect this person suffered as a child made it necessary for him to "go it alone." He doesn't need others in his life.

2. **Detached Active** — This individual needs protection. His social style is that of avoidance, and his self-image is one of alienation. Millon suggests that this personality style is the result of a parenting style of rejection.

3. **Dependent Passive** — This person needs attachment and with his social style of submission they tend to latch onto one other individual at a time. Their attachment may resemble the "fatal attraction" syndrome. This personality style comes from a parental style of over-protection. This child was not allowed to think or act for himself.

4. **Dependent Active** — This personality type is quite unique. From the age of birth to eighteen months there tends to be adequate parental bonding, except the word "no" never really meant no. Boundaries in relationships were never clearly established. These people usually have a tremendous need to have someone else's approval. They tend to be the charmer and the life of the party with many relationships, but they do not tend to form lasting bonds. They develop very superficial relationships. This person exhibits a histrionic or hysterical type of personality and behavioral style. In Millon's terms, the need of this person is for approval. The social style is gregarious, and they see themselves as sociable. This style of personality is the result of an over submissive parental style.

5. **Independent Passive** — The basic need of these individuals is self-gratification with a social style of narcissism. They have a self-image of seeing themselves as admirable.
This personality style is one in which things in life become most important, and these individuals tend to be led about by their impulses. As children grow up with virtually all of their needs met, they tend to feel very good about themselves, except that they tend also to be rather self- absorbed. Because they have always received everything that they might want, they tend to become angry when someone refuses them or says "no." They are the result of an over-indulgent parental style.

6. **Independent Active** — The basic need here is that of power. They are the product of a parental style of domination. The child is criticized at a very early age and grows up believing there are only winners and losers that one either dominates or is dominated. They strive,

therefore, to win over or dominate others. They are considered independent because they do not bond or create close relationships, and they are willing to get the job done, whatever the cost. These people often become the dictators of the world. Their self-image is one of assertiveness, with a social style of aggressiveness.

7. **Ambivalent Passive** — These people need to have control. Their social style is conforming, and their self-image is conscientious. They could easily fit into the characteristics of the Pharisees in the Bible. They have a feeling that they must measure up to the full measure of the law and tend to be the nicest people and the best of friends. They do everything that people expect of them, because they have a need to be perfect. With a parental style of perfectionism it is easy to see why these individuals become the way they are.

8. **Ambivalent Active** — Here the need is resistance. The social style is negativistic and the self-image is discontented. All of this coming from a parental style of over coercion. These people tend to be independent on the outside but very dependent on the inside. They tend to offend others during their first five minutes of contact. They tended to get a certain amount of resistance when they were young, such as a nagging mother. They may have received important bonding, but still have difficulty with relationships. There are many positive aspects to their personality, once one is able to wade through their normal resistance and hostility.

An easier definition of some of the terms used above may help the reader to better understand the concepts.

- Passive — non-initiating in relationships

- Active — initiation in relationships

- Detached — active and passive

- Dependent — focus on others

- Independent — focus against others

- Ambivalent — a mixture of focus

It is important to note that these descriptions are clinical generalizations, and that no one individual is a "pure" personality type according to these theories.

Human Development

Research Methods

How human development is studied is of real importance. Much of the early research had very little scientific method to it. It is a wonder that some of the early theory proved to be so accurate. A theory is a set of related statements about data, most of the information obtained through research. Theories are important in helping scientists to explain, interpret, and predict behavior. Theories help scientists find a coherent structure in the data.

Theories help researchers to form hypothesis to guide further research, to explain certain phenomenon and are used to predict the outcome of an experiment. Theories, hypotheses, and further research depends on the various methods of study conducted. The term "scientific method" refers to certain underlying principles that characterize scientific inquiry in any field. Careful observation, recording of data, testing of alter-native hypotheses or different alternatives for the data, and wide spread dissemination of the findings and conclusions are all a part of this process. This helps other observers learn from, analyze, repeat, and build on the results. There are various techniques used in research. The following are called non-experimental methods.

Non-experimental methods

Case Studies — Case studies are studies of a single case or individual life. Much of the support for Freudian theory comes from the use of case studies. Freud kept careful notes on each of his patients and then drew conclusions from the interpretation of those notes. The earliest data on the development of infants comes mostly from this type of study.

Naturalistic Observation — In this method of study, researchers observe subjects and record their behavior in their real life settings (pre-school, nursing home, etc.). No effort is made to manipulate the environment or to alter behavior. This type of study is to gain norms for various behaviors.

Clinical Studies — The clinical method combines observation with flexible, individualized questioning. Piaget developed this method to find out how children think. This method is tailor-made for each individual as opposed to the use of standardized tests.

Interview Method — In this method, instead of being observed, the subjects are interviewed and asked to directly state their attitudes and opinions. This method requires the interviewing of large numbers of people in order to be able to get a broad picture of what the people being interviewed say they believe.

Correlation Studies — Correlation studies show the direction and magnitude of a relationship between variables. The point is to see whether two or more variables relate positively or negatively. Correlations are reported as numbers ranging from -1.0 (a perfect negative, or inverse, relationship) to +1.0 (a perfect positive, or direct relationship). The higher the number + or - the stronger the relationship.

Experimental Methods

An experimental method is a rigorously controlled procedure in which the researcher, called the experimenter, manipulates variables to determine how one affects another.

Variables and Groups — In an experimental study, the experiment would have an independent variable and a dependent variable (sometime more than one). The independent variable is the one over which the experimenter has direct control. The dependent variable is the characteristic that may or may not change as a result of changes in the independent variable.

Sampling and Assignment — In the experimental study it is necessary to start with a sample population that is representative of the entire population. An experiment done with a sample of upper socio-economic class males would not produce results that could be applied to children living in the ghetto. The sample should also be a random sample, meaning that each member of the population has an equal chance of being selected. Next the random sample is to be randomly assigned to either experimental or control groups.

Types of Experiments

There are three principal types of experiment: those conducted in the laboratory; those conducted in the field; and those that make use of naturally occurring experiences.

The matter of conducting experiments with human beings in the process of development is complicated by the fact that the experiments would normally take a lifetime to complete.

Personal Reflections

After many years of study and work in the field of human behavior and human development, I can honestly say that there are some real truths in all of the theories mentioned in this chapter. It is equally true that some of the material presented by most of the researchers must be "taken with a grain of salt."

I did not include a discussion of the humanistic theory of the development of the person because of the strong resistance to any mention of the term humanism. I must admit however, that I have found some very important insights in the work and writings of men such as Abraham Maslow (1954 and 1968) and C. Buhler (1933 & 1968).

In 1962, a group of psychologists founded the Association of Humanistic Psychology. The reason for the formation of the new association was in protest to what they considered to be the essentially negative beliefs underlying behaviorist and psychoanalytic theories.

This new breed maintained that human nature is either neutral or good and that any bad characteristics are the result of damage that has been inflicted on the developing self. The fact that these psychologists viewed people as being able to take charge of their lives and foster their own development, made it easier for me to accept some of the findings they presented. I do not in any way accept what has come to be known as "secular humanism."

Any truth about human development and human behavior should be tested in every way possible. I believe that too much of our un-derstanding of the nature of adolescence, for example, is based on either ignorance of pure religion taboos. Just to suggest this possibility would cause some people to conclude that I am in some way saying the all religious taboos are wrong. This is simply not the case. I do believe that each and every belief is subject to research. If our faith or our political convictions cannot stand up under objective research, there may be something wrong with those convictions.

In my opinion there is a need for more Christian counselors to become involved in research concerning human development and human behavior. It is one thing to minister to those who are hurting, but there is a need to seek for more knowledge and wisdom concerning the reasons for their hurts.

Review for Chapter 3

- The three major theoretical approaches to studying human development are: Heredity, Environmental influences, and a combination of the first two.

- Locke was a pure environmentalist.

- Rousseau was considered a romantic naturalist.

- Maria Montessori developed an educational program based primarily on the environmental philosophy.

- This chapter deals with the various theorists and their theories of human development.

- All of the theorists would agree that the stage theory is simply a convenient way of studying human development.

- Characteristics of a rigorous stage theory include the following characteristics:

    1. The stages will always be in an invariant sequence.
    2. The stages are divided into qualitatively different periods.
    3. The stages refer to general characteristics rather than specific ones.
    4. The stages represent hierarchic integration.
    5. The stages unfold in the same way in all cultures.

- Sigmund Freud was considered as the father of modern psychology.

- Freud theory of development consisted of five major stages.

    1. Oral stage
    2. Anal stage
    3. Phallic or Oedipal stage
    4. The Latency stage
    5. The Genital stage

- Freud wrote very little about adolescence. This was left to his daughter, Anna.

- The most important concepts that Freud offered were fixation and regression.

- Freud believed that a person could become fixated at any of the stages.

Stage Theories of Human Development

- Freud also believed that a person could regress to an earlier stage later in life.
- Jean Piaget presented the most important work in the area of intellectual development or cognition.
- Piaget's general stages of development are:
  - Period I. Sensorimotor intelligence
  - Period II. Preoperational Thought
  - Period III. Concrete Operations
  - Period IV. Formal Operations
- Kohlberg presented a stage theory that dealt with moral development.
- Kohlberg's theory is as follows:
- Level I Preconvention Morality
  - Stage 1. Obedience and Punishment Orientation
  - Stage 2. Individualism and Exchange
- Level II Conventional Morality
  - Stage 3. Good Interpersonal Relationships
  - Stage 4. Maintaining Social Order
  - Stage 5. Social Contract and Individual Rights
  - Stage 6. Universal Principles
- Jack Wintz suggested 6 stages of development of faith:
  - Stage 1. Imaginative Faith
  - Stage 2. Literal Faith
  - Stage 3. Group Faith
  - Stage 4. Personal Faith
  - Stage 5. Mystical Faith
  - Stage 6. Sacrificial Faith
- Fowler also suggested six stages of the development of faith.
  - Stage 1. Intuitive Projective
  - Stage 2. Mythic-literal
  - Stage 3. Synthetic-conventional
  - Stage 4. Individualistic-reflective
  - Stage 5. Conjunctive

- Stage 6. Universalizing
- Erik Erikson's stages of development were called psychosocial stages and are eight in number:
  - Stage 1. Oral Sensory Stage
  - Stage 2. Muscular Anal Stage
  - Stage 3. Locomotor Genital Stage
  - Stage 4. Latency Stage
  - Stage 5. Puberty Stage
  - Stage 6. Young Adulthood
  - Stage 7. Adulthood
  - Stage 8. Maturity
- Each of Erikson's stages was identified by a definite psychosocial encounter as follows:
  1. Trust vs Mistrust
  2. Autonomy vs Shame and Doubt
  3. Initiative vs Guilt
  4. Industry vs Inferiority
  5. Identity vs Role Confusion
  6. Intimacy vs Isolation
  7. Generativity vs Stagnation
  8. Ego Integrity vs Despair
- Arnold Gesell developed a theory that he said unfolded according to nature's inner plan or timetable.
- Gesell also introduced the concept of Reciprocal Interweaving, out of which the concept of bonding developed.
- John Bowlby's major contribution had to do with the theory of attachment in infants:
  - Phase 1. Indiscriminate Responsiveness
  - Phase 2. Focusing on Familiar People
  - Phase 3. Active Proximity-seeking
  - Phase 4. Partnership Behavior
- One of Carl Jung's major contributions was the concept of Universal Consciousness.

- Noam Chomsky worked in the area of language development.
- Theodore Millon's personality scale suggested eight personality styles:
    1. Detached Passive
    2. Detached Active
    3. Dependent Passive
    4. Dependent Active
    5. Independent Passive
    6. Independent Active
    7. Ambivalent Passive
    8. Ambivalent Active
- The various experimental methods were discussed.
- Non-experimental methods
- Case studies
- Naturalistic Observations
- Clinical Studies
- Interview Method
- Correlation Studies
    - Experimental Methods
- Variables and Groups
- Sampling and Assignment
    - The three types of experimental research are:
- Laboratory
- Field research
- Natural surrounding

Glossary for Chapter 3

Glossary of Terms

Accommodation — Piagetian term for a change in an existing cognitive structure to cope with new information.

Achieving Stage — Second of Schale's five cognitive stages, in which young adults use knowledge to gain independence and competence and do best on tasks relevant to life goals they have established for themselves.

Acquired Adaptations — In Piagetian terminology, reorganized schemes for particular behavior earned by accommodation.

Adaptation — Piagetian term for effective integration with the en-vironment (problem solving) through the complementary processes of assimilation and accommodation.

Anal stage — According to Freudian theory, the psycho-sexual stage of toddlerhood (12-18 months to 3 years), in which the chief source of sensation gratification is moving the bowels; toilet training forces the child to delay this gratification.

Animism — Attribution of life to inanimate objects; according to Piaget, characteristic of Pre-operational thought.

Assimilation — Piaget's term for the incorporation of new information into an existing cognitive structure.

Attachment — Active affectionate reciprocal relationship specifically be-tween two persons (usually infant and parent), in which interaction reinforces and strengthens the link.

Authoritarian Parents — Baumrind's terminology - parents whose child-rearing style emphasizes the values of control and obedience and who use forceful punishment to make children conform to a set of standards of conduct. Compare with authoritative parents

Authoritative Parents — Parents, whose method of child-rearing blends respect for a child's individuality with an effort to instill social values in the child.

Basic Trust vs Basic Mistrust — Erikson's theory that the first critical balancing of alternatives in psychosocial development (from birth to 12-18 months), in which the infant develops a sense of whether or not the world can be trusted; the quality of interaction with mother in feeding is a primary determinant of the outcome of this stage.

Cognitive Development — Changes in thought processes that result in a growing ability to acquire and use knowledge.

Concrete Operations — Third stage of Piagetian cognitive development (about age 5-7 to age 11), during which children develop logical but not abstract thinking.

Fixation — In Freudian theory, an arrest in development that occurs be-cause a child has been gratified too much or too little during a particular psychosexual stage.

Generativity vs Stagnation — According to Erikson, the seventh critical alternative of psychosocial development in which mature adults develop concern with establishing and guiding the next generation or else experience stagnation (a sense of inactivity or lifelessness).

Gerontologists — Persons engaged in gerontology, the study of the aged and the process of dying.

Humanistic Perspective — View of humanity that sees people as having the ability to foster their own positive, healthy development through the distinctively human capacities for choice, creativity, and self-realization.

Identity vs Identity Confusion — According to Eriksonian theory, the fifth critical alternative of psychosocial development, in which an adolescent must determine his or her own sense of self (identity), including the role he or she is to play in society.

Industry vs Inferiority — Erikson's fourth critical alternative of psychosocial development, occurring during middle childhood, in which children must learn the productive skills their culture requires or else face feelings of inferiority.

Initiative vs Guilt — In Eriksonian theory this is the third psychosocial stage of development occurring between the ages of 3 and 6, in which children must balance the urge to form and carry out goals with their moral judgment about what they want to do. Children develop initiative when they try out new things and are not overwhelmed by failure.

Integrity vs Despair — Erikson's eighth and final critical psychosocial alternative is development in which people in late adulthood either accept their lives as a whole and thus accept death, or yield to despair because their lives cannot be relived.

Intimacy vs Isolation — Erikson's sixth critical alternative of psychosocial development, in which young adults either make commitments to others or face a possible sense of isolation and consequent self-absorption.

Language Acquisition Device — In Chomsky's theory, an inborn mental structure that enables children to build linguistic rules by analyzing the language they hear.

Morality of Autonomous Moral Principles — In Kohlberg's system, the highest level of moral development, normally reached after the age of 12 (if it is ever reached at all), in which people follow internally held moral principles and make choices between conflicting moral standards.

Morality of Conventional Role Conformity — Second of Kohlberg's three levels of moral reasoning, normally reached between the ages of 10-13, in which children have internalized the standards of authority figures and obey rules to please others or to maintain order.

Naturalistic Observation — Method of research in which people's behavior is studied in natural settings without the observer's intervention or manipulation.

Personality — A person's collective pattern of character, behavioral, temperamental, emotional, and mental traits.

Phallic Stage — According to Freudian theory, the stage of psychosexual development between the ages of 3 and 6 in which the child receives gratification chiefly in the genital area.

Piagetian Approach — Study of intellectual development by describing qualitative stages, or typical changes, in children's and adolescent's cognitive functioning; proposed by Piaget.

Preconvention Morality — According to Kohlberg, the first level of moral development, in which children aged approximately 4 to 10 years obey rules or standards set by others, in order to gain rewards or avoid punishment.

Programmed-aging Theory — Theory that bodies age in accordance with a normal development pattern built into every organism of a particular species; compare with wear-and-tear theory of aging.

Psychosexual Development — In Freudian theory, an unvarying sequence of stages of personality development during childhood and adolescence, in which gratification shifts from mouth to the anus and then to the genitals.

Psychosocial-Development Theory — Theory of Erik Erikson that societal and cultural influences play a major part in healthy personality development. According to this theory, development occurs in eight maturational predetermined stages throughout the life span, each revolving around a particular crisis or turning point in which the person is faced with achieving a healthy balance between alternatives of positive and negative traits.

Reaction Formation — In Freudian theory, a defense mechanism characterized by replacement of an anxiety-producing feeling by the expression of its opposite.

Reintegrate Stage — Fifth of Schale's cognitive stages, in which older people choose to focus energy on tasks that have meaning for them.

Responsible State — Third of Schale's five cognitive stages, in which middle aged people are concerned with long range goals and practical problems often related to their responsibility for others.

Sensorimotor Stage — First of Piaget's stages of cognitive development, when infants (from birth to 2 years) learn through their developing senses and motor activities.

Social-Learning Theory — Theory, proposed chiefly by Bandura, that behaviors are learned by observing and imitating models and are maintained through reinforcement.

Superego — According to Freudian theory, the aspect of personality representing values that parents and other agents of society communicate to a child. It develops around the age of 5 or 6 as a result of resolution of the Oedipus or Electra complex.

Temperament — Person's characteristic style of approaching and reacting to people and situations. Considered to be an innate character, genetic predisposition.

Tertiary Circular Reaction — A baby's purposeful variations of behavior to test novel ways of producing desired results; characteristic of the fifth sub-stage described by Piaget.

"What's done to children, they will do to society."
—Karl Menninger

Chapter 4

Ages 0-2

In Erikson's terminology, this is the period that deals with the basic issues of **Trust vs Mistrust**. In the Freudian framework, this first stage is the **Oral Sensory Stage**. This period begins with the actual birth of the infant and lasts until about 2 years of age.

Birth

Of all the wonders of the world, birth should, in the opinion of many, be listed as the greatest wonder. Anyone who has experienced, first hand, the process of the birth of a human child can testify to the wonder of such a process.

The fetus has for the past nine months been confined to the womb of the mother, floating in amniotic fluid, being nourished through the umbilical cord and rather quickly running out of living space. "In the fullness of time," to borrow a phrase from the Bible, (266 days after conception) things begin to happen. It is generally accepted that it is very important to have support during delivery, either by the husband, medical staff, or even untrained persons as they can help reduce the complications of childbirth.

There are a number of things that can happen to harm the infant and/or the mother. This text will not go into these deviations from normal birth as that is a separate study of its own. Some of the problems, however, are the result of too much or too little speed in the delivery process. One method of speeding up delivery is by use of the drug OxyContin. This and all other drugs can pass through the placenta wall and cause harm to the fetus. Normal delivery takes place in two stages.

The first stage is appropriately called labor. It is hard physical work. During labor there are three stages: 1) the cervix expands or dilates so that it will be large enough for the infant to pass through; 2) the infant passes through the birth canal and is born; 3) the placenta or "after-birth" is expelled.

Occasionally, an infant will not be able to pass through the birth canal in the proper manner. Normally, the infant passes through the canal head first. If this does not happen and the infant cannot be turned, a number of problems can occur. The physician may elect to deliver the infant by cesarean section (CS or C section), in which the delivery is made through the abdomen and the uterus is opened surgically.

There are several methods of avoiding some of the problems of delivery. Fetal monitoring is one of those ways. Fetal monitoring can be done manually with the aid of a monitoring device that records the heartbeat of the infant and of the mother. This procedure will identify any extremes of stress that the infant may be experiencing. Other methods of monitoring involve invasive techniques that can present some serious danger to mother and child.

At times, it may become necessary for the obstetrician to assist the birth with the use of instruments. Under normal circumstances, the use of instruments will not cause any serious damage. However, there is always the possibility that the use of forceps and/or vacuum extraction, may result in some disfiguring of the infant. Usually, the damage is temporary and the physical marks will disappear. Occasionally, serious damage can be done that will have a lifelong effect on the individual.

Even though the entire birth process may be considered normal and without any serious complications, there is still the trauma of birth that can have an effect on the newborn. Rank (1929) in his research reported in his book *The Trauma of Birth*, suggests that all anxiety and pleasure may originate in this experience.

In the womb there is safety and warmth. The experience is apparently peaceful (except in certain situations). During the birth process many changes take place. The struggle through the birth canal, the bright lights of the delivery room, the cold metal table used to clean and attend to the infant and the noise of the personnel in the room can all be rather traumatic.

Fortunately, many of the larger hospitals are now using birthing centers where the mother and father stay during the entire birth. These rooms are much like a family bedroom at home and are almost self-contained. Everything that will be needed is in the room. With a simple turn of a knob the bed becomes the delivery table. After the infant is born, he is not allowed out of the room until the whole family is discharged from the hospital. The father can stay in the room during the entire process and for a day or so afterwards.

Health officials believe that the trend toward birthing centers will facilitate the bonding between infant, mother and father. Freud (1936) believed that all anxiety of adult life was due to an infant being flooded with too much stimulation in the absence of adequate defense apparatus. Freud continued to add that "all efforts to reduce anxiety are efforts to return to the safety of the womb."

Most psychoanalytic theorists agree with Rank that "birth is probably the most important psychological event in life."

Birth trauma and low birth weight can influence a child's early adjustment to life outside the womb and may even exert an influence on later development. It is believed that a supportive postnatal environment can often improve the outcome and effects of birth trauma.

Low birth weight is the major factor in infant mortality. Although the infant mortality rate in the United States has improved, it is still disturbingly high, especially for black babies. Drug and alcohol can contribute to low birth weight.

Sudden infant death syndrome (SIDS) is the leading cause of death in infants between 1 month and 1 year of age, affecting some 7000 infants each year in the United States. There are many theories about the cause of SIDS, and no one theory is universally accepted.

At one minute and 5 minutes after birth, the **neonate** is assessed medically by the **Apgar scale** which measures five factors. They are appearance, pulse, grimace, activity, and respiration. These indicate how well the newborn is adjusting to extra uterine life. The neonate may also be screened for one or more medical conditions.

Other tests used to determine the state of development of an infant include **The Bayley Scale of Infant Development** and **Deavers Developmental Screening Test**.

The Brazelton Neonatal Behavior Assessment Scale may be given to assess the way a newborn baby is responding to the environment and to predict future development.

Temperament

The use of temperament, used in reference to infants, is not the same as the temperament theory used in modern terminology. However, different infants do seem to exhibit different temperaments. One test that assesses infant temperament is known as the Toddler Temperament Scale, in which parents of the infants are asked to rate the infant's activity level (AL).

The test is used more frequently with toddlers but has been used with infants as young as five months. Conclusions drawn from the tests show strong individual differences from prenatal life throughout infancy and beyond. Parents, caretakers, and scientists agree on the differences shown by this test. Data from studies of twins showed some genetic or biological basis for individual differences in activity.

Two main temperament characteristics were formulated from the studies and are emotional/distress and soothability and inhibited and uninhibited (shy - social). Much more could be said about temperament in infants, but the reader is referred to Fullard et al., 1984 for a more complete discussion on this topic. It is important, however, to note that the difference in infant temperament may well be an indication of neonatal circumstances or genetic inheritance and most likely, both. The major studies are those which followed up on infants into older childhood and even into adulthood.

A New York Longitudinal Study (NYLS) followed 133 people from early infancy into early adulthood. The researchers identified nine different aspects or components of temperament that showed up soon after birth. In general these aspects of temperament remained rather stable, though some people did show considerable change (Papalia & Olds, 1989. p. 158-159). The nine components of temperament are:

1. *Activity level* — how and how much a person moves

2. *Rhythmicity, or regularity* — the predictability of biological cycles such as hunger, sleep, and elimination.

3. *Approach or withdrawal* — how a person initially responds to a new stimulus, such as a new toy, food, or person.

4. *Adaptability* — how easily an initial response is modified in a desired direction.

5. *Threshold of responsiveness* — how much stimulation is needed to evoke a response?

6. *Intensity of reaction* — how energetically a person responds.

7. *Quality of mood* — whether a person's behavior is predominantly pleasant, joyful, and friendly, or unpleasant, unhappy, and unfriendly.

8. *Distractibility* — how easily an irrelevant stimulation can alter or interfere with a person's behavior.

9. *Attention span and persistence* — how long a person pursues an activity and continues in face of obstacles.

Three patterns of temperament emerged for the study: the easy child, the difficult child, and the slow to warm-up child. (for more on this, see Papalia and Olds, 1989, pp. 158-159).

Temperament appears to be inborn and largely genetic (Chess, 1977, 1984). There is some research, however, that suggests that it is not exclusively genetic. It is suspected that some of these differences were shaped by prenatal chemical or physiological influences on the brain. Newborns with lower levels of the enzyme **monoamnine oxidase**, are more active, more excitable and crankier than neonates with higher MAO levels (Sostek & Wyatt, 1981). The temperament of a child seems to be largely innate, but changes that take place in temperamental style may be triggered by unusual events, such as the death of a parent, and sudden emergence of a talent, or peer-induced use of drugs. (Thomas and Chase, 1984).

Temperament can affect children's adjustment in life. Excessive stress occurs when children are frequently expected to behave in ways inconsistent with their basic temperament. When parents have little influence on a baby's natural temperament style, "goodness of fit" between children's temperament and parents' expectations is important. If a mother recognizes that fussiness reflects an inborn tendency, she will be better able to accept a "difficult" child, and the child will probably be better adjusted (Papalia & Olds, 1989, p. 159).

Normal physical growth and motor development occurs in a largely preordained sequence, according to three principles:

1. The **cephalocaudal** principle, development proceeds from the head to the lower body parts.

2. The **proximodistal** principle dictates that the development is from the center of the body outward.

3. Development usually proceeds from simple to complex behavior.

The first few weeks of the infant's life are spent sleeping, feeding, crying (the infant's only means of communication), and soiling themselves. During the first few days they excrete a substance call **meconium**, which is the substance that has accumulated in the intestines while in the womb. Considerable research has been done in the area of bonding to include the father, extended family (grandparents, etc.) and other non-related care givers.

From the scientific field of ethnology (the study of animal behavior), theorists have developed the concept of bonding. Konrad Lorenz (1903-1989) and Niko Tinbergen (1907-1988), who work in Lorenz's shadow, observed that many young birds and mammals "seem to be innately disposed to follow their mother, but actually follow her because she was the first object they saw and followed during a specific time in infancy." When Lorenz raised goslings from birth, they took him for the "mother." They followed him about in a single file wherever he went, ignoring the other geese. They had **imprinted** on him (Lorenz, 1935, p.124). **Imprinting** has since been related to the concept of bonding in humans. Although there are some differences of opinion as to the total psychological impact on the infant related to **bonding**, the major opinion is that the process is of inestimable value, not only psychologically, but with respect to physical development as well.

An even more monumental research was conducted by John Harlow with young monkeys. He discovered that very young monkeys actually languished if they were denied access to a mother. In his famous experiment, Harlow created surrogate mothers constructed of mesh wire and covered with a soft cloth material. A bottle for nursing was attached to the surrogate mother and the infant monkey would accept them as they would a real mother. Even if the bottle was attached to another wire model almost out of reach, the young monkeys would cling to the surrogate model and reach over to nurse.

Although there is a certain danger in applying too completely the findings of ethnology to human development and human behavior, these findings about imprinting did lead to the research that brought understanding the importance of the bonding process.

Research done with orphans raised in institutional settings have shown that they usually develop more slowly both physically and emotionally. One of the findings of all of the research is that infants need the benefit of tactile relationship in order to develop properly. In all too many cases, before this important information was available and before the societal demands for more humane treatment of infants in certain institutions, infants actually died from the lack of human touch and attention. This type of death is referred to as **Marasmus**, a failure to thrive because of the lack of touch.

Physical Development

Breast feeding seems to offer physiological benefits to the infant. It is believed that the infant will develop some of the mother's immunities to certain diseases through ingesting the mother's natural milk. Breast feeding is also thought to facilitate the formation of the mother-infant bond. However, the quality of the relationship between mother and child is more important than the feeding method in promoting healthy development. When breast feeding causes serious pain and frustration on the part of the mother, or the infant has serious difficulty in gaining the nourishment needed because of some problem in breast feeding, the alternative use of baby formula would seem to be justified.

During the first year of the infant's life the baby grows rapidly and triples its birth weight. He becomes mobile in that he is able to move about in his or her own way (crawling, etc.). Also, during this time the baby is able to sit and stand. All of these actions indicate a constant and rapid growth and coordination of muscle and brain.

Early in the stage, birth to one month, infants exercise their inborn reflexes and gain some control over them. They do not coordinate information from their senses. They are not able to grasp an object that they are looking at. According to Piaget (1926), "they have not developed object permanence."

After this first stage, physical development begins to move very rapidly. At about 12 weeks, the baby has gained enough muscle development to support his head when in a prone position. He is able to rest on his elbows, but still may not have any noticeable **Moro** or grasping, reflex.

At sixteen weeks, the child is able to play with a rattle placed in his hands, and by the time he is 20 weeks old he can sit up with props.

By six months of age the infant is sitting. He is able to bend forward and use his hands for support. He can bear his own weight when put into a standing position but cannot yet stand while holding on. His reaching becomes unilateral. He will release one cube when handed another.

The infant can stand holding on to something by about the eighth month. He begins to show thumb opposition at this time and can pick up a small object with his thumb and finger tips. By the tenth month the child is creeping rather efficiently and can take side steps while holding on. A child can usually pull himself up to a standing position. Walking can begin between now and the twelfth month if held by the hand.

The child continues to grow and by the time he reaches the age of two years he has attained one half of its adult height.

Psychosexual Development

This beginning stage is what Freud called the Oral Stage, in which the infant's major preoccupation and source of pleasure (**autoerotic**) is "the act of sucking at his mother's breast." The sucking reflex is not, however, related only to satisfying the need for food. This can be seen in the apparent satisfaction that an infant receives from a "pacifier" substitute for the nipple, even when the infant is not hungry.

Freud also noted that because the infant's world is in an objectless state, he exists in what Freud called a state of **primary narcissism**. This occurs during the first few months.

The second part of the oral stage begins at about six months. Babies begin to develop a concept of others, especially the mother, as a **separate necessary** person. They experience separation anxiety when she leaves or when they encounter a stranger in her place (Freud, 1936a, p. 99).

At about this same time, the baby begins to develop teeth and the urge to bite. One theorist suggested that "babies dimly form the idea that it is they, with their urge to bite and devour, who can drive their mothers away (Karl Abraham (1924). Life for the infant and the mother becomes very troubling at this stage of life. Major conflicts at this stage can create long lasting problems for the infant, who longs to return to the earlier oral stage, when things seemed to be much simpler and more gratifying.

The Problem of Fixation and Regression. Freud insisted that all humans go through the oral stage and all of the other stages of psychosexual development. Problems that develop can include fixation and regression.

By fixation, Freud meant that no matter how far an individual advances beyond a stage, it is possible to continue to be lastingly preoccupied with the pleasures and issues of the earlier stage. This concept has been used to explain such habits as nail biting, sucking on pencils, biting other objects, smoking tobacco and drinking alcohol partly because of the oral pleasure involved (Freud 1905, Abraham; 1924b). It is believed by many psychoanalysts that fixation is the result of excessive frustration at the stage in question (Abraham, 1924b. p. 357). For example, an infant who is not able to receive oral gratification because of the inability of the mother to nurse could become very frustrated. As mentioned earlier, infants confined to institutions who are fed by placing a bottle in their crib and leaving them to "do the best they can" suffer significant frustration, especially without the added pleasure of a mother to hold and cuddle them while they nurse.

Adults show few oral traits until they are frustrated, at which time they may **regress** to an oral fixation point. In a later chapter, some attention will be given to such problems as overeating, binging, etc., as a probable sign of regression to the oral stage by an adult when experiencing some frustrating event in his life. It should be noted that this type of regression can occur in any "normal" adult and is not to be necessarily considered neurotic behavior.

The Anal Stage

The anal stage, suggested by Freud, actually begins at about one and a half years old and lasts until the age of three years. At this stage children become increasingly aware of the pleasurable sensations that bowel movements produce on the mucous membranes of the anal region. One of the problems that develop at this stage is that children become fascinated with the product of their own bowel and will at times play with or smear the feces.

According to Freud children will fight back at parents who try to "pottytrain" them. They do this by deliberately soiling themselves (Freud 1905, p. 59). They also can rebel by becoming wasteful, disorderly, and messy, traits that occasionally persist into adulthood, resulting in what has become known as the **anal expulsive** character trait.

Freud also noted that the opposite reaction is experienced by many children who become excessively preoccupied with cleanliness, orderliness, and reliability (1908a). These children felt it was too risky to rebel against the parent's demand. As adults, they develop a compulsive need to be clean and orderly and are referred to as **anal compulsives**. These people usually are resentful over submitting to authority and develop a passive obstinacy (sometimes called **passive-aggressive** behavior).

To the parents of children, the theories of Freud concerning this stage may present some serious considerations with regard to methods of toilet training.

Psychosocial Theory

Erik Erikson's first stage is called the Oral Sensory Stage and covers about the same period of Freud's theory, birth to 2 years. Erikson tried to add to Freud's concept by suggesting that for each **libidinal zone** there is also an **ego mode**. He also added the concept that the early part of this first stage was one of "taking in" not only by the mouth but through the eyes and ears.

Erikson considered this first stage as the most general stage with the major encounter of **Basic Trust vs Mistrust**. The main issue here is the general encounter between the child's maturing ego and the social world. The infant is looking to his social environment to meet all of his needs. The question is, "Can my world be trusted to feed me when I am hungry, change me when I am soiled, comfort me when I am hurting, keep me warm and comfortable, and let me get the sleep I need so desperately?" Erikson did not mean that the infant experienced either trust or mistrust to the exclusion of the other. Actually, infants experience some trust and some mistrust which, as Erikson would put it, "is clear that the human infant must experience a goodly measure of mistrust in order to trust discerningly..."(1976. p. 23).

Erikson sees a favorable ratio as being the most beneficial for healthy growth. If, on the other hand, the environment is more hostile or indifferent and the child's basic needs are constantly not met, the balance will swing to the mistrust side.

Because the basic virtue in this stage of development is hope, parents need to keep the daily routine of the infant on a level of continuity and consistency. A lifestyle that is very flexible can create instability and mistrust in a child. When a child does not receive the nurturing he needs, he will develop a sense of estrangement or abandonment.

According to Millon (1981), the mistrust that results from an infant's social environment can be caused by a parental style of neglect or rejection. In the case of neglect, the individuals usually develop a personality style of **Detached Passive**, in which children can develop a social style that is characterized by indifference to others. They tend to have a need to be distant from others, and their self-image is one of complacency. All of this is caused by a lack of emotional bonding.

A parental style of rejection has a similar effect on the child resulting in a personality style of **Detached Active**. These are individuals who develop a need for protection. They have a social style of avoidance and a self-image of alienation. Of course, infants, in the first stage of life, will not be able to discern cognitively the difference between neglect and rejection as such, but they will, as they move into later stages of devel-opment, recognize that something is missing in their lives. The real results of the basic mistrust may not be realized thoroughly until the child becomes an adult. In extreme cases the personality could actually become **schizoid**.

There has been considerable research in recent years concerning the effects of working mothers or single parents on infants. Many mothers return to work very soon after the birth of the baby, leaving the child in the care of some other caretaker. All of the findings are not in as yet, but there is enough evidence that children are often damaged psychosocially or emotionally by being deprived of the mother's care at too early an age. The evidence also indicates that boys are more affected than are girls.

The exceptions to the findings seem to be in cases where the infant is left in the care of close and loving grandparents, who often make better parents than the real parents do.

One further observance regarding the findings of John Bowlby (1907-1990), who developed a theory of the Phases of Attachment, needs to be mentioned before leaving the concept of bonding. Bowlby lists four phases of attachment.

Phases of Attachment

Phase 1 (birth to three months) — Indiscriminate Responsiveness to Humans. In this phase babies showed various kinds of responsiveness to people, but this responsiveness is unselective: babies react to most people in fairly similar ways.

Right after birth, babies like to listen to human voices and to look at human faces (Frantz, 1961; Freedman 1974. p. 23). In recent studies it was observed that right after birth, infants preferred to look at a human face than at a sheet or other indiscriminate object. It is during this time that the infant develops what Bowlby called the social smile that serves to stir love and attachment in the adult.

The social smile is not the same as the smile that babies less than five weeks old often present, usually just before falling asleep. These smiles are not yet social. The social smiling begins at about five weeks according to Freedman, (1974. pp. 180-81).

Phase 2 (three to six months) — Focusing on Familiar People

Beginning at about the age of three months, there is a change in many of the baby's behaviors. Reflexes including Moro, grasping, and rooting, drop away. This is the time when infants begin to restrict their smiles to the people most familiar to them. They will simply stare at strangers as a rule. This is also the stage when babies will begin to reach out and grasp on to parts of adults' bodies such as the hair, but only if they know the adult. Babies tend to attach most strongly to the individual who is most attentive to their needs and their signals (1969. pp. 306-16).

Phase 3 (six months to three years) — Active Proximity-seeking

Babies show a deep concern for the attachment figure's presence at about the age of six months. At first they can only cry in distress at the departure of the parents, but by the time they reach eight months they are able to crawl after the departing parent.

Babies become much more active in monitoring the parent's whereabouts and are constantly, through what Bowlby called a **goal-corrected system**, keeping track of where the parent is. They will occasionally move away from the attachment figure, but this behavior is one of exploring and usually ends in a hasty return (i.e., rapprochement).

Occasionally, a child will develop a pattern of attachment in which he or she rarely cries when separated from the primary caregiver and avoids contact upon the caregiver's return. The extreme of this behavior has been thought by some to be only one step away from **infantile autism**, a developmental disorder that begins within the first 2 1/2 years of life. It is characterized by a lack of ability to respond to people or situations from the beginning of life, severely impaired communications skills, and a compulsive insistence on consistency or sameness. Bruno Bettelheim referred to these children as "empty fortresses."

They avoid eye contact, in addition to not responding to visual or auditory contact. Mothers say about such children, "He was never cuddly," or "He never noticed when I came into or left his room." A fine motion picture was produced many years ago that portrayed an adult autistic individual. The film was titled, *Rain Man*.

Theories about the **etiology** of infantile Autism range from organic causes on one end of the spectrum to parent-child relationship factors on the other. There has been a tendency in the past to place the blame on certain familial interpersonal factors.

Certain diseases have also been suspected as being contributing factors. Diseases such as **maternal rubella**, **phenylketonuria**, **encephalitis**, **meningitis**, and **tuberous sclerosis** lead the order.

The other phases of attachment, according to the age to which they apply, will be noted in the chapter to follow

Moral Development (Spiritual)

At this age children are dependent on the parents to interpret right from wrong. As a child approaches the "terrible twos" the one word that they use most is the word "no!" This annoying practice may well be a result of the many times that parents must say "no" to the infants in the course of a day. It is one of the first words that they learn to imitate.

Kohlberg (1958b) agrees with Piaget when he refers to this age as the stage of Obedience and Punishment Orientation. Children at this age are basically amoral. They do or do not do things simply because they assume that powerful authorities hand down a fixed set of rules which he or she must unquestioningly obey.

These younger children regard rules as fixed and absolute. They believe that rules are handed down by adults or God and that one cannot change them. It is true that this level of morality actually is most noticeable a little later in life than in the stage 1 period. It can safely be said that the attitude toward rules, and what is right or wrong, begins at a very early age and is most likely the result of a style of parenting.

Psychological Development

Mentally from birth to about age one it is a time for discovery. Emotionally the baby is sensitive and capable of such emotions as anger and joy. In Piagetian terms this is the Period I level that he referred to as the **Sensorimotor Intelligence** period. The entire period covers from birth to about 2 years of age but is divided into several stages.

This is the time when babies organize their physical action schemes, such as sucking, grasping, and hitting for dealing with the immediate world. Piaget's first developmental level consists of six stages.

Stage 1 (birth to one month) — The Uses of Reflexes

Piaget used the terms **scheme** or **schema** when talking about an infant's action-structures. A scheme can be any action pattern for dealing with the environment. The first schemes consist primarily of inborn reflexes, the most prominent of which is the sucking reflex. Reflexes imply a certain amount of passivity according to Piaget. He suggests that the or-ganism lies inactive until something comes along to stimulate it. If an infant's mouth is touched, he will usually begin to suck. However, it has been noticed that at times the infant will suck even without any outside activity. Babies will suck on almost anything that comes near the mouth such as blankets, pillows, their own fingers, etc.

Stage 2 (one to four months) — Primary Circular Reactions

A circular reaction occurs when the baby chances upon a new experience and tries to repeat it (1936a. p.55). An example would be thumb sucking. By chance the infant gets his thumb near or into his mouth and, when the hand falls away, he will try to return it to his mouth. At first the child may fail in repeating the action, even after several tries, but even-tually he will succeed in organizing the sucking and hand movements and master the art of thumb sucking.

Since the baby must adjust the head and lip movements to accomplish this task, Piaget suggests that the beginnings of accommodation can be seen here, although it is more a part of stage 2 (1926a. pp. 29-31, 39).

This circular reaction is a good illustration of what Piaget means by intellectual development as a "construction process." The baby actively "puts together" different movements and schemes (Crain. 1985. p. 92).

Stage 3 (four to 10 months) — Secondary Circular Reactions

Secondary circular reactions are so called because instead of involving coordination of parts of baby's own body, this stage involves interesting events discovered and reproduced *outside* himself or herself (1936a. p. 154). Piaget gives the example of his own daughter, who one day while lying in her bassinet, made movement with her legs which stirred the dolls hanging overhead. She stared at the dolls a moment and then moved her legs again, watching the dolls move again. Over the next few days, she repeated this action again and again (pp. 157-59).

Stage 4 (10 to 12 months) — The Coordination of Secondary Schemes

In stage 3 the infant performs a single action to get a result, but in stage four the infant's actions become more differentiated; he or she learns to coordinate two separate schemes to get a result. Children may, for example, try to ignore a parent's hand that is hiding an object they desired. They may try waving their hand, shaking themselves and wagging their head from side to side (1936a. p.217). Finally, after a few days of trying they will strike the hand out of the way before grabbing the object, thus, coordinating two separate schemes, striking and grabbing, to obtain the object.

Stage 5 (12 to 18 months) — Tertiary Circular Reactions

At this stage children experiment with different actions and observe different outcomes. Piaget tells of a twelve month old boy sitting in a bathtub watching the water pour from the faucet. He put his hand under the faucet, and water sprayed outward. He repeated this action twice, making the interesting sight last. He then shifted the position of his hand, sometimes nearer, sometimes farther away from the faucet, observing how the water sprayed out at different angles. He varied his actions to see what new and different results would follow (Crain. 1985. p. 94).

It is interesting to note that these children were learning on their own, developing their schemes solely out of an individual curiosity about their surroundings.

Stage 6 (18 months to two years) — The Beginning of Thought

At stage 6 children seem to think out situations more internally, before they act. Piaget illustrates this stage by telling about his daughter, Lucienne and the matchbox. Piaget had placed a chain in the box which Lucienne immediately tried to recover. She possessed two schemes for getting the chain: turning the box over and sticking her finger in the box's slit. However, neither scheme worked. She then did something curious. She stopped her actions and looked at the slit with great attention. Then, several times in succession, she opened and shut her mouth, wider and wider (1936a. p. 344). After this, she promptly opened the box and obtained the chain.

This is also the stage when the child's efforts at imitation can be seen. Children will also develop the ability called deferred imitation. They can imitate absent models.

Personal Reflections

While writing this chapter I became very much aware of the fact that I was using the masculine for personal pronouns when referring to a singular noun such as child or baby. I suppose this is because of the recent birth of my fourth grandchild, who just happens to be a boy. Much of the material in the chapters dealing with prenatal development, birth and the first few weeks of life have undoubtedly affected my perspective. The experience of seeing my new grandson has without question made the writing of these chapters more important to me be-cause I am living the very experiences of which I write.

My other three grandchildren are all in their early teens, so I expect that when I get to the chapter about adolescence, I will again experience some nostalgia.

The whole process of birth and development is so fascinating that one can forget to take advantage of the really important things such as the love and sweetness one finds in the face of a newborn infant.

What also drives me to write and teach about human development is the fact that so many of the findings of the various theorists present important implications for parenting and later for education. I do not wish to cause any alarm to new parents. Most of us knew very little in the years when we were having and raising our children, but for the most part they seemed to survive our ignorance.

I have, however, in the past few years wished that I had known what I know now. I do not know for sure how I would characterize the parental style that my wife and I used, but I am sure that had we known what damage that could be done to a small infant, we would have been much more aware of our treatment of them.

As I recall at this time (some forty years later), we were both so involved in what was happening in our own lives that, although we dearly loved and thoroughly enjoyed all of our children, we were more concerned about what they ate and that they were properly clothed. We treated for any illnesses and properly educated our children and were less concerned about whether certain behavior on our part could be interpreted as being neglecting or rejecting by any of them.

There is such a difference among our four children that I must accept that a part of the way a child develops is due to an inheritance factor. Each of the four is of an entirely different emotional temperament, and each has achieved a very different level of success in life.

I guess the advice I would give to new parents (although many of the baby-boomer parents of this day think they know all there is to know about the process of raising children) would be to become as aware of all of the factors that influence the development of a child. Then love them with all the love possible, making sure that, in the words of the medical profession, you "Do No Harm."

Although I do not necessarily agree with all of the findings of all of the theorists mentioned in the text, I have come to believe that there is much truth to be gleaned from their theories. We should never "throw the baby out with the bathwater" as the saying goes, because we (especially Christians) have been taught certain beliefs about child rearing. "Spare the rod and spoil the child," is only one of those concepts that I am sure has been misused. I agree with modern medical observers, a new born cannot be spoiled. As the child grows, there is certainly a need to develop standards and teach values, but the child must have some room to grown on his own as long as the liberty to grow independently is not actually a form of neglect.

I can recall my early years and my family of origin. My mother was not what one would call a warm caring person, although, I never doubted that I was loved. I was born at home and my mother breast-fed me until I was weaned. About all I can remember about my father is that he was always away at work. He lived at home, but was usually gone to work before I was awake, and when he came home from work, he usually worked in the garage on cars to earn extra money (we were just coming out of the great depression). By the time he quit working in the garage, I was already in bed for the night. All of this must have impressed me as neglect or rejection, because there is no way I could have appreciated my father's need to work so much in order to take care of his family. I don't remember ever going hungry or being without any of the necessities of life, but I now realize that my problems with intimacy may have come from the parental style of my family.

Review for Chapter 4

- Birth, the greatest wonder of mankind.
- A number of things can happen to harm the fetus.
- The first stage of birth is labor.
- Extremely difficult births may require a C section.
- Fetal monitoring can reduce the dangers of difficult births.
- At times birth must be assisted with the use of instruments.
- Many larger hospitals have birthing centers designed to make the delivery more natural.
- Rank felt that birth is the most important psychological event of life.
- Birth trauma and low birth weight can influence a child's development.
- Low birth weight is a major factor in infant mortality.
- Sudden Infant Death Syndrome (SIDS) is the leading cause of death among infants between 1 month and 1 year.
- The Apgar scale is used to test the infant's adjustment during the first few minutes of life.
- The Braselton Neonatal Behavioral Assessment Scale is used to assess the way a baby is adjusting to its environment.
- Temperament is used to evaluate infants according to 1) Emotional/Distress and Soothability and 2) Inhibited - Uninhibited (Shy - Sociable).
- The New York Longitudinal Study found nine components of temperament:

    1. Activity level
    2. Rhythmicity or regularity
    3. Approach or withdrawal
    4. Adaptability
    5. Threshold of responsiveness
    6. Intensity of reaction
    7. Quality of mood
    8. Distractibility

        9. Attention span and persistence
- Temperament seems to be largely genetic.
- Temperament can affect a child's adjustment to life.
- There are three theories of normal growth patterns:
    1. Cephalocaudal
    2. Proximodistal
    3. Simple to complex
- Ethology has taught science much about the development of infants.
- Research done with orphans has shown how much children depend on touch and care to survive.
- Breast feeding seems to add certain physiological benefits to the infant.
- The infant triples his birth weight during the first year.
- Growth is very rapid during the first few months of life.
- The new infant is in stage one, according to Freud and Erikson, which is the oral stage.
- If the infant is frustrated during the oral stage they may become fixated at that stage.
- Some people regress to the early oral stage later in life if their needs are not sufficiently met at that early stage.
- At one and a half to three years of age the child is in the anal stage. This is the time of the dreaded potty-training.
- Other psychological problems can have their roots in the frustrations experienced in the anal stage such as the anal compulsive and the anal expulsive.
- According to Erikson this period is a struggle between trust and mistrust. The infant who learns that his environment is hostile will learn to be distrustful later in life.
- According to Millon, certain parental styles can contribute to the basic personality of the child.
- This is the period of life when attachment is important.
- At this stage children are dependent on their parents for their sense of morality which largely is a matter of reward and punishment.
- Piaget's stage theory of intellectual development is discussed.

Ages 0-2

Glossary for Chapter 4

Glossary of Terms

Accommodation — Piagetian term for a change in an existing cognitive structure to cope with new information.

Active Proximity Seeking — According to the attachment theory, stage three is characterized by the infant now being able to seek out the primary care-taker and avoid separation anxiety.

Anal Compulsive — A Freudian concept that describes those individuals that have developed compulsive behavior as a result or problems during the anal stage of development. These are very neat and clean individuals.

Anal Expulsive — These are the same as the compulsives except that they develop a pattern of messiness during the anal stage.

Apgar Scale — Standard measurement of a newborn's condition; it assesses appearance, pulse, grimace, activity, and respiration.

Autoerotic — Freudian term that suggests that certain areas such as the mouth, anus or genitals are highly sensitive to pleasurable sensations.

Avoidant Attachment — Pattern of attachment in which an infant rarely cries when separated from the primary caregiver and avoids contact upon his or her return.

Basic Trust vs Basic Mistrust — The first of Erikson's stages involving a critical balancing of alternatives in psychosocial development (from birth to 12-18 months), in which the infant develops a sense of whether or not the world can be trusted; the quality of interaction with the mother in feeding is a primary determinant of the outcome of this stage.

Bayley Scale of Infant Development — Standardized test for measuring the intellectual development of infants; the test consists of a mental scale and a motor scale. Each of these yields a development quotient (DQ) computed by comparing what a particular baby can do at a certain age with the performance of a large number of previously observed babies at the same age.

Birth Trauma — Birth-related brain injury caused by oxygen deprivation, mechanical injury, or infection or disease at birth. The term is also used to describe the physical trauma of the birthing process itself.

Brazelton Neonatal Behavioral Assessment Scale — Neurological and behavioral test to measure neonates' response to the environment; it assesses interactive behaviors, motor behaviors, physiological control, and response to stress.

Cephalcodal — Refers to the theory that the fetus develops from the head to the lower extremities (head to tail).

Clinical Method — Study done in a controlled situation instead of simple observation in natural surroundings.

Deaver's Developmental Screening Test — Test given to children 1 month to 6 years old to determine whether or not they are developing normally; it assesses gross motor skills, fine motor skills, language development, and personal and social development.

Detached Active — According to Million's theory a personality type resulting from a parental style of reject. **Detached passive** — In Million's theory a personality style that is the result of a parental style of neglect.

Distractibility — One of the nine components of temperament suggested by the New York Longitudinal Study that describes how easily an individual can be distracted.

Encephalitis — An inflammation of the brain.

Etiology — A division of medical science dealing with the systematic study of the causes of mental and physical diseases.

Failure to Thrive — An apparently healthy, well-fed baby's failure to grow, often as a result of emotional neglect.

Fetal Alcohol Syndrome — (FAS). Mental, motor, and developmental abnormalities (including stunted growth, facial and bodily malformations, and disorders of the central nervous system) affecting the offspring of some women who drink heavily during pregnancy.

Fixation — In Freudian terms, an arrest in development that occurs because a child has been gratified too much or too little during a particular psycho-sexual stage.

Hospitalism — Decline in a child's intellectual and psychological functioning resulting from long institutionalization.

Imprinting — Instinctive form of learning in which, after a single encounter, an animal recognizes and trusts one particular individual.

Infant Mortality — Death during the first year of life. The most common is SIDS: Sudden Infant Death Syndrome.

Infantile Autism — Developmental disorder that begins within the first 2 1/2 years of life and is characterized by lack of responsiveness to other people. Bruno Bettelheim referred to these children as "empty fortresses."

Low Birth-Weight Babies — Babies who weigh less than 5 1/2 pounds at birth because they are premature or small for date.

Maturation — Unfolding of a biologically determined, age-related sequence of behavior patterns programmed by the genes, including the readiness to master new abilities.

Meninges — Any of the three membranes that envelop the brain and the spinal cord.

Meningitis — Bacterial disease in which inflammation of meninges occurs.

Miconium — Fetal waste matter excreted during the first few days after birth. Medicated delivery — Childbirth in which the mother receives anesthesia.

Mother-Infant Bond — A mother's feeling of a close, caring connection with her newborn.

Neonate — A newborn baby.

Oral stage — In Freudian terms, the psychosexual stage of infancy (birth to 12-18 months) characterized by a sensual gratification in the oral region, chiefly through food (sucking).

Phenyketonuria (PKU) — A congenital metabolic disorder resulting from the inability of the body to convert phenylalanine, an essential amino acid.

Reflex Behaviors — Automatic responses to external stimulation. Reflexes, by their presence or disappearance, are early signs of an infant's neurological growth.

Regressive — Having to do with going back psychologically to an earlier stage of emotional development.

Rubella — Maternal rubella is a disease that the mother contracted while infected with German measles.

Scheme — In Piagetian terminology, a basic cognitive structure that the infant uses to interact with the environment; an organized pattern of thought and behavior.

Schizoid — A personality disorder characterized by withdrawal, reservation, and reclusiveness.

Self-Awareness — Realization, beginning in infancy, of separateness from other people and things, allowing reflection on one's own actions in relation to social standards.

Self-Recognition — Children's ability to recognize their own physical image; occurs at about 18 months.

Separation Anxiety — Distress shown by an infant, usually beginning in the second half of the first year, when a familiar caregiver leaves; it is commonly a sign that attachment has occurred.

Stranger Anxiety — Phenomenon that often occurs during the second half of the child's first year (in conjunction with separation anxiety), when the infant becomes wary of strange people and places; commonly a sign that attachment has occurred.

Stress — The organism's physiological and psychological reaction to demands made on it.

Temperament — Person's characteristic style of approaching and reacting to people and situations.

Vernix Caseosa — Oily substance on a neonate that protects against infection. It dries within a few days after birth.

"Children have more need of models than of critics."
—Joseph Joubert

Chapter 5

Ages 2-3

This stage, which is stage 2 of Erikson's stage theory, has as its main features Autonomy vs Shame and Doubt, while Freud referred to this age group as **Muscular Anal**.

Physical Development

By the time a child is two years old, he has reached half of his adult height. The child has gone from crawling to walking and running, but may fall in sudden turns. He or she can quickly alternate between sitting and standing and walk up and down stairs using one foot only.

By 30 months, infants should be able to jump into the air with both feet. They can stand on one foot for about a second or two. They can take a few steps on tiptoes. They are able to jump from a chair and have developed good hand and finger coordination with the ability to move digits independently. The manipulation of objects has become much improved and they can build towers with about six blocks.

By the beginning of the third year growth begins to slow a little and there is a noticeable improvement in the coordination of the large muscles.

As the infants become more and more physically able, they tend to want to do more things for themselves. They also tend to "get into everything" so that parents are constantly placing dangerous objects out of their reach. Between two and three years of age many children begin climbing everything and anything that can be climbed, but often they are not able to climb down.

The physical growth of the infant from birth to the age of two years has been phenomenal, but the growth that occurs from age 2 to 6 is even more of a wonder. On an average a boy will grow from 34 1/2 inches at two years to about 46 1/2 inches at 6 years old. Girls will go from about 34 inches at 2 years to about 45 1/2 inches at the age of six. Boys will gain about 20 pounds in that same time frame, while girls will gain about 19 pounds.

Ages 2-3

The rate of gain for any child during his or her first year is greater than it is during the years between 2 and 6.

The baby fat that gave infants their babyish look gradually disappears during the second year of life.

Until the age of two, there are few gender differences between boys and girls. Even though adults tend to treat boy and girl babies differently, the infants themselves tend to play and behave in very similar ways. It is only later in their lives that they learn to behave in different ways, mostly as a result of the way adults react to them. In one study, if adults saw a boy crying they assumed that he was angry, but if they saw a girl crying they assumed that she had been hurt.

Freud's Anal Stage

Freud's anal stage of psychosexual development actually begins at about age 18 months and continues into three years of age. There is a certain amount of overlapping in all of the stage theories, it is important to note that each stage is qualitative rather than quantitative, that is, infants do not suddenly change at a certain age from oral to anal in focus. The anal stage is that stage when the child's focus of sexual interest is that of the anal zone. The content of this theory has been presented briefly in Chapter 3, and the main dangers of not recognizing the significance of the research of this period can result in lasting personality and behavioral characteristics. Chapter 3 pointed out the possibility of a child becoming either anal compulsive or anal expulsive. Either of those two Freudian conditions, if developed in the extreme, can result in a serious psychological condition that will affect the individual for the rest of his or her life if not treated.

Anal Expulsive individuals become wasteful, disorderly, and messy in their own life situations and in their relations with others. Most importantly, anal expulsives will behave in a messy, disorderly, wasteful manner in their marriage and also in child rearing.

The opposite of the anal expulsive is the anal compulsive who becomes characteristically clean and orderly. They may become very frugal and stingy (a variation of, that is mine, I will not let go). Many people would consider this type of behavior at times as being desirable. These individuals can be very effective as librarians, record keepers, etc. because they will never lose a thing.

Some anal compulsive individuals may become very rich if they were baseball card collectors years ago. However, it would be almost impossible to convince some of them to sell their cards, even if it meant receiving considerable wealth.

Freud felt that toilet training could be very traumatic to a child, especially if the training was started too early. Munroe (1955, p.287), posited that toilet-training probably arouses sufficient anger and fear to produce some measure of fixation in most children, especially in the United States, where parents tend to be strict about this matter.

Freud also believed that frustration and trauma, at this stage, particularly when associated with toilet-training, are likely to produce lifelong problems with obstinacy, frugality, or compulsive behavior.

The problem is that, especially in the United States, parents feel pressured to have their child perform this unpleasant function in a socially acceptable manner and will many times attempt to force toilet-training too early in the child's life. Another cause of the difficulties arises from toilet-training being taught by an obstinate parent who feels that the child is willfully resisting. The other half of the difficulty results from parents who makes too few demands on the child in this training. Whatever the manner of training, it is to be noted that the real factor is the presence of conflict in the process between the infant and the parent.

At times, the traits of the anal explosive and the anal compulsive will have little serious impact on one's life. Crain noted, (1995, p. 144) problems can emerge in a more pronounced way when one becomes anxious about his or her work.

It has also been suggested that the great success of all of the laxative companies is contributable to the number of anal compulsive individuals in modern day stressful living.

According to the Million personality theory, the types of parental style that are usually very negative at this stage are 1) domination; 2) perfectionism, 3) over-coercion and 4) overindulgence. The parents that exhibit any of these parental styles help to create, in an infant seeking to "do things his own way," a personality style of either Independent Passive, Independent Active, Ambivalent Passive, or Ambivalent Active. Each of these personality styles may not be obvious to the casual observer, but in their more extreme levels they can create deep-seated emotional problems in the individual.

Independent personality patterns, according to Millon, are characterized by a reliance on the self. The individuals have learned that they obtain maximum pleasure and minimum pain if they depend on themselves rather than others. In this study, during stage two, that would refer to either the overindulgent or the dominant parental style.

The independent active has a need for power, because most of the initiative he wanted to use as a toddler was denied him by the dominant parent or parents. The independent active child is one who has become aggressive in interpersonal relationships and has developed a self-image of assertiveness. A parental style of domination can cause an individual to rebel against the domination and develop a need for power to control his own life circumstances. The parent in this scenario forced the infant to sit until he had dutifully performed on the potty. The child, consequently, will spend the rest of his life feeling no need for others in his life and will actively seek to control others and his own world with his own power.

The independent passive personality is similar to the independent active in respect to the fact that there is a feeling that whatever they are going to get out of life will come from themselves rather than others, The exception is that the passive person is more interested in self-gratification than power. The overindulgent parental style leads to feelings of narcissism in relation to others and a self-image of being admirable, superior and of considerable worth. The parent that is overindulgent is one that allows the child to "do as he pleases with such matters as the evacuation of the bowels."

For the most part these individuals seem to be rather well adjusted in that they appear to be confident, calm and self-satisfied. They seem to be untroubled by the minor irritations of life, and consider such mundane concerns as beneath them. They seem to be unaware of the societal rules for reciprocity in interpersonal relationships. They expect the world and personal relations to gratify their desires, with nothing in return.

As a child, the independent passive does not view himself as having faults, so they seldom enter therapy. But their lives can be very dysfunctional because others tend to avoid them.

All of the damage done by the overindulgent parent is not confined to this stage but, in view of the basic issue of stage two, it is not too unreasonable to conclude that this stage is where the real patterns begin to form.

According to Millon (1981), ambivalent refers to individuals who "remain unsure as to which way to turn; that is, they are in conflict regarding whether to depend on themselves for reinforcement or on others." Millon goes on to describe the ambivalent passive personality as the compulsive personality. These individuals manifest extraordinary consistency, a rigid and unvarying uniformity in all significant settings. He says that "they accomplish this by repressing urges toward autonomy and independence" (the very psychosocial issue of children at stage 2).

These individuals are resistant to change and new ideas. They are also threatened by having to make decisions, since this process involves an element of uncertainty about what to expect. A lifestyle built around conformity does not allow for the development of a rich individual personality (Benner, 1985).

The ambivalent active person is one whose parents exhibited a parental style of over coercion and are sometimes described as the negativistic personality individual. They are subject to sudden and extensive mood swings, from despondent and distraught to spiteful and accusatory. They seem to have a need to show resistance and for the most part have a self-image of discontent. These persons usually come from a family background of schismatic persons. The very dysfunctional state of the family was most likely the reason the parents were so over-coercive.

Later in life the ambivalent-active individual may need institutional care. The most frightening finding by Millon is that "The active-ambivalent personality pattern is particularly insidious because it is so easily self-perpetuating" (1985). The prognosis for these individuals is not good.

Some practical suggestions for parents are presented by Papalia and Olds (Papalia, Daine E. and Olds Sally W. *Human Development*. NY: McGraw-Hill Book Company. 1989. p. 121). They suggest that the parent should wait until the infant is about 20 months of age at which time they should test for physical readiness. If the child can dress and undress himself and is able to readily take instructions, he may be ready to start toilet-training. Otherwise, the parents should wait another few weeks and test again.

The authors go on to say that the parents should become models in dressing and undressing and of the use of the toilet. Children learn by modeling after their caregivers.

Parents need to accumulate an assortment of small snack items and drinks to use as reinforcers. They also need to use praise, hugging, smiling, and applauding as reinforcers. The kind of reinforcement used will depend on the nature and temperament of each individual child.

Other practical suggestions include getting a potty chair that the child can empty, using a doll that wets, using training pants, and the "big boy" "big girl" phrases to encourage the child to dress him/herself.

Teaching each of the various steps to be followed in the process will also help. Praise and encouragement to relax while on the potty will help to eliminate some of the stress and trauma. The main element in the entire process is that of reward and encouragement. Punishment or ridicule for accidents will not, for the most part, have a positive effect and will only result in more frustration for both the child and for the parent. The practice of placing a child on the potty with a stern warning that he is not to get up until he has "produced" and then simply leaving him there alone will only prolong the training period and create some undesirable effects on the child.

Freud insists that a baby's Id operates under the pleasure principle, striving for immediate gratification. When gratification is delayed, the ego develops and operates under the reality principle, striving to find socially acceptable ways to obtain gratification.

Whether the anal zone focus is indeed a matter of autoerotic sensations or not, there is no doubt that toilet-training can be a traumatic experience for everyone involved. The conflict between parent and child at this stage of development must be recognized for the basis of at least some personality impact on the child. In Freudian theory, fixation in or regression to this stage of development could very well explain some adult problems of adjustment and dysfunctional behavior at times.

Psychosocial Development

Erikson agreed with Freud when he said that the basic modes of this stage are retention and elimination, or holding on or letting go. He also believed that the basic conflicts in the set of social modalities associated with this stage could lead, in the end, to either hostile or benign expectations and attitudes. Erikson, however, suggested that the modes of this stage go beyond the anal zone. At this age, children are able to hold on to objects or even throw them away. They learn to pile blocks and other objects one second and tear them down the next. They behave in the same way with people — sometimes holding on and at other times pushing away.

Erikson called this stage **Autonomy vs Shame and Doubt**. In all of the holding on to and throwing away there is a pattern of the child making choices. There is a beginning of the exercise of the will, or as, Erikson phrased it, their autonomy.

Because children are now able to stand up and move around more effectively, they begin to explore their world on their own. They express their autonomy quite often by the constant use of the word "no!" Parents often become frustrated because children at this age do not seem to be able to say, "Yes!" As mentioned in another section of the text, the fact that parents must constantly say no to the infant, makes it the word that he is most likely to remember.

In some societies, parents feel a need to make the adventurous 2 year old "mind." Here again is the conflict of the dreaded "toilet-training" as many parents feel a sense of urgency for the child to be potty-trained. It is embarrassing to many parents to discover that a child of an acquaintance is several months younger and is already potty-trained and theirs isn't.

Erikson suggests that autonomy comes from within; biological maturation generates the ability to do things on one's own (Crain. 1985. p. 165). The control of one's sphincter muscles is only a part of the story, and in the child's efforts to be autonomous and do things on his own, there is a possibility of failure with accompanying shame or guilt. In some cultures, that may not have the advantage of all of the wisdom of Dr. Spock and others, parents seem to try to help children at this age learn acceptable social behavior without crushing the child's will. However in other cultures, a child who soils himself or breaks some other social law, may be severely scolded and shamed excessively, or the child may be ridiculed when he attempts to do something on his own.

Erikson believed that the ridicule and shaming could do lasting damage to children by creating a feeling of shame and doubt that can last into adulthood and result in dysfunctional behavior. Erikson suggested, however, that "shame is an emotion insufficiently studied, because in our civilization it is so early and easily absorbed by guilt." He also added that "Too much shaming does not lead to genuine propriety, but to a secret determination to try to "get away" with things, unseen — impulsively" (Erikson. 1963. p. 252-253).

Erikson also suggested that because shame is the brother of doubt, it often leads to some form of compulsive doubting, which ultimately finds its expression in adult expressions of "paranoiac fears concerning hidden persecutors and secret persecutions threatening from behind (and from within)" (1963. p. 254).

Adults who are reluctant to attempt anything new, who are more comfortable doing simple routine things, and who are not in the least adventurous are usually those individuals who still suffer considerable shame and doubt about their abilities. To some individuals, failure of any kind is the fear that paralyzes them in personal and business relationships.

A number of writers, such as John Bradshaw, have written extensively about the problems of shame and doubt that are carried from childhood into later life.

Another issue that comes into play in children that have been subject to excessive shame and doubt, because they were not encouraged to become autonomous or were ridiculed and shamed, is the issue of self-esteem. A large portion of the individuals who fail in interpersonal relationships, fail because of a poor self-image. Low self-esteem is at the root of an alarming percentage of people who find themselves failing in almost every venture in life.

A considerable amount of damage to the personality of children occurs in the first two years because of the lack of proper bonding, neglect, or other trauma. Although children of different primary temperaments may respond differently to negative relationships, the fact remains that the struggle for autonomy without shame and guilt is considered to be most important to healthy emotional maturation.

The family may well be the largest single influence on children's development, and children also influence other family members in many important ways. Much of research focuses on relationships between children and their fathers and siblings, as well as their mothers (Papalia & Olds, 1989. p.159). (see the discussion of temperament in the preceding chapter.

Disturbance in Family Relations

The problem of unstable or broken family relations applies in both the first and second stage of a child's life. There are a number of factors that can create a disturbance in a family situation and all of those factors can cause considerable damage. Such factors as parental deprivation, that is, a family situation where one or both of the primary parents are not in on the bonding process. Fathers who are just too busy or for some reason are unable to relate to an infant deprive the child of the need for both male and female relationships.

Ages 2-3

Many single parent families are the result of either death or divorce. Mothers working outside of the home are a factor in the changes in family structure. Although little is known about the actual effect on infants because most of the research in this area has been done with older children, we do know that toddlers will exhibit certain symptoms of stress or distress such as sleeplessness, whining, etc., when one parent, with whom there has been some bonding, suddenly disappears. It is assumed that children at this early age do not understand death (or divorce) and tend to think of the separation as temporary.

Institutionalization has long been considered as a potential source of damage in the younger child. When orphanages were in common usage as a means of providing for children whose parents may have died or simply abandoned them, many of the children, especially the very young, died during their first year (Spitz, 1945). The children who did not die declined in intellectual functioning and developed many psychological problems.

Some of the same damage can occur in a necessary hospitalization of a child. Premature infants who must stay in the hospital after the parents go home may, in years to come, be found to have some of the same psychological problems. However, in modern hospitals, much more personal attention is given to these hospitalized infants than in years gone by. Children who are hospitalized in later childhood are also in better hopes of avoiding such psychological damage because of the attention they receive from various professional and volunteer attendants. Many hospitals provide for parental housing in or near the hospital so that the parent can be with the child as much as possible.

Hospitalized babies 15-30 months old have been observed to go through three stages of separation anxiety (Bowlby, 1960).

1. **Protest** — Babies actively try to get their mothers back by shaking the crib and throwing themselves about.

2. **Despair** — Babies become withdrawn and inactive, crying monotonously or intermittently. Because they are so quiet, it is often assumed that they have accepted the situation.

3. **Detachment** — Babies accept care from a succession of nurses and are willing to eat, play with toys, smile, and be sociable; but when their mother visits, the babies remain apathetic and even turn away.

Personality Style

In the terms of Millon's personality development, the parenting style of neglect and rejection can be difficult to differentiate as the causal factor in the development of the detached passive and the detached active. Very young children are not always or hardly ever able to distinguish between neglect or rejection, and because these children have no way of comparing their situation with that of other children they respond to their situation in the only way available to them.

In situations of child abuse and neglect, the child may think that his situation is perfectly normal. However, the child abuse or neglect results in the formation of psychological needs in the child that will later show up in interpersonal relationships. The child, who at this young age is abused, physically, emotionally, sexually, or simply through neglect, will most often become an adult with a need to distance himself from others. He will have learned the art of survival and become complacent in his image of self. Social relationships will not be of much importance, and the child grows up to be somewhat of a loner (often a hermit). Because of the pain of the abuse and neglect the individual learns to distance himself from others to avoid the possibility of being hurt yet again.

In the case of rejection (this can be real rejection or in the case of death or abandonment may be perceived rejection) the usual personality style that results is that of detached active, whose needs include protection. This individual develops a social style of avoidance and develops a self-image of alienation (remember the discussion of separation anxiety mentioned earlier).

A very important observation needs to be inserted at this time. What is most important in any life situation, especially with very young children, is that what is the true situation (neglect, rejection, abuse, etc.) is not as important as what the individual perceives the situation to be.

Critics of some of the recent therapies that base most of an adult's psychological problems on events that occurred early in infancy, point to the fact that many of the individuals who are involved in such therapy cannot remember the events in their early life that may have been the roots of their problem. There is no suggestion that the negative events never really took place, but that the patient was made to believe them by the suggestions of the therapist.

Infantile amnesia

Freud introduced the concept of infantile amnesia as being a product of repression. He thought that the mind simply repressed into the unconscious those negative or unpleasant happenings that were a threat.

Schachtel (Schachtel, 1959, p. 286) defines infantile amnesia as the inability of children to remember most events of their first five or six years. He agreed with Freud partly, but he pointed out two problems with the repression hypothesis. He said that, first, childhood amnesia is quite pervasive; we forget not only sexual and hostile feelings that we might have had cause to repress but almost every other aspect of our early childhood as well. Second, even psychoanalytic patients, who sometimes can get beneath the repression barrier, are still unable to remember much of their lives during their first few years (Schachtel, 1959, p. 285).

Schachtel posited that childhood amnesia has to do with *perceptual modes of experience* as opposed to the memories of adults that are based on verbal categories. Childhood experiences are largely preverbal, but based largely on the senses, making the tagging of those experiences almost impossible.

Schachtel divided infancy into two stages which he called autocentric or allocentric. The first stage he called infancy (birth to one year), in which the senses were autocentric, being mostly in the body such as taste, thermal sense, smells and touch.

These autocentric senses are to be distinguished from the allocentric senses such as hearing and sight, in that the senses are directed outside the body (1959, pp. 81-84, 96-115). Both the autocentric and the allocentric senses are intimately bound up with feelings of pleasure and unpleasure, of comfort and discomfort, etc.

The second stage (ages one to five years) is characterized by the change in the concern of the children. From about one year old on they are less concerned about their security and move on to a more active interest in their world. They begin to use the pure allocentric senses — hearing and sight. They experience new objects by looking at them. Schachtel does not deal too extensively with the problems of perception of situations as opposed to the reality experiences.

Crain (1985, p. 193) summarizes the findings of Schachtel by saying that "neither the autocentric experiences of the infant nor the allocentric experiences of the young child fit into the adult's way of categorizing and remembering events. The infant's world of tastes, smells, and touch, as well as the young child's fresh and open experience of things in all their fullness, are foreign to the adult and are not subject to recall.

Minimizing Negativity

Papalia and Olds (1989, p. 181) believe that one of the most important issues of this age group is the avoidance of negativity. They make some very practical suggestions in view of the fact that the "terrible twos", a period in which children seem to express their urge for autonomy by resisting almost everything they are told to do, is a perfectly normal stage that often continues through the preschool years. But not all children in this stage are equally negative. Indeed, many seem to wish to tease or 'play with' their parents, not to be taken seriously. Flexible parents who view a child's expressions of self-will as a striving for independence, not as stubbornness, are more likely to have compliant preschoolers. A certain amount of opposition is undoubtedly healthy. Parents can avoid excessive conflicts and contribute to a child's sense of competence by following these suggestions" (From Haswell, Hock, & Wernar, 1981).

1. Don't interrupt an activity unless the interruption is necessary; try to wait until the child's attention has shifted to something else.

2. If an activity must be interrupted, give advance warning: "In ten minutes, it will be time to put your toys away and come to dinner." This gives the child time to adjust and perhaps to finish what he or she is doing.

3. Suggest, don't command. Accompany requests with smiles or hugs, not criticism, threats, or physical control.

4. Wait a few moments before repeating a request when a child doesn't immediately comply.

5. Give the child a choice — even a limited one. That way, the child feels in control. ("Would you like to have your bath now, or in 5 minutes?")

6. Be consistent in discipline.

7. When you and the child get into a power struggle, take time out. Leave the child alone for a few minutes; the resistance may diminish or even disappear.

Much of the child's self-control reflects the way in which his parents or caregivers treats him and talks to him. Parents need to remember that this is the stage when a child is seeking to become autonomous. He is seeking to explore his own ability to function in his world. It is the responsibility of the parents to seek to reinforce the needs of the child by recognizing the needs and to avoid the temptation to constantly control the efforts of the child to develop his own self-control.

Some other practical considerations offered by Papalia and Olds include:

Parents need to learn to respond to the signals that children give. Answering cries, responding to apparent agitation, taking time to listen and care are all practical ways that parents can support the efforts of a child to develop a meaningful self-image and a healthy will.

Parents need to provide a meaningful, interesting, and stimulating environment for the child. The whole theory of the Montessori Method is that the child will grow in a healthy manner if he is subjected to the proper environment. What may seem like an interesting environment to an adult may seem all too boring to a child.

A great deal of patience is necessary in taking care of a child at this stage, or at any other stage for that matter. At times young children will throw things out of their beds or off of their high chair. This is only one way of exploring their boundaries. If parents become too annoyed with this type of behavior, it may only serve to promote even more of the objectionable actions.

Children must be given freedom to explore. The parents must be careful to keep the environment free of harmful objects, but beyond that the child will benefit from the freedom to explore his own space freely.

Prelinguistic speech

At about the age of 18 months, the child has an average repertoire of 3 to 50 words. Patterns of sound and intonation resemble discourse, and the child has made good progress in understanding.

Two year olds usually have a vocabulary of over 50 words, and use two-word phrases frequently. The child becomes very interested in verbal communication and infant babbling usually stops.

By the age of 30 months, new words are learned almost every day. Utterances consist of three or more words. The child at this age has excellent comprehension but makes many mistakes in grammar.

The average child has learned about 1000 words by the time he is 3 years old, and about 80% are intelligible. His grammar is close to adult colloquial speech, and his syntactic mistakes are fewer.

Personal Reflections

There is no doubt in my mind that the first two stages of human development, including the prenatal nine months, are by far the most crucial in an individual's life. Many of the problems that develop in the years to come will, to a large degree, be a result of what happened during these years.

There is a danger of young parents developing a real sense of guilt when they realize that some of the problems that their children are experiencing in the present are the effects of the wrong things they did when the children were young. I have long ago prayed for the Lord's forgiveness for some of the unintentional parenting errors my wife and I made in the rearing of the children.

I have come to believe, after years of working with children in public schools and in the church, that it is not reasonable to assume that all children are so fragile and that the development of their personalities. their social adjustment, and their happiness, is tied completely in the hands of their parents. Most children have an amazing, innate ability to survive in even the most trying situations. That is not to say that they will not suffer in some way, but at least their problems will probably not be totally damaging or permanent.

Still, it would be foolish to ignore all of the findings presented in research. Children can be damaged. The problem is that there are so many seriously damaged children who are the products of very dysfunctional families, that those who are only mildly disturbed are overlooked because they are not as dysfunctional as their counterparts.

Parents do have an effect on their children. In recent years there has appeared on the scene the concept of parent training programs. The main purpose of these programs is to teach parents to be more authoritative (firm, democratic, reasonable, respectful) rather than authoritarian (harsh, controlling, demanding, dogmatic, powerful) or permissive (*laissez-faire*, non-controlling, weak). The idea is to teach parents to become authoritative.

The problems with parent training programs, as I see them, are that the concepts taught are too simple for the very complex job of raising children.

It would seem that the most important thing that parents can do is to provide lots of love and care, while exhibiting great patience in dealing with children in any stage but especially in those stages that present the most difficulty for the child. There are periods in the child's life when things run much smoother than at other times. As we shall see in the chapter dealing with pre-adolescence and teenage, there are some stages in development that are very stormy.

It has been well demonstrated that in training children, punishment is not nearly so potent in bringing about change in behavior as reinforcement and praise. One of the most objectionable practices in my mind is that of "reverse psychology" (or deceit, if you will). To attempt to make a child behave in a certain manner by pretending to want him to act in the opposite manner (because of the negative responses of the toddler) is nothing more than trickery. Sooner or later the child will realize what is going on and may actually develop some distrust toward the parents.

At one time, my wife and I took on a foster child. She was brought to us in the evening with no clean clothes (the ones she was wearing were stained with milk, urine and fecal matter), one bottle, matted hair and little else. The story as related to us by the social worker was that she had been left in her crib for hours on end without any attention or care. She would be given a bottle of milk or formula, and left to her own. She was about six months old when we got her and could not, or would not, smile or respond in any way to either my wife or me, or to any of our four children. Her father was in prison for murder. He had shot his wife and her lover and had left the infant alone in her crib.

It took months before we were able to get any response from her at all. We gave her all of the love and care possible, even though she did not seem to understand or accept our efforts. Finally, after many months, we began to see some new light in her eyes. She began to respond to all of us with smiles. I tell this story only to emphasize the fact that with love and care, even some of the most damaged children can begin to show some small gain toward recovery from the most horrendous family background.

Ages 2-3

I have not taken time to introduce the worse scenarios. These are the stories that result in the most damaged and usually unrecoverable, human beings. M. Scott Peck wrote a book entitled, People of the Lie, in which he records stories of families that were so dysfunctional that they could only be considered as evil. The progeny of these families have no hope of living a normal life aside from a miracle from God Himself. Every Christian who is interested in becoming a counselor should read Peck's book.

Review for Chapter 5

This chapter covers ages 2-5 years.

- By two years old the child has reached one half of his adult height.

- The growth of a child from 2 to 6 years old is even more phenomenal than during the first two years.

- Freud referred to this stage as the anal stage.

- Anal compulsion and anal expulsive are two of the psychological personality types that can develop due to problems during this stage.

- Freud felt that toilet training could be a very traumatic experience for the child.

- According to Millon, the types of parental styles that are usually very negative at this stage are 1) domination; 2) perfectionism; 3) overcoercion; and 4) overindulgence.

- Independent personality patterns are characterized by a reliance on self.

- The independent active has a need for power.

- The independent passive personality is similar to the independent active in that they feel that whatever they are going to get out of life, they must depend on themselves and not others.

- All of the damage done by the negative parental styles is not confined to this stage.

- Ambivalent personalities are resistant to change and new ideas.

- Some practical suggestions were noted from Papalia and Olds on positive parental care.

- Erikson agreed with Freud that the basic modes of this stage are retention and elimination.

- Erikson called this stage Autonomy vs. Shame and Doubt.

- Autonomy comes from within and the biological maturation generates the ability to do things on one's own.

- Erikson believed that ridicule and shaming could do lasting damage to children by creating a feeling of shame and doubt that could last into adulthood.

- Adults who are reluctant to attempt anything new, who are more comfortable doing simple things, and who are the least adventurous are usually those individuals who still suffer shame and doubt.
- The shame and doubt at this stage is the beginning of a poor self-image that may last a lifetime.
- The family is the most single influence on a child's development.
- Unstable family situations are damaging in both the first and second stages of life.
- Some serious questions are unanswered about the long term effects of the single parent family.
- Institutionalization and hospitalization can have very serious effects on a young child.
- The importance of parental styles according to Millon are discussed.
- The concept of infantile amnesia in Freudian belief is a product of repression.
- Schachtel felt that infantile amnesia has to do with perceptual modes of experience.
- Schachtel divided infancy into two stages: autocentric or allocentric.
- The most important issue of this stage is the avoidance of negativity in the parental style.
- This is a period of linguistic growth.
- By the time that a child is 3 years old he has learned about 1000 words.

Glossary for Chapter 5

Glossary of Terms

Allocentric Senses — Hearing, and especially sight; coming from outside the body.

Ambivalent Passive — One of Millon's eight personality patterns.

Ambivalent-Active — One of Millon's eight basic personalities.

Anal Stage — According to Freudian theory, the psychosexual stage of toddler hood (12-18 months to 3 years), in which the chief source of sensual gratification is moving the bowels; toilet training forces the child to delay this gratification.

Autocentric Senses — According to Schachtel, these are senses felt in the body, such as taste or smell.

Autonomy — Independent self-determination.

Autonomy vs Shame and Doubt — According to Erikson, the second critical pair of alternatives in psychosocial development (from 12-18 months to 3 years), in which toddlers develop a balance of autonomous control (independence, self-determination) over shame and doubt.

Dependent-Active — One of Millon's basic personalities.

Dependent-Passive — One of Millon's basic personalities.

Gender Roles — Behaviors, interests, attitudes, and skills that a culture considers appropriate for males and females and expects them to fulfill.

Independent-Active — One of Millon's basic personalities.

Independent-Passive — One of Millon's basic personalities

Infantile Amnesia — According to Schachtel's theory, our inability to remember most of the events of our first five years. Freud's explanation was that it was a product of repression.

Morality of Conventional Role — One of Kohlberg's sub-stages of morality development.

Morphemes — The smallest element of speech that has meaning.

Prelinguistic Speech — Sounds that young children make that resemble speech that they have learned by imitation, accidental or deliberate.

"Children need love, especially when they do not deserve it."
—Harold S. Hulbert

Chapter 6

Ages 3-5

Pearce (1977) referred to this age growth as *magical* in terms of thinking and thoughts. That is, the thinking of a 4 year old "does not always need to be checked against reality. In these early years, thinking is autistic, wishful, fantastic."

This chapter examines the child as a preschooler. In modern society, many children are placed in preschools as young as 2 or 3 years old. Early enrollment in preschools and day care centers is usually necessary because both parents work, or in the case of a single parent home, there is no one else to care for the child during the day.

Physical Growth

Between the ages of 3 and 5 years the average boy will grow about eight inches and will gain an average of 16 pounds. Girls will grow about 8 inches and gain an average of 15 pounds in weight. This growth, as striking as it may seem, is not nearly as striking as the physical growth experienced by infants from birth to 2 years of age. There is a marked slowing of growth during this early childhood stage.

Different growth rates for different parts of the body help explain some of the changes that occur between the ages of 2 and 6. Most of the layer of fat that is noted in very young infants will have disappeared almost completely. The youngsters begin to look more like little adults.

Guy R. Lefrancois (1989) points out that one of the reasons for the differences has to do with the more rapid growth of muscle and bone tissue during this stage than earlier stages. The waist of younger infants is at least the same size as hips or chest, creating what seems like a squat appearance. Six year old children, by contrast, begin to develop a waist that is smaller than their shoulders and hips. This will become even more apparent in adolescence.

Ages 3-5

The larger size of the young infant's waist is due in part to the relatively large size of their internal organs. As they grow in height there is more room for the organs, and the stomach does not protrude as much.

Another thing that is responsible for the difference in appearance of the six year old is the difference in the ratio of the size of the head to the body size. The head of a 2 month old infant is equal to approximately half of the length of the rest of his body. By the age of 6 years, the head is about one-eighth of the total body size. It is this difference in fat and head size that result in the 6 year old looking remarkably like an adult.

Physically, this is also a time of motor development. Most children have learned to walk during stage 2, but they continue to learn to coordinate other motor activities, such as picking up objects, stacking blocks, unlacing shoes, and many more. Piaget explained the close relationship between motor and cognitive development during infancy in explicit theories.

As mentioned in the chapter on stage 1, infants from birth to age two had difficulty separating action from thought. Piaget posited that for infants, thought is internalized, whereas from the age of three on, their motor and cognitive development moves more to externalization. One of the more noticeable motor skill refinements in this stage is the change from the wide-footed stance of the toddler to a more sure-footed movement. There is also a perceivable improvement in equilibrium with their arms and hands being held closer to the body.

With this newly acquired stability of equilibrium comes the ability to climb stairs while standing up straight, a more steady walk, and the ability to hop with both feet.

There is also a noticeable improvement in the motor skills involving smaller muscles. The child can now begin to hold a pencil or crayon and is able to do rough tracing and copying of various designs. The work of Gessell (1925) pointed out that a two year old is incapable of copying a circle or even a horizontal line. The average three year old can do so quite easily. Gessell discovered that by the age of 4 years the child was able to copy a cross and trace a diamond, and button his own shirt. A five year old can copy a triangle or a prism and is able to lace or unlace his shoes.

Gessell's findings are confirmed by Cratty (1970), who used a sample of 170 middle-class children in an attempt to determine the order of difficulty in copying various geometric designs. Cratty did not include subjects younger than four years. All of this research confirms that during the stage 2 years there is a continuing, almost predictable, development of smaller muscles and cognitive ability (or hand-eye-mind coordination).

The Revised Stanford Binet Intelligence test for younger children was developed largely on the basis that the order of difficulty of the various geometric forms is the same for every reported study. The test is used to determine the advancement of motor skills, indicating the subsequent advancement of the cognitive development.

It has been noted by some researchers, especially in the social sciences, that part of the motivation for development of motor and cognitive skills may be related to a child's need to be accepted by other children into their games, etc.

For example, a child who is not able to jump, run, or perform other motor skills will not be chosen by his peers to play in games. Game playing is one of the important means of socialization (this becomes even more obvious in the chapters on adolescence and teenagers).

The muscular, skeletal, nervous, respiratory, circulatory, and immune systems are maturing, and all primary teeth are present.

Proper growth and health depend on proper nutrition, and because children eat less than before it is important to be sure that they receive a well-balanced diet with all of the essential nutrients needed. Various minor illnesses help to build immunity to disease and may also have cognitive and emotional benefits. Major contagious diseases are rare, especially when the children have been vaccinated.

There is a possibility of an increased risk to the health and care of children at this stage because of exposure to other children, stress in the home, poverty and hunger.

Stage Three was called the **Locomotor Genital** stage by Freud, while Erikson suggested that this stage is characterized by the issues of **Initiative vs Guilt**.

Psychosexual Development

In Freudian theory, this is the Phallic Stage, the time of "family romance"—the Oedipus complex in boys and the Electra complex in girls. Here the zone of gratification shifts to the genital region. The mistaken idea that children at this stage are very sexually motivated has led many writers to be critical of Freudian theory.

The more accurate interpretation is that the genital gratification of this stage is in terms of gender relations rather than actual sexual activity. Boys at this age become attached to their mothers in a different way than before.

The boy's oedipal crisis begins when the boy starts to take an interest in his penis, an organ that he has discovered is "so easily excitable and changeable, and so rich in sensations" (Freud. 1923. p. 246). At this age the boy wants to compare his penis to those of other males and of animals, and he tries to see the sexual organs of girls and women. He may also visualize himself as an aggressive heroic male with particular direction of his intentions toward his mother (his primary love object). This is the time when boys begin kissing their mother in a more aggressive manner and many of them wish to sleep with their mothers. He is, of course, not interested in sexual intercourse, but he fantasizes being in bed with mother and doing whatever it is that adults do in bed together.

As a rule, fathers are not too thrilled with the young boy's "unnatural" attachment to their wives, and they will object, calling the behavior either infantile of just a nuisance. This can be seen at the beginning of the oedipal conflict. The boy cannot take the place of the father, but that does not stop the rival wishes. Freud suggested that the frustration of this conflict is the cause of the boy's fear of castration by the father, who is, after all, much bigger than he.

According to Freud, this is the point at which a boy will begin to masturbate. In Freud's day, parents actually threatened their boys with castration if they were caught masturbating. The boy, in turn, would develop a greater fear of castration, because he may have noticed that his sister and other girls are missing a penis. He naturally concludes that they once had one but had it cut off, and that the same thing could happen to him. Thus, said Freud, "the oedipal rivalry takes on a new, dangerous dimension, and the boy must escape the whole situation" (Freud. 1923). Freud said that the boy resolves the oedipal conflict through a series of defensive maneuvers (Freud. 1923, 1924). The procedure is somewhat like this. The boy represses the oedipal feelings and, although he still loves his mother, he begins to identify with his father. Instead of fighting the father, he attempts to be more like him and to enjoy vicariously the feelings of being a man. Crain (1985) noticed that it is like the old saying, "If you can't beat him, join him."

The Girl's Oedipus Complex

Freud believed that girls have their own oedipal conflict. Freud's view on the topic is something like this. He noted (1933, pp. 122-27) that the girl, by the age of five years or so, becomes disappointed in her mother. She feels deprived because her mother no longer gives her the constant love and care that she required as a baby, and so, if new babies are born, she resents the attention they get. Furthermore, she is irritated by the mother's prohibitions, such as that of masturbation. Finally, and most upsetting, the girl discovers that she does not have a penis — a fact for which she blames the mother, "who sent her into the world so insufficiently equipped" (1925a. p. 193). These feelings lead to what Freud called "penis envy."

The conflict with mother over the thought that the lack of a penis was the mother's fault, eventually leads to a new discovery. The girl rediscovers her femininity. She learns to appreciate the love and attention she receives from her father. She begins to spin romantic fantasies about herself and her father. At first, the fantasies include wanting to have a penis like his, but before long she simply wants to have a baby and give the penis to him as a present.

Like the boy, the girl soon discovers that she cannot have sole ownership of the father. She cannot marry him, nor can she cuddle, hug and sleep with him. Freud called this complex in the girl the Electra complex.

Freud found the resolution of the Electra complex rather more puzzling than the oedipal complex in the boy. The boy was motivated by the fear of castration. He finally admitted that he did not know the answer, but made what he called his best guess. He said that the resolution of the Electra complex may well have been the result of the girl's fear of losing the love of both of the parents. Freud did not believe that the defensive move on the part of the boy or the girl ended the conflict. Although it was repressed from conscious thought, it was ever present in the unconscious. This is one of the major conflicts that Freud saw in the struggle of the Id and the Ego.

For example, Freud felt that in the case of the girl's inner conflict there may develop a "masculinity complex" in which a woman may avoid intimate relationships with men, since these only remind her of her inferior state, and instead, try to outdo men by becoming very aggressive and assertive" (1933. P. 126).

Psychosocial Development

Erikson maintained that the chief developmental crisis of early childhood is the development of a balance between initiative and guilt. He referred to the stage as the Phallic (Oedipal) Stage) agreeing with Freud in that the child's concerns at this age shifted from the anal zone to that of the genital zone. He also agreed with Freud that children now focus their interest on their genitals and become curious about the sex organs of others. They begin to see themselves in adult roles and dare to rival one parent for the love of the other.

Erikson calls the primary mode of this stage intrusion. The word intrusion describes the activity of the boy's penis, but as a general mode it infers much more. He suggested that in both sexes, the "maturation of physical and mental abilities impels the child forward into a variety of intrusive activities. These include the intrusion into other bodies by physical attack; the intrusion into other people's ears and minds by aggressive talking, the intrusion into space by vigorous locomotion, the intrusion into the unknown by consuming curiosity" (1950. p. 87).

The General Stage: Initiative vs Guilt.

Initiative, like intrusion, connotes forward movement. The child at this stage makes plans, set goals, and perseveres in attaining them. One only needs to observe the average 4 or 5 year old to realize the number of activities they will engage in during one day's time.

The crisis comes, however, when the child realizes that his greatest plans and hopes are doomed for failure. Again, Erikson is referring to the oedipal wishes and plan. As the child discovers that his (oedipal) plans are far too dangerous, he will begin to internalize social prohibitions — a guilt-producing superego — to keep such dangerous impulses and fantasies in check (Crain. 1985).

The result is a new form of self-restriction that produces in the individual a lifetime of self-observance, self-control, and self-punishment.

Erikson felt that the creation of a superego was one of the great tragedies of life. Although the superego is necessary to insure ac-ceptable social behavior, it also stifles the bold initiative with which the child met life at the phallic stage.

Erikson saw that three to six year olds were, more than at any other time, able to channel their ambitions into socially useful pursuits (1950). His suggestion for parents was that they ease their authority somewhat by permitting children to participate with them as equals on interesting projects. Thus, children do not need to give up their ambitions altogether and can begin to attach them to the goals of adult social life (Crain. 1985). Parents do play an important role in the outcome of this stage.

Identification

Identification is the adoption of the characteristics, beliefs, attitudes, values, and behaviors of another person or a group. It is an important personality development of early childhood.

In Freudian terms, the child identifies with the same sex parent at the resolution of the Oedipus or Electra complex. According to social learning theory, identification occurs when the child observes and imitates one or more models.

Gender Identity

The cognitive development theory maintains that gender identity and moral development are related to cognitive development. In other words, as the mind and cognition develop, the individual is able to discern and adapt to the behavior expected of him or her from the clues given by society.

The gender-schema theory, a variation of cognitive development theory that draws on aspects of social learning, holds that children fit their self-concept to the gender schema for their culture, a socially organized pattern of behavior for males and females. According to this theory, the gender schema of a culture or an individual can be changed. Sex differences are physical differences between males and females. Gender differences are differences between sexes that may or may not be based on biology. In some cultures, the responsibility of providing food for the family is the responsibility of the mother, while the father is the caretaker of the children. Gender roles are the behavior a culture deems appropriate for males and for females. Gender typing refers to the learning of culturally determined gender roles.

There are actually few differences between the sexes. After about the age of 10 or 11, girls do better in verbal abilities and boys do better in math and spatial abilities. Boys are more aggressive than girls from early childhood, and girls are more empathic. It is believed that these differences are the result of societal and family influences.

Despite these relatively minor gender differences, our society holds strong ideas about appropriate behavior for the two sexes, and children learn these expectations at an early age. The way that family and adults in general respond to children, teaches them how they are expected to behave. "Boys do not cry," "Girls can't throw a ball right." These are only two examples of the many clichés that are common in western society.

Gender stereotypes, exaggerated generalization that may not be true of individuals, have the potential to restrict the development of both sexes. **Androgynous** child rearing, which encourages the expression of both "male" and "female" characteristics, is being fostered by many individuals and social institutions. Mention has already been made to the theory of Jung that posits that all humans are part male and part female. His terms were anima and animus.

Society is not completely ready to accept males, who behave in a feminine manner, nor females that are too masculine, but there has been a preponderance of literature that expresses the concept that men need to learn to be more feeling and that women need to become more logical, and so forth.

Cognitive Development

Piaget puts this age group in what he called the preoperational stage, which is actually divided into two stages. The first stage covers ages 2-4 and is referred to as pre-conceptual, while stage 2 covering ages of 4-7 years is thought of as intuitive. The entire preoperational stage (2-7 years old) is characterized by egocentric thought.

Younger infants, who were in Piaget's sensorimotor stage, had a representation of the world and reasoning about it on the basis of sensation and action, but by the end of the second year of life, the child, especially because of the advent of language, begins to symbolize. They begin to represent their actions mentally, to anticipate consequences before the action actually occurs, and to develop some notion of causes of actions as means to an end.

According to Piaget, because of the development of recall, thought is not limited to events in the immediate environment as in the sensorimotor stage. The child, however, cannot yet think logically as in the next stage, concrete operations.

The symbolic function, as shown in deferred imitation, symbolic play, and language, enables children to mentally represent and reflect upon people, objects, and events through symbols and signs. Symbolic activity refers to the use of one object to represent an absent one. The child is thinking symbolically when he pretends that a mud pie is real food.

Children in the sensorimotor stage can learn to imitate the faces adults make while the adult is present and actually making the face. In the preoperational stage, they are able to imitate faces and other actions even when the adult is absent.

Some psychologists believe that children learn to think more logically as they master language, but Piaget disagreed with them. He felt that even though language is important and provides children with the symbols of communication, it does not provide in itself the structure of logical thinking (1966. pp.86-90).

Emotional Development

In terms of Millon's parental style for this stage, rejection would seem to be the most devastating. Because of the attachments that are made as a result of the oedipal complex, both in boys and in girls, to be rejected by either parent, or both parents, would lead to a less than desirable personality style of **detached active**. The child could very well grow to be an individual with a great need for protection, an avoidant social style, and a self-image of alienation.

The great danger in this stage is for the child to be convinced that there was something very wrong with their feelings toward their parent. This is one of the reasons that Erikson suggested that guilt was the alternative outcome in the child's struggle to express initiative.

It is generally accepted by psychologists, and others in the mental health profession, that feelings of guilt are central to the understanding of psychological maladjustment. Guilt is one of the major emotions (anxiety being the other) that sets in motion the various psychological defense mechanisms. Because guilt is painful, people, especially children, tend to repress the feelings of guilt. This repression is the first step on the road to the formation of neurotic symptoms (Benner. 1985).

Preschool children show many fears of both real and imaginary objects and events. Sometimes these fears develop into phobias, which are irrational, involuntary, and inappropriate to the situation. Conditioning and modeling can help children overcome fears and phobias. (Papalia. 1989).

Unfortunately, parents do not realize the seriousness of the phobias and fears, and because of their own ignorance choose to ignore or simply hope that they will disappear in time.

Feelings of guilt (often referred to as punitive guilt feelings) are based on attitudes of self-punishment, self-rejection, and low esteem. They develop over a period of years within the context of the child's relationship with parents and significant others. Benner lists four dynamics that appear to be central in the development of the guilt feelings: 1) the child's innate capacity for self-observation and judgment, 2) the taking in of the standards and expectations of others, 3) the taking in of the punishments and corrective attitudes of others, and 4) the child's anger over the frustration of his or her needs and wishes.

Theorists all seem to agree that the development of guilt feelings and other aspects of moral functioning are central to the child's innate potential for cognitive development, without which the child would be unable to accurately evaluate their actions and the consequence of them or to profit from the socialization process (Benner. 1989).

The second factor in the development of guilt feelings, mentioned by Benner, is the child's taking in of the standards of parents or significant others. This process is called internalization, and it takes place as children begin to adopt parental and societal values which are often in conflict with their own base feelings and needs. The result of this need to accept parental values is the fear of punishment or rejection for disobedience, and children take their parent's standards as their own, usually repressing their own feelings.

When the child feels angry with his parents and others, he naturally assumes that they are also angry with him. When parents punish a child, he or she will see the parent as being angrier than they usually are. This situation of confusion leads to a stronger feeling of anger in the child with the accompanying feelings of guilt. This is why many adults with loving parents still have serious problems with guilt.

Social Development

The child at this stage, due to his increased mobility, becomes more social. With his new social contacts come new problems for parents. Some of the old behavior of the terrible twos will still be present as the child continues to protect what he feels is "Mine" and is not to be shared.

New aggressive social behaviors will begin to be expressed towards others outside of the family. Whether this aggressive behavior is a result of the parental style, a product of modeling of parent's action, or the influence of the media is still in the process of research.

The question of the effect of siblings on the development of children has been a point of discussion for students of child development for many years. There is evidence that children raised as an only child tend to fare better emotionally and intellectually than do children with siblings. As siblings move through early childhood, most of their interactions are positive. As they mature their interaction is often less physical and more often verbal. Older siblings tend to be dominant and are more aggressive and more prosocial.

Children who are aggressive or withdrawn tend to be less popular with playmates than children who act friendly. The type of attachment the child had in infancy, as well as their parents' attitudes, disciplinary techniques, and child rearing style, affect the ease with which young children find playmates and friends (Papalia. 1989).

The Ever Widening Environment

Many children between 3 and 6 years of age attend day care centers, preschool and kindergarten. Some of these programs are changing to meet the needs of working parents, as well as children's intellectual and developmental needs. Little is known yet about the effects of most day care. Studies of the highest quality day care centers suggest that good day care enhances children's social and emotional development. Preschool and kindergarten prepares children for formal schooling. Some programs focus more on structured cognitive tasks, and others on activities of the children's initiating. In the past 30 years, the academic content of the kindergarten curriculum has increased.

One study showed that the compensatory preschool programs can have a long-term positive outcome. However, it is important not to put too much academic pressure on children 3 and 4 years old. One of the most successful programs has been the Montessori schools, in which children are able to learn at their level of interest without preconceived norms being set by the teachers. It should be noted here that not all Montessori schools are alike. Theoretically, all of the schools are supposed to follow the same methods, using the materials produced by Montessori. For economic reasons or because some of the teachers are not adequately trained in the Montessori system, many of the schools use a modification of the original and official Montessori methods.

Lefrancois (1989) observed that all of the experiences of children, from birth to school age, compose their preschool education. The language they hear, the people who serve as models for their behavior, those who control some of their rewards and punishments, television programs, books, stories, movies, visits to different places such as museums or even Disneyland, the activities in which they engage — all of these are teachers. Life is the curriculum, adaptation is the major objective; development becomes the teaching process, and the child is the learner at the center of the process.

Lefrancois also pointed out that the most striking feature of the preschooler's environment is its haphazard, unstructured nature; yet the strides preschoolers make from birth to school age are enormous. This is, in the opinion of many, another argument for the Montessori method, which in turn goes all the way back to the original premise of Rousseau and his theoretical work of fiction, "Emile." It would seem that there is support for the notion that children learn more efficiently when the environment is rich in stimulus, and the child is allowed to learn on his or her own time table.

Kohlberg (1968) noted that the Montessori Method represents three distinct things: a set of ideas, a set of materials, and an ideology. Each aspect is examined briefly in turn.

Maria Montessori's ideas are complex, far reaching, highly speculative, somewhat poetic, frequently unscientific, and relatively difficult to summarize (Lefrancois. 1989). Montessori speaks of the "absorbent" nature of the child's mind. She suggested that society had a responsibility for providing a structured education as early in the child's life as possible. However, her ideas of structured programs differed considerably from what comes to mind for the modern educator.

Montessori developed an impressively large number of physical materials that were used in teaching. One such material consisted of large letters made with sandpaper on one surface. She claimed to have taught a large population of slum children in Rome to read effectively with the use of these letters and the assistance of a phonetic reinforcement. She believed that while the child simultaneously felt the texture of the letter with the fingers of one hand getting the tactile sensation of it, and repeated the phonetic sound, and looked at the shape of the letter, the child was learning by three senses: touch, vision, and hearing.

Montessori also maintained that the method fostered moral development by emphasizing order, patience, self-control, responsibility and cooperation.

For more information about the Montessori teaching methods, see, Montessori, Marie. *The Absorbent Mind.* New York: Holt, Rinehart & Winston. 1967.

One preschool effort, a Project Head Start program developed in Ypsilanti, Michigan was based directly on Piagetian theory. Teaching emphasized the development of the child's understanding of the world and the development of reasoning in direct relation to their developmental readiness. For more information on this project see Kamii (1972).

Personal Reflections

This stage of development presents many of the same problems of the first two stages. The preschool child is at a very impressionable age and is dealing with some explosive issues in his life, most of which he is not able to fully understand. Parents need to be aware of the issue of the Oedipal complex and Electra complex and develop an understanding, loving, and non-judgmental attitude toward their child at such an important time in the early development.

Ages 3-5

In the counseling office, it is not unusual to deal with a client who has suffered considerable trauma during the preschool years. Some of the trauma may have developed in some rather irritating phobias and fears that, although not completely debilitating, may cause considerable discomfort in the individual's daily life.

The greater problem with which many counselors must deal stems from a heinous behavior that may seem beyond possibility to some. I speak here of the situation in which a father (or mother) is so totally ignorant of the dynamics of the Oedipal Complex, especially the Electra Complex, that they truly believe that the attraction of the girl to the father is a sensual seductive response. I was once told by a friend in the probation department of a large city that the defense a father used, for his molestation of his five year old daughter, was that the five year old had seduced him.

I have no idea what happened to the little girl as she grew into adulthood, but I can almost say without reservation that she has or will seek the help of a professional counselor sometime in her lifetime.

Since John Bradshaw published his first book dealing with abusing parents and adults who were abused as children, literally thousands of hurt, damaged people have realized that what they experienced as young children was wrong, and the guilt that they had experienced all of their lives was the repressed fear and guilt suffered at the hands of a cruel father, and often an ignorant mother as well.

Review of Chapter 6

- Pearce called this stage a time of magical growth.
- These children are the preschoolers.
- Children continue to grow physically but not as rapidly as before.
- Much of the growth at this stage has to do with muscle and bone.
- Children begin to take on a different overall look at this stage due to the difference in the size of the head to the rest of the body.
- This is a time of motor development.
- There is a new stability of equilibrium.
- Finer motor skills are not yet noticeable.
- Part of the reason that motor skills develop more rapidly is that the children want to be accepted by other children.
- Freud called this stage the locomotor genital stage.
- Erikson maintained that the psychosocial issue of this stage was Initiative vs Guilt.
- Freudian theory referred to this stage as the phallic stage that was the beginning of the Oedipus complex in boys and the Electra complex in girls.
- Both the Oedipus and the Electra complex, although very problematic for the parents and the children, find resolution with the children changing their alliance to the parent of the same sex.
- Erikson saw this stage as a time of intrusion.
- Erikson thought that the development of the superego was one of life's great tragedies.
- Freud's use of the term identification had to do with a child identifying with the parent of the same sex.
- The cognitive development theory maintains that gender identity and moral development are related to cognitive development.
- Sex differences are physical differences between male and female and gender differences are differences between sexes that may or may not be based on biology.
- There are actually very few differences between the sexes biologically.

- The main differences are in the gender differences fostered by society.
- Gender stereotypes tend to exaggerate the differences.
- Piaget placed this age group in the preoperational stage.
- Piaget disagreed with those psychologists who believed that children learned to think more logically as they mastered language.
- According to Millon and others, the great danger of this stage is that children might feel that there is something wrong with their feeling toward their parents.
- Feelings of guilt are central to an understanding of psychological maladjustment.
- Preschool children show many fears of both real and imaginary objects and events.
- Theorists all seem to agree that the development of guilt feelings and other aspects of moral functioning are central to the child's innate potential for cognitive development.
- When a child feels angry with his parents, he naturally feels that they are also angry with him.
- Children at this stage are becoming more social.
- New aggressive social behaviors will begin to be expressed towards others outside the family.
- Siblings play a very important role in the development of the child.
- The environment of the child at this stage becomes ever widening.
- One study showed that compensatory preschool education can have a long-term positive outcome.
- Kohlberg noted that the Montessori Method represented three distinct things: a set of ideas, a set of materials, and ideology.
- The development of the Project Head Start program emphasized the development of the child's understanding of the world and the development of reasoning in direct relation to their developmental readiness.

Glossary for Chapter 6

Glossary of Terms

Aggressive Behavior — Hostile actions intended to hurt somebody or to establish dominance.

Ambivalent Attachment — Pattern of attachment in which an infant becomes anxious before the primary caregiver leaves, is extremely upset during his or her absence, and both seeks and resists contact upon his or her return; also called resistant attachment.

Androgynous — Personality type integrating positive characteristics typically thought of as masculine with positive characteristics typically thought of as feminine.

Attachment — Active, affectionate reciprocal relationship specifically between two persons (usually infant and parent), in which interaction reinforces and strengthens the link.

Authoritarian Parents — In Baumrind's terminology, parents whose child-rearing style emphasizes the values of control and obedience and the use of forceful punishment to make children conform to a set standard of conduct. Compare with authoritative parents and permissive parents.

Behavior Modification — Changing undesirable behavior by rewarding desirable behavior. Based loosely on the theories of Pavlov and B.F. Skinner.

Castration Complex — Phenomenon described by Freud in which a male child, seeing that girls do not have a penis and overwhelmed by guilt about his Oedipal feelings and fear of his father's power, becomes fearful that he will be castrated by his father.

Childhood Depression — Affective disorder characterized by a child's inability to form and maintain friendships, have fun, concentrate, and display normal emotional reactions.

Cognitive Development — Changes in thought processes that result in a growing ability to acquire and use knowledge.

Cognitive Play — Forms of play that are real and that enhance children's cognitive development.

Concrete Operations — Third stage of Piagetian cognitive development (approximately from 5-7 to age 11), during which children develop logical but not abstract thinking.

Decenter — In Piagetian terminology to consider all significant aspects of a situation simultaneously. Decentration is characteristic of operational thought.

Defense Mechanisms — According to Freudian theory, way in which people unconsciously combat anxiety by distorting reality.

Deferred Imitation — In Piagetian terminology, reproduction of an observed behavior after the passage of time by calling up a stored symbol of it.

Ego — In Freudian theory, an aspect of personality that develops during infancy and operates on the reality principle, seeking acceptable means of gratification in dealing with the real world.

119

Electra Complex — According to Freudian theory, the female counterpart of the Oedipus complex, in which the young girl in the phallic stage feels sexual attraction for her father and rivalry toward her mother.

Gender — Significance of being male or female.

Gender Conservation — Realization that one's sex will always stay the same.

Gender Differences — Difference between males and females that may or may not be based on biological differences.

Gender Identity — Awareness developed in early childhood, that one is male or female.

Gender Roles — Behavior, interests, attitudes, and skills that a culture considers appropriate for males and females and expects them to fulfill.

Gender Stereotypes — Exaggerated generalizations about male or female role behavior.

Gender Typing — Socialization process by which a child, at an early age, learns the appropriate gender role.

Id — In Freudian theory, the instinctual aspect of personality (present at birth) that operates on the pleasure principle, seeking immediate gratification.

Identification — Process by which a person acquires characteristics, beliefs, attitudes, values, and behavior of another person or of a group; an important personality development of early childhood.

Initiative vs Guilt — According to Erikson, the third stage of crisis of psychosocial development, occurring between the ages of 3 and 6, in which children must balance the urge to form and carry out goals with their moral judgments about what they want to do. Children develop initiative when they try out new things and are not overwhelmed by failure.

Introjection — In the development of the superego, it is the process by which values are incorporated.

Invisible Imitation — Imitation with parts of one's body that one cannot see, e.g., the mouth.

Oedipus Complex — Phenomenon described by Freud in which the young boy in the phallic stage feels sexual attraction for his mother and rivalry toward his father.

Penis Envy — Phenomenon, described by Freud, in which a girl envies the male's penis and wants one of her own.

Permissive Parents — parents whose child-rearing style emphasizes the cause of self-expression and self-regulation. Compare with authoritarian parents and authoritative parents.

Phallic Stage — According to Freudian theory, the stage of psychosexual development between the ages of 3 and 6, in which the child receives gratification chiefly in the genital area.

Phobias — Irrational, involuntary fears inappropriate to the real situation. Pre-conventional morality : According to Kohlberg, the first level of moral development, in which children aged approximately 4 to 10 years obey the rules or standards set by others, in order to gain rewards or avoid punishment.

Preoperational Stage — In Piagetian theory, the second major period of intellectual development (approximately from age 2 to 7), in which children can think about things not physically present by using mental representation but are limited by their use of logic.

Pretend Play — Play involving imaginary situations; also called fantasy play, dramatic play, or imaginative play.

Private Speech — Talking aloud to oneself with no intent to communicate, common in early and middle childhood.

Project Head Start — Compensatory preschool education program begun in the United States in 1965.

Prosocial Behavior — Behavior intended to help others without external reward.

Schema — According to Sandra Bem (1983, 1985) it is a mentally organized pattern of behavior that helps a child sort out perceived information.

Self-esteem — Person's self-evaluation or self-image.

Superego — According to Freudian theory, that aspect of personality representing values that parents and other agents of society communicate to a child. It develops around the age of 5 or 6 as a result of resolution of the Oedipus or Electra complex.

Symbolic Function — In Piaget's terminology, ability to learn by using mental representations (symbols or signs) to which a child has attached meaning; this ability characteristic is shown in deferred imitation, symbolic play and language.

Symbolic Play — In Piaget's terminology, play in which a child makes an object stand for something else.

Systematic Desensitization — An experiment involving gradual exposure to the feared object in phobias.

"There are two lasting bequests we can hope to give our children. One of these is roots, the other, wings."
—Hodding Carter

Chapter 7

Ages 6-12

Freud referred to this stage as the **Latency Period**.
Erikson described the conflict of this period as **Industry vs Inferiority**.
The middle childhood years are the elementary school years. Children make great strides in development during the age between 6 and 12 years.

Physical development

During these years children grow taller, heavier, and stronger. They become better at things that they have already been doing. They can throw a ball farther and more accurately. They can run faster and for a longer time.

There are three important considerations of physical development during these years. They are nutrition, obesity, and the improvement of children's fitness.

The development of children at this stage can best be called "slow and steady." Physical growth slows down considerably, and while motor skills continue to improve, the changes are not nearly so dramatic as before (Papalia. 1985). These years between 6 and 12 are considered to be the healthiest in the life span. Papalia notes, however, that children are not as healthy nor physically fit as their counterparts of the 1960's.

At this stage, there is a wide variety of sizes and shapes to be seen in an elementary schoolyard full of children. Some are tall, some short, some chubby, some thin, but most of them would be exhibiting a considerable amount of energy. Some of the children would actually be considered as obese or fat.

Both boys and girls gain an average of 7 pounds and 2 to 3 inches a year until the adolescent growth spurt, which comes for girls about age 10, out distancing boys physically until the boys have their spurt and overtake them at age 12 or 13 (Papalia. 1989).

Of course, these figures are presented as averages. Each child grows at his own rate and in a group of 13 year old boys, one would expect to find a difference of several inches in height and several pounds in weight. However, most of the boys would fit within what might be called a normal limit. Another consideration is that growth rates vary with race, national origin, and socioeconomic level.

Because of the wide variations between sexes of middle childhood children, care must be taken not to make judgments concerning children's health on size alone. It is true, however, that nutrition can make a great difference in the physical development of children at this age.

Because the child between the ages of 6 and 12 doubles his average body weight and because these children are much more active using more energy than at any other time in their life up until now, nutrition plays a very important role in health and physical development. The average child at this period in life needs about 2400 calories per day, 34 grams of protein a day, and high levels of complex carbohydrates, such as found in potatoes and cereal grains. The one food type that they do not need much of is the refined carbohydrates (sugars).

It is no secret that poor nutrition can slow growth. If a child is not getting enough calories to meet the energy and growth needs of his body, his growth will be slowed considerably. If, on the other hand, most of a child's calories come from sugar products, not only will growth slow down, but serious health and behavior problems may develop.

One of the health problems of modern society is that of obesity. It is estimated that there is 54 percent more obesity among 6 to 12 year olds (39 percent more common for 12 to 17 year olds) in the United States than two decades ago. The problem stems most likely from the amount of sugary foods and fast foods eaten each day by the average child. A second part of the problem is that children are not as active in today's society as their counterparts 20 years ago.

Obesity is more common among the lower socioeconomic groups, especially among females. There is evidence that there is a correlation between obesity and the time spent in front of a television. Children who watch more television eat more snacks (usually those advertised in commercials) and play less than other children. It also follows that obese children often grow up to be obese parents (Kolata. 1986), and of course obesity in adulthood puts individuals at greater health risk.

There are many programs aimed at improving the health of children, especially in this age group. Probably the most well-known is the President's Fitness Program. Unfortunately, these programs do not carry over into the pre-teen years, where they are equally as important.

Studies that were done some 20 years ago, when children were more active, suggested that motor abilities improve with age. These studies also found sex differences: boys tended to run faster, jump higher, throw farther, and show more strength than girls did (Espenchade. 1960 Gavotos. 1959).

A chronological summary of the physical development of boys and girls ages 6 to 12 is presented in Papalia as adapted from Cratty. 1979. p. 222.

Age 6. Girls are superior in accuracy of movement; boys are superior in forceful, less complex acts. Children can throw with proper weight shift and step.

Age 7. Balancing on one foot without looking becomes almost possible. Children can walk 2 inch-wide balance beams. They can hop and jump accurately into small squares, such as in the jumping-jack exercises.

Age 8. Children's grip strength permits steady 12 pound pressure. The number of games participated in by both sexes is greater at this age. Children can engage in alternate rhythmic hopping in a 2-, 2-3, or 3-3 pattern. Girls can throw a small ball about 40 feet.

Age 9. Girls can jump vertically to a height of 8 1/2 inches and boys can jump to about 10 inches. Boys can run 16 1/2 feet per second and throw a ball about 70 feet.

Age 10. Children can judge and intercept pathways of small balls thrown from a distance. Girls can run 17 feet per second.

Age 11. A standing broad jump of 5 feet is possible for boys, 6 inches less than girls.

Age 12. A standing high jump of 3 feet is possible.

Major health problems are rarer at this age, and the death rate in middle childhood is the lowest in the life span. If the child does become ill with a serious illness, the duration is relatively short. They do experience many minor illnesses, such as colds, allergies, upper respiratory infections, viruses, or eczema. Most of the minor illnesses in this age group are no doubt attributable to the increased activity and increased association with other children in school.

Cognitive Development

Between the ages of 5-7, according to Piaget, children enter the stage of **concrete operations**, when they can think logically about the present, but not yet about abstractions. This stage lasts until about the age of 11 years.

Operational thinking is the term that Piaget used to mean that children can use symbols to carry out operations, or mental activity, as opposed to the physical activities that were the basis for most of their earliest thinking. The children are much more able to make mental representations of objects and events that are not immediately present. They can classify, manipulate numbers, deal with concepts of time and space, and distinguish reality from fantasy.

A detailed study of the development of cognitive abilities can best be understood by referring to the complete writings of Piaget (1955). For the purposes of this text, only an overview is possible.

One of the major considerations of Piaget's theory has to do with the concept that he called **conservation**. Conservation is the ability to recognize that two equal quantities of matter remain the equal — in substance, weight, or volume — so long as nothing is added or taken away.

Children at this age will go through three basic stages in mastering conservation. In the first stage, preoperational children fail to conserve, because they focus on one aspect of the situation. In one of the illustrations used by Piaget, a child is shown two equally sized lumps of clay. If one of the lumps is rolled into a snake, they will think that the now longer piece of clay is larger (they will not be able to reason that it is also thinner). Neither do these children understand the concept of **reversibility** or the concept that the long thin piece of clay can be returned to its original mass.

The second stage in conservation is transitional in that children will vacillate, sometimes conserving and sometimes not. In the third stage children conserve and give logical **justifications** for their answers. They may, for example, justify their position by saying that if the snake were to be reshaped into a ball it would be the same as before, reversibility. Another form of justification is called identity, in which the child would reason, "It's the same clay, you haven't taken away or added any to it," or they may employ what Piaget called **compensation** ("The ball is shorter than the worm, but the worm is thinner than the ball, so they both have the same amount of clay").

Piaget insisted that children develop the ability to conserve when they are neurologically mature enough. The children who learn conservation skills earliest are children who have higher IQs (and non-dominant mothers) (Papalia. 1989.)

Moral Development

Papalia adapted a summary of Piaget's two stages of moral development. Kohlberg's work on moral development is similar in form. The following is an abbreviated review of those concepts.

Piaget believed that moral development parallels approximately the preoperational and operational stages of cognition development. The first stage of moral development is **morality of constraint** (also called **heteronomous morality**). It is characterized by rigid, simplistic judgments where everything is either black or white. There are no gray areas. Because of the egocentricity of children in this stage, they cannot imagine that there could be more than one way of looking at a moral question. This child views an act as either totally right or totally wrong. They cannot put themselves in the place of others.

In the first stage, children judge acts in terms of actual physical consequence, not the motivation behind them. They obey rules because they are sacred and unalterable, handed down by the powerful adult or even God.

In stage one, children are led to feelings or obligation to conform to adult standards and obey adult rules.

Stage one children favor severe punishment. Because they feel that punishment itself defines the wrongness of the act. An act is bad if it will elicit punishment. (One cannot help but make the connection to Millon's overindulgent parental style).

These children often confuse moral law with physical law. They believe that any physical accident or misfortune that occurs after a misdeed is a punishment willed by God or some other supernatural force. There are many adults apparently fixated at this stage, who feel that any serious accident or illness is God's punishment for some wrong act on their part.

Stage two in moral development is referred to as the morality of cooperation (or autonomous morality) and can be identified by the following:

Piaget called this stage the **morality of cooperation**. At this stage, children can put themselves in the place of others. They are not absolutist in judgments but see that more than one point of view is possible. They now judge acts by intentions not consequences. Children recognize that rules were made by people and can be changed by people. They consider themselves just as capable of changing rules as anyone else.

At this stage children begin to gain a mutual respect for authority and peers. They allow others to value their own opinions and abilities and to judge other people realistically. Children at this stage favor milder punishment that compensates the victim. They believe this also helps the culprit recognize why an act was wrong, thus leading to reform (or at least repentance). By this time, the child no longer confuses natural misfortune with punishment.

Kohlberg's Theory: Moral Reasoning

Kohlberg tells the following story to a group of boys ranging in age from 10 to 16. Although the ages here extend beyond the range of this chapter, it is interesting to see the results of this research.

A woman is near death from cancer.

A druggist has discovered a drug that doctors believe might save her. The druggist is charging $2000 for a small dose which is 10 times what it costs him to make the drug. The sick woman's husband, Heinz, borrows from everyone he knows but can scrape together only $1000. He begs the druggist to sell him the drug for less or let him pay later. The druggist refuses, saying, "I discovered the drug, and I'm going to make money from it." Heinz, desperate, breaks into the man's store and steals the drug. Should Heinz have done that? Why, or why not? (Kohlberg, 1969).

The boys were asked to respond in relation to 25 fundamental moral ideas. From their responses, Kohlberg formulated his six levels of moral reasoning. The levels were further divided into stages of reasoning. For the purposes of this text the levels and stages of moral reasoning will be greatly abbreviated. For a more complete study, see Kohlberg, 1969.

Levels and Stages of Moral Development

Level 1 Pre-conventional (ages 4-10)

Emphasis in this level is on external control. The standards are those of others, and they are observed as whether to avoid punishment or to reap rewards.

Stage one of moral reasoning is an orientation to punishment and obedience. "What will happen to me?" Children obey the rules of others to avoid punishment. They ignore the motives of an act and focus on its physical form (such as the size of the lie) or its consequences (for example, the amount of physical damage). Typical answers to the story are:

Pro: "He should steal the drug. It isn't really bad to take it. It isn't as if he hadn't asked to pay for it first. The drug he'd take is worth only $200; he's not really taking a $2000 drug."

Con: "He shouldn't steal the drug. It's a big crime. He didn't get permission, he used force and broke and entered. He did a lot of damage, stealing a very expensive drug and breaking the law."

Stage 2 is characterized by instrumental purpose and exchange: "You scratch my back, I'll scratch yours." Children conform to rules out of self-interest and consideration for what others can do for them in return. They look at an act in terms of the human needs it meets and differentiates this value from the act's physical form and consequence. Some typical answers are:

Pro: "It's all right to steal the drug, because his wife needs it, and he wants her to live. It isn't that he wants to steal, but that's what he has to do to get the drug to save her."

Con: "He shouldn't steal it. The druggist isn't wrong or bad: he just wants to make a profit. That's what you're in business for — to make money."

Level II: Morality of conventional role conformity (ages 10 to 13)

Children now want to please other people. They still observe the standards of others, but they have internalized these standards to some extent. Now they want to be considered "good" by those persons whose opinions are important to them. They are now able to take the roles of authority figures well enough to decide whether an action is good by their standards.

Stage 3 is characterized by maintaining mutual relations, approval of others, the golden rule: "Am I a good boy or girl?" Children want to please and help others. They can judge the intentions of others, and develop their own ideas of what a good person is. They evaluate an act according to the motive behind it or the person performing it, and they take circumstances into account. Typical answers to Heinz's dilemma:

Pro: "He should steal the drug. He is only doing something that is natural for a good husband to do. You can't blame him for doing something out of love for his wife. You'd blame him if he didn't love his wife enough to save her."

Con: "He shouldn't steal. If his wife dies he can't be blamed. It isn't because he is heartless or that he doesn't love her enough to do everything that he legally can. The druggist is the heartless or selfish one."

Stage 4 and stages 5 and 6 of level III will be considered in the next chapter, because they relate more to the next age level.

Psychosexual Development

Children at this age (6 to 12) enter what Freud called the latency period, having established strong defenses against oedipal feelings. The strong sexual aggressive fantasies are now largely latent; they are kept firmly down in the unconscious. Freud thought that the repression of sexuality at this time is quite sweeping; it includes not only oedipal feelings and memories, but oral and anal ones as well (1905. pp. 580-85). The latency period is one of relative calm now that the impulses and fantasies are repressed. This is the time of the child's life when he or she can redirect their energies into concrete, socially acceptable pursuits, such as sports, games and intellectual activities.

Based on such facts that an eight year old boy may still be interested in girls' bodies, some of Freud's followers (Blos. 1962. pp.53-54), suggest that not all of the sexual aggressiveness and fantasies are completely repressed. This is the age at which many children learn about the real facts of life. However, most Freudians believe that most of the furor concerning sexual issues is considerably dissipated during the latency period.

Benner (1985) points out that "We now know that sexual interest still exists, but it is no longer at center stage, as is the case during the earlier years of oedipal struggle. The latency period is a time of consolidating and integrating previous attainments in psychosexual development. The most important of these attainments are gender identity and sex roles. Latency years are therefore characterized by a predominance of same-sex relationships that serve to solidify gender identity and basic sex roles."

It is interesting to note that less has been written about this psychosexual stage than some of the others. It is not that the stage itself is not interesting, but the problems and conflicts of this stage are not as dramatic as in other stages. Because of the changes taking place in modern society, some of the "normal" behavior of boys and girls at this stage are changing at least in outward behavior. In years past, the same-sex relations were much more defined. Boys often acted as if they would rather die than be caught playing with a girl. Of course, the thought of actually kissing a girl romantically was total anathema.

Another way of looking at this period in life is that it is the calm before the storm, as mentioned earlier. Anyone who has worked with elementary school children will agree that for the most part these children seem to be experiencing a wonderful time in their lives. These are truly the Wonder Years just before the entrance into puberty.

Psychosocial Development

Erikson agreed with Freud that this stage was one of latency. He noted, however, that this stage may not be entirely free of conflict. The birth of a sibling may arouse intense jealousy. As far as the instincts and drives, nothing much is going on.

Siblings tend to quarrel or fight more than peers outside of the home. The main difference is that siblings tend to make up, whereas peers may fight and never be real friends again.

Another problem that has become more prevalent in recent years is the problem of **blended children**. Blended children are children in a home where there has been a divorce and remarriage. Each of the parents, who were married before, bring their own children to the new marriage and often have children together creating the "yours, mine, and ours" syndrome. There has not been enough time for meaningful research to be complete on the effects of these combination families.

Many questions remain unanswered. What effect does the merging of stepchildren into a new family system have on each of the children? Is it possible for the new father (or mother) to treat the offspring of someone else with the same love and care as they do their own? Will children who felt secure in the position of the firstborn child in a family, feel as secure when a step-sibling comes along who is older and the first-born of another family group?

With most of these questions, only time will tell.

Although many children may suffer emotionally, physically, and/or spiritually from dysfunctional families, there are some youngsters that are considered as **resilient children**. These children are able to bounce back from circumstances that would totally overwhelm others. These are the children of the ghetto who go on to become professional people. They are the neglected and abused children who go on to form intimate relationships and to lead fulfilling lives. They are winners, in spite of the negative circumstances of their lives.

There are some questions about why some children are so resilient. Erikson did see this stage as a most decisive stage for ego growth. Children master important cognitive and social skills. The crisis is **Industry vs**

Inferiority. Children forget their past hopes and wishes, which were often played out within the family. Now their attention is focused on learning the useful skills and tools necessary in the wider culture. Erikson noted that in the rural society of preliterate culture, this was the time when children learned to hunt, fish, farm, and make utensils. In modern culture, children are expected to attend school and master the more cerebral skills — reading, writing, and arithmetic. In both early and modern cultures, the children are learning to do meaningful tasks and are developing the ego strengths of "stealth attention and persevering diligence" (1930. p. 259).

Erikson saw the danger of this stage as excessive feelings of inadequacy and inferiority (1950. p. 260). Most adults can remember the hurt of failures during the elementary school years in the classroom or on the playground. A deep sense of inferiority may have deep and various roots, and sometime children have difficulty at this stage because they have not successfully resolved the conflicts of earlier stages.

Dr. DeKoven (1992) tells a story in his book entitled, *I Want to be Like You, Dad*. The story follows:

> "It was a hot August morning, and my dad had asked me to paint our white picket fence. As with most eight year olds, my dad was my hero. I would have done anything to prove myself worthy of his affection. For him to be proud of me was my highest desire. I could demonstrate my worth by painting the fence just for him.
>
> I remember so vividly putting on my old clothes (which is somewhat redundant since we were so poor, all my clothes were old), gathering the paint and brush, and setting out to transform our old picket fence into a beautiful showpiece.
>
> Needless to say, I got nearly as much paint on my clothes and the grass as on the fence. Eight year olds are not the most skilled at such things. About halfway through the day my Mom brought me some finger sandwiches and Kool-Aid (like she did for my dad). An extra special touch for what was shaping up to be a most excellent day.
>
> About 5:00 pm, I started cleaning up the paint brushes and putting away the supplies in anticipation of my dad's arrival home. After tidying up, I sat down on my front porch, like a little Buddha, waiting for dad's arrival.
>
> A few minutes later my dad drove up, pulling his old but faithful car into the vacant lot next to our old house. After

inspecting the rocks (a daily ritual, to make sure that new ones had not grown or been thrown at the house), he walked toward the house. I sat with positive expectations. He came through the front gate, and walked past me without acknowledgment. My heart beat a bit faster, though this was a fairly common routine. After work, my dad would typically enter the house, pat my mom on the head, kiss the dog, and change his clothes. Honest! How my mom could tolerate playing second fiddle to the dog I'll never know.

After changing, my dad came back outside, again without seeming to notice me, and began to inspect the fence. My heart really began to beat. At times my dad could be quite angry. I had hopes that today would not be one of those days. As

my dad began to approach the front of the house, I heard him speaking to himself. He was mumbling loud enough for me to hear some comments that would impact the course of my life for many years to come. He stated, in no uncertain terms, "If you're to do a man's job, you need a man to do it. Stan, you're never going to amount to (expletives)!" Pow."

It is not too difficult to see how Stan's experience could leave an eight year old with real and painful feelings of inferiority. Erikson said that the virtue of this stage was **competence**, there was no competence inspired in the above story.

Theodore Millon would suggest that this parental style was **perfectionism**. The individual who was raised under a perfectionist parental style most often would develop a personality style of **ambivalent passive**.

The ambivalent passive personality needs control, because as long as he can control every situation he has a greater chance of not failing. Socially, this person is conforming. He is still trying to please dad (or mom) and almost everyone becomes a dad or mom figure. He will do everything he can to get people to accept and love him and to see him as competent. He sees himself as being extremely conscientious in all that he does in an effort to be perfect. "The ambivalent passive individual can easily fit the characteristics of the Pharisees in the Bible. They have a belief that they must measure up to the full measure of the law and tend to be the nicest people and the best of friends" (DeKoven. *On Belay!: Introduction to Christian Counseling.* Ramona: Vision Publishing. 1991.)

Ambivalent passive people do everything that people expect of them in an effort to be accepted.

Introduction of the Gospel

According to studies reported by Grunlan in his book, *Marriage and the Family: A Christian Perspective* (Grand Rapids: Zondervan. 1984), children at this stage of development are able to respond to the Gospel and are open to accepting Christ. They are eager to please, which would indicate that this is an excellent time to present concepts of Christian values. They are concerned with relating truth to life and are able to grasp the implications of biblical teachings. The implications for the church and Sunday school programs are staggering.

From about the age of 12 on children may still be open to spiritual challenges, but they are also looking for purpose and are beginning to be influenced by their peers.

Intellectual Developmental

During this stage memory improves considerably because children become more adept at using memory strategies such as rehearsal, organization, elaboration, and external aids. Children's understanding of complex syntax develops up to and perhaps even after age 9. Although the ability to communicate improves, even older children may not have a complete awareness of the processes of communication.

The intelligence of school-aged children is assessed by group tests, such as the Otis-Lennon Mental Ability Test, and individual tests such as the WISC-R.

Critics claim that psychometric intelligence tests overlook practical intelligence and creative insight and falsely equate mental efficiency with speed. New methods are being devised to test and train intelligence.

In the past, some researchers felt that black Americans tended to score lower that white Americans. In more recent studies, it has been pointed out that the difference more likely reflects environmental rather that innate racial difference in intelligence. It was also noted by a number of researchers and educators that many of the intelligence tests used terminology and referred to social situations that would not have been a part of a black child's environmental background.

Developers of intelligence tests have been trying to devise "culture free" tests: tests that focus on experiences common to different cultures. The attempts have met with little success.

Implications for Education

Teachers have considerable influence on the success or failure of elementary school children and the resulting self-image. Papalia (1989) suggests that "self-fulfilling prophecies often limit the achievement of poor and minority children." These children have seen older brothers and sisters fail in school and expect that they too will fail, because failure is a characteristic of their socioeconomic status. Teachers are becoming more aware of the need for much positive support of the underachievers who are failing because of their poor self-image.

Educational systems need to do all that is possible to secure and make use of the latest in educational resources. The use of computers has opened many vistas for students who otherwise might fail.

The educational system needs to find more ways to involve parents in the educational process. It has been shown that when parents work with the teachers and especially with their children, there is a definite improvement in the quality of work produced by the children.

Educational systems need to reevaluate some of their programs for those children who seem to be underachievers. The problem may not be a lack of intelligence or some learning disability. The problem may come from damage that has been done to the child emotionally because of neglect, physical and/or mental abuse, and sexual abuse. The problems of the slow learner may also be traced at times to poor nutrition, illness, or a negative parental influence.

Unfortunately, too many schools are overcrowded and the student-teacher ratio is so high that teachers do not have the time to evaluate each student properly. Until schools are able to reduce the ratio significantly and train teachers in the problems of human development, society will continue to see good children fall through the cracks and end up as failures for the rest of their lives.

Personal Reflections

> "To be or not to be, that is the question."
> —Shakespeare, Hamlet.

One of the things that has impressed me most over the years that I have studied human development and human behavior is the substance of the quote from Hamlet. Too much time is wasted on becoming and too little time on just being. The U.S. Army advertises, "Be all that you can be, in the Army." What they mean by that slogan is that the Army will make you into the kind of person you should be.

In the church, we talk about becoming more like Christ as a goal in life. It can be conceded that to be like Christ is a noble goal, but, it is all but unattainable in this life. In the words of the Apostle Paul, "Not as though I had already attained, either were already perfect: but I follow after, if that I may apprehend that for which I also am apprehended of Christ Jesus."

Not that I have already obtained it or have already become perfect, but I press on so that I may lay hold of that for which also I was laid hold of by

Christ Jesus; however, let us keep living by that same standard to which we have attained (Phil. 3:12, 16 NAS).

Each stage in life has its own particular problems and joys. The reality of life is that we are all moving toward the same goal. "And inasmuch as it is appointed for men to die once and after this comes judgment" (Heb. 9:27 NAS).

I do not mean to infer that we should not strive to better ourselves through whatever means are available. I do mean to infer that man has lost the art of enjoying "whatsoever state" (stage) he is in. It is so sad to know individuals who spend all of their adult lives trying to change things that cannot be changed or trying to make themselves into something other than what they are, only to die without ever attaining their goal. Goals are good only if they are attainable.

The plight of most children is to grow up. Little do they know that each new stage of development will have problems of its own. I have often thought how utterly stupid I was as a teen not to realize how wonderful life was. I spent most of my teen years drinking alcohol and running with the wrong crowd. I left high school in the middle of the 10th grade to seek my fame and fortune, both of which were ever elusive.

Parents and schools need to develop programs that teach children how to live and enjoy life right where they are in the process of development. The sad story is that most parents (and teachers) are so bitter about their own lost youth, that they spend much of their time either trying to regain some of the pleasures or to forget the pains of that youth. Then they have little time left to teach their children how to avoid the dismal trap called discontent.

There are so many good things about this life, especially for those who have given their lives to Christ, that I just want to be and not spend so much precious time trying to become. At the age of 71 years, there is little time left for me to change what I have become. I shall therefore concentrate on just being who I am. It took me many years to really like myself. I was one of the foolish ones who believed all of the negative lies my parents and teachers tried to teach me about myself. But no more.

When I started kindergarten, I could not speak or understand any English. I am sure that must have caused some problems, but it was not until about the second or third grade that I was really damaged. My teacher at the time must have thought that I was either lacking in intelligence or that I was suffering from some form of learning disability. She sent me to the Sunshine Annex.

The Sunshine Annex was a "special school" where children with low IQs, learning difficulties, or some form of physical handicap were sent. I was of course very confused. I was not told why I was being sent to the annex, but I knew it must have something to do with my inability to do the class work.

I was only in Sunshine Annex for a couple of days. Someone there sent me back with a note saying that I did not belong there. I am sure this made a real good impression on my teacher. I went on to complete the eighth grade, but the damage had been done. I was already convinced that I was not as bright as other kids.

I entered high school, and because of the records that were sent from the elementary school, they placed me in a track called general (reserved for those who had no chance of ever attending a college). I simply wasted my time for the first year, barely passing courses. In the tenth grade I failed all of my courses, except Geography (I still have very warm feelings for my geography teacher who did not see me as a failure). After receiving my report card for the first half of the tenth grade, I decided to give up.

It was several years later while serving in the U.S. Navy that I decided I should go to college and get an education. When I left the Navy at the end of World War II, I attended one year of Bible College and then went into the ministry. While pastoring a church in Detroit, a friend convinced me to attend Wayne State University. I had to take the G.E.D. test to get my high school diploma. I passed the test with such a high score that I was given 18 units of college credits. All of this did not in any way change my low self-esteem. I guess I must have thought that I was lucky and just guessed the right answers. I did not lose that poor image of myself until many years, and two college degrees later. I decided to apply for the doctoral program in a university in San Diego, where I had been teaching in public schools. Prerequisite for admission into the doctoral program was a passing grade on the Miller's Analogies Test, an adult test of intelligence.

On the day that I was to meet with the admissions committee, I was seated in the lobby of the offices where they were interviewing prospective students. The student who preceded me did not close the door completely when he left the interview room. I could hear the panel of professors discussing the next candidate. One of the committee mentioned my name, and I heard another member say, "Isn't he the guy that scored so high on the Miller's?" Another replied, "He got the highest score ever recorded." I got in, and got my Ph.D., but most of all, that night I realized after all of those years of self-doubt, that I was not a dummy, or that I was doomed to failure.

All of the lies that I had believed for so many years were now seen for what they really were: lies. The real shame is that it took me until I was nearly fifty years old. I missed so much in my youth and for so much of my life. There is no way to go back and undo what had been done. I thank God that from the time of my enlightenment, I have learned to live and enjoy my life as God has intended. The answer to Hamlet's query is TO BE!

The Road to Healing

One of the most effective ways of dealing with past hurts, especially the lies that have controlled your life for many years is to simply confess the hurts, pains, shame, feelings of anger, or whatever else might be bothering you, to the Lord first and then to someone whom you trust and know will be understanding.

Your author has bared his soul in confessing to you the hurts and shame that he experienced as a child in elementary school. It took him many years to finally find release and healing. You need not wait any longer. Healing is for you.

If you cannot confess to someone else, the next best thing is to write about those things that cause you such pain or lack of self-esteem in much the same way that the author did in this chapter. At some date in the future, you may wish to share what you write with someone else.

After you finish writing or confessing to a friend, then it is time to pray.

"Lord, I have been able with your help to discover and confess those things that were so painful in my childhood. Your Word declares that if I confess my sins, you are faithful and just to forgive me and to cleanse me for all my faults.

I am weary of carrying the load of shame and guilt that has been mine because of the lie that I, as a child, was not wise enough to understand were just that, LIES.

I trust you to heal me and deliver me from all of the oppression of the devil. Set me free to serve you without any of the weights and sin that long entangled me.

In the Name of the Father, and of the Son, Jesus Christ, and of the Holy Spirit, I pray. Amen¡'

Now believe what you have prayed and go forth in the Name and Power of the Lord to achieve all that the Lord has planned for your life. You are now ready to help those who, like you were in bondage to the lies of Satan.

Ages 6-12

Review of Chapter 7

- Freud referred to this stage as the Latency Period.
- Erikson saw the social conflict as Industry vs Inferiority.
- These are the elementary school years.
- During these years the child grows heavier, and taller.
- The development of children at this stage can be thought of as slow and steady.
- At this stage one would see a wide variety of sizes and shapes on the average school ground.
- Both boys and girls gain an average of 7 pounds.
- Children between 6 and 12 double their average body weight.
- Nutrition is a major factor in the growth and health of children at this age.
- Obesity becomes more of a problem at this stage.
- There are some differences between boys and girls concerning physical skills at this stage.
- Between the ages of 5-7 children enter the cognitive stage of concrete operations.
- Concrete operations means that children are now able to use symbols and think logically.
- According to Piaget, children at this stage will go through three basic stages in mastering conversation.
- Moral development at this stage consists of two stages: morality of constraint and the morality of cooperation.
- Kohlberg identified this stage of moral development as moral reasoning.
- In Freudian terminology, this stage is called the latency period, a period of relative calm.
- Sexual interests still exist, but it is no longer center stage.
- This stage can be considered as the calm before the storm (adolescence).

Review of Chapter 7

- Erikson agreed with Freud that this was a stage of latency, but added that the psychosocial issues were Industry vs Inferiority. An important point was made about blended children and resilient children.
- Erikson saw the real danger of this stage as excessive feelings of inadequacy and inferiority.
- Dr. DeKoven's story of the white picket fence serves to illustrate the hurt that can be inflicted on a child at this stage.
- Millon suggests that a parental style of perfectionism at this stage results in a personality style of ambivalent passive.
- This is considered as the best age to introduce children to the Gospel.
- At this stage memory tends to improve considerably.
- In the past, black Americans tested lower on the traditional intelligence tests because the tests were skewed in favor of the white middle class child.
- Several implications were made regarding the course of education, public and private.

Glossary for Chapter 7

Glossary of Terms

Blended Children — Children in a marriage to which one or both parents bring children from a previous marriage, and then may have children of the new marriage.

Compensation — The Piagetian term meaning that a child has learned to reason that one change cancels out another.

Concrete Operations — One of Piaget's stages of cognitive development.

Conservation — A Piagetian concept in which a child is required to respond to two or more dimensions of a stimulus simultaneously.

Gender Identification — The concept of identity popularized by Erickson in which the individual learns gender identity through relationships in family and society.

Heteronomous Morality — Piaget's concept that children tend to view morality from a egocentric point of view.

Industry vs Inferiority — Erikson's fourth stage of psychosocial development: ages 6 - 12.

Justification — Piagetian term to describe the action of a child in reasoning that if nothing has been taken away and nothing added, a substance is the same regardless of how it is reshaped.

Latency Period — Freudian term for the elementary grade child.

Morality of Constraint — First of Piaget's two stages of moral development, characterized by rigid, simplistic judgments; also called heteronomous morality.

Resilient Children — Children who in spite of severe difficulties in the developmental process are able to overcome and do more than simply survive.

Reversibility — A Piagetian term used to describe a child's ability to reverse a cognitive observation in the Object Permanence stage of cognitive development.

"To be nobody but yourself — in a world which is doing its best, night and day, to make you everybody else — means to fight the hardest battle which any human being can fight, and never stop fighting." —E.E. Cummings

Chapter 8

Ages 12-18

The central issue of this age group is **Identity vs Role Confusion**.

In Freudian terminology this is the time of **Puberty and Adolescence**. Much of the more significant contributions in this area were made, not by Sigmund Freud, but by his sister Anna.

This is the stage that is best described as a roller coaster ride because of the many major changes that take place in a child's life. There are major hormonal and physical changes as well as a significant growth spurt. Coupled with the sexual development, this can be at the same time, the most exciting and most depressing time of development.

Traditionally, puberty signaled the passage from child to adult. However, because puberty is beginning earlier than it did a hundred years ago, children, especially in the Western cultures, are beginning the journey at an earlier age.

In some of the more so called "primitive" societies, the passage from childhood to adulthood is clearly marked by certain rites of passage involving rituals and ceremonies. In these rites, there are clear steps that are intended to assist the child in the transition.

The first step in the rites of passage might be called separation, in which the child is removed from the rest of the group (in some cultures this especially includes sisters and mother). Often the boys are sent to live in a separate building, cut off from the rest of the group.

The second stage prior to induction into adulthood is that of training. This training for boys is conducted by elders in the tribe or older relatives (uncles, etc.). The training leaves very little doubt as to what is expected of the child as an adult. Certain childish behavior will no longer be tolerated.

The third step is the initiation itself, which includes certain rituals. Often these rituals are a time of suffering and pain but at the same time, a time of celebration and rejoicing. In some cultures the ritual includes circumcision. Other practices such as scarring, fasting, walking on fire, etc., are a part of the initiation. The final step of passage is induction. The child now knows that he/she is a full adult member of the group (tribe) with all the rights and privileges of full membership.

Rites of passage differ somewhat for girls in these primitive groups, but for all intents and purposes serve the same end: the induction into society as an adult.

In Western culture we have such things as the senior prom, Bar or Bat Mitzvah (the religious rite of passage for the Jewish boy or girl in which they are accepted into the religious and social responsibilities of adults). Most children in modern Western cultures do not have any such rites of passage. Consequently, adolescence is, for most of these youngsters, very difficult.

Biologically, adolescence usually indicates the time from the onset of puberty to adulthood, although it more accurately should include pubescence, because that is where the whole process begins. Puberty is the beginning of sexual maturity, while pubescence refers to the changes that result in that process of sexual maturity. Another way of defining puberty is "the ability to make babies" and is sometimes called nubility.

For girls pubescence starts officially with their first menstrual period (called menarche) and usually begins at about the age of 12. Girls are frequently infertile for about a year after the beginning of the menstrual cycle. The cycle itself may not be as regular in the beginning as it becomes later.

Among the first signs of pubescence is the appearance of pigmented pubic hair. At about the same time as the pubic hair begins to appear, the testes of the boy begin to grow and the girl begins to experience some growth of her breasts. The girls then experience rapid growth and actually become taller than the boys of the same age. The boys will catch up within a year or two and actually pass the girls.

Puberty development in boys — In addition to the enlarging of the testes there is a change in the texture and color of the scrotum. These changes begin on the average in the middle of the 11th year, although it is not until the age of 14 that there is a steep rise in the size of the testes. The penis begins to enlarge in size and is fully developed around the age of 14 1/2, but there are wide individual differences, and it may not occur until the boy is 16 1/2. At about the age of 14 the pubic hair is complete, and soon thereafter underarm hair begins to appear. Male facial hair and body hair usually develops more slowly and is not complete until several years later. Another physical change in the boy is the deepening of his voice, which is the result of the enlargement of the larynx and lengthening of the vocal cords.

At about the same time that the penis is growing, the **prostate gland** and the **seminal vesicles** enlarge, and about one year later, at about the age of 15, **spermarche**, the first spontaneous ejaculation of seminal fluid occurs. The first fluid produced contains few sperm, so like the girls, the boys have a period of infertility. It is believed by some theorists that spermarche is as psychologically significant an event for the boys as the menarche is for girls (Gaddis & Brook-Gunn. 1985).

Pubertal development in girls — After the onset of menarche, the first menstrual period and the budding of breasts with the general growth spurt, there is an expansion of the pelvis. In the year following the appearance of pubic hair and the enlargement of the breast, the underarm hair begins to appear. The average time for pubertal development for girls is about 3 years. Some develop much faster, some take longer.

For the boys and girls who have had no teaching to prepare them for the events of pubescence, this can be a very frightening time. Mild to major psychological problems can develop. Some of the psychological struggles will be discussed in the section of this chapter dealing with psychosexual and psychosocial development. However, it should be noted that most research that has been done in this area deals with the problems experienced by girls with relation to the menarche period. No significant studies have been made to look at the difference across social classes and ethnic groups, and to date we know little about the psychological significance of puberty for boys (Brooks-Gunn. 1984).

It is important to remember that the times and duration of the events of pubescence vary greatly among cultures and even within any one culture, but the physical, emotional, spiritual and social implications are much the same in all cultures.

Many of the concerns of adolescents would seem to be rather minor. The greatest worries that boys express are such things as the presence of blackheads or pimples, irregular teeth, oily skin, glasses, and other slight physical problems. Boys (apparently more than girls) also become concerned about the fact that other parts of their bodies begin to grow rather rapidly. The nose and ears grow considerably and often appear to be too big for the face. In time the face seems to catch up. Girls, like the boys, are concerned about blackheads and pimples, but also about freckles, scars, birthmarks, and moles in addition to the oily skin.

It would appear that the problems that adolescents express in answer to questionnaires are not in reality the major issues. The increasing number of teenage suicides, mental break-downs and juvenile delinquency problems would indicate that there are emotional problems of major proportions being experienced by this age group.

Psychosexual Development

Freud referred to this stage as Puberty or the Genital Stage. As noted at the end of the last chapter, the latency period, with all of its calm, is only the lull before the storm. Freud centered on the sexual energy that appears in full adult force and threatens to disrupt the established defenses. The Oedipal feelings that had been repressed are now back in full force, and the child is big enough to do something about them in reality instead of in fantasy. Freud said that the great task of the individual from the time of the beginning of adolescence is beginning to "free himself from his parents" (1920. p. 345). The son must free himself from his mother and find a woman of his own. The boy also must resolve his rivalry with his father and free himself from his father's domination. The daughter must separate from the parents and establish a life of her own. Freud noted that this freeing of one's self from parents does not come without stress and anxiety. Both boys and girls have built up strong dependencies on the parents over the years making separation emotionally painful. For most people, the goal of genuine freedom and independence is never completely attained (1920. p. 346).

Anna Freud continued the work of her father in the study of adolescence and provided many insights into the stresses and behavior patterns of this stage that he left out. Anna's studies found that much of what her father wrote was correct but not complete. She particularly agreed that the teenager experiences a resurgence of the Oedipal feeling of early childhood. She pointed out that the young person becomes most aware of a growing resentment against the parent of the same sex. Incestuous feelings toward the other parent remain more unconscious.

Anna noticed that the first impulse that the adolescent has when confronted with the resurgence of the old Oedipal feeling is to take flight. She said that teenagers feel tense in the presence of the parents and feel safe when apart. This theory may well explain why teens so often run away from home. Those who do stay in the home begin to act more like a boarder than a member of the family (A. Freud. p. 269).

Anna Freud went on to suggest that sometimes teens escape parents by developing a blanket of contempt for them instead of admitting any dependence and love. The independence that teenagers may feel at this time coupled with the fact that the parents still dominate their lives is at the root of most of the family's stress. Meanwhile, the teen is expending a great deal of energy deriding their parents. They have no way of understanding that the real battle is within.

Anna also suggested that teenagers will attempt to defend themselves against feelings and impulses altogether. One strategy is asceticism, that is, the teenager tries to avoid all physical pleasure through strict diets, avoiding attractive clothing, dancing, or music, or anything else fun or frivolous (A. Freud. 1958. 1936).

Another defensive approach is the use of **intellectualization**. The adolescent tries to transfer sex and aggression into an abstract, intellectual plane. Although they intellectualize about love, the family, and freedom, these intellectualizations are only disguised efforts to deal with the oedipal issues on a purely intellectual level.

Anna Freud did not feel that the struggles of the teenager indicated the need for therapy. She felt that they should be allowed to work through the struggles on their own with nothing more than support and empathy from the parents.

Psychosocial Development

Erikson theorized that the basic issues to be resolved at this stage are **Identity vs Role Confusion**. He agreed with Freud that this could be considered the genital stage. He agreed with Sigmund and Anna Freud in that this stage was one of considerable turbulence because of the dramatic physiological changes taking place. Sexual and aggressive drives, which lay dormant during the latency period, now threaten to overwhelm the ego and its defenses. The genital zone in particular is infused with tremendous sexual energy and the adolescent is overwhelmed by the return of the oedipal feeling.

Erikson, however, sees all of this as only a part of the problem. He postulated that adolescents become overwhelmed and confused with new social conflicts and demands. The adolescent is in the process of establishing a new sense of ego identity.

The adolescent suddenly feels as if his impulses have a will of their own. Also, the rapid physical growth at this stage creates a sense of identity confusion. It is almost like waking up and discovering that one is in a different body. The adolescent looks different, feels different and is being treated differently by family and peers. He is at times controlled by impulses that he has never experienced before. He may have been taught that some of the feelings and some of the behavior that is now almost beyond his control is sinful in the eyes of God.

Because adolescents are so uncertain about who they are, they anxiously tend to identify with "in groups." They tend to become clannish, intolerant, and cruel in their exclusion of others who are different (1959. p.92). Some youths will align themselves with ideologies — national, political, or religious — which provide them with a group of identity and clear-cut images of good and bad in the world.

Erikson felt that humans form their identity over a lifetime through a process he called **identifications**. Problems occur when teens try to identify too quickly with almost any group that seems to offer a resolution to their confusion. Even though identity-formation is a lifelong process, it reaches its peak during adolescence.

In modern Western cultures, teens will often find their new sense of identity in conflict with the ideals of their parents. In fact, at times teens will take on an identity that is diametrically opposed to "everything" that the parents stand for and believe.

There are some teens who will declare a sort of identity moratorium or "time out" to postpone any commitment and identity foreclosure. The search for identity has been dramatically demonstrated by such men as

Piaget, Freud, and Erikson, who spent some time searching for their own true calling.

Health Problems

Adolescence is a healthy time of life for most teens. The most common health problems are often related to the problems of identity confusion. Among the most common health problem are eating disorders, drug abuse, and sexually transmitted diseases. There are always some risks involved when an individual is going through such dramatic changes in adolescence.

Nutrition

The appetite of the teenager takes a dramatic change over the eating habits of the middle childhood years. Most teens have a ravishing appetite that may not always include the best of foods. Boys need about 2800 calories per day, while girls only need about 2200 calories. Teenagers tend to eat a lot of "junk food" such as French fries, soft drinks, ice cream, and potato chips. Adolescents need a higher amount of protein, but with the ingestion of junk foods they receive the largest portion of their calories from fats and refined carbohydrates (sweets).

The most common mineral deficiencies in adolescence are of calcium, iron, and zinc. Calcium is needed for the increased growth of bones. Milk is one of the best sources of calcium, but the large amount of butterfat in whole milk makes it advisable for them to drink nothing except skimmed milk.

Among girls the lack of iron can lead to a common health problem, iron deficiency anemia, which is partly due to the loss of blood during the menstrual period.

There are three serious eating disorders that are most common among teenage girls. Two are **anorexia nervosa** and **bulimia**. Both of these disorders are probably a result of modern society's stringent standards of female beauty, in which slenderness is exalted above all else. The third disorder is that of **obesity**. Obesity is defined as being 20 percent overweight. By this standard some 15% of adolescents are obese. The real problem is that obese teens most often become obese adults. Obesity is often considered to be caused by overeating. Evidence exists that the condition may be the result of the inheritance or genetic regulation of the body's metabolism (obesity often runs in families). Physical inactivity and emotional stress may also contribute to the problem of obesity.

The emotional pain that young teens experience when seen as or perceived as being "fat" may have a profound effect on their self-esteem.

Anorexia nervosa, or self-starvation, is most likely to occur in bright, well-behaved, appealing females between puberty and the early twenties.

A well-known singer died at the height of her career many years ago as a result of this condition. There doesn't seem to be any known cause of the disorder. It is thought that there may be some kind of chemical imbalance in the hypothalamus that causes the individual to avoid food. Others think that it may be an emotional disturbance that is related to a dysfunctional family background.

Treatment involves nutritional and behavioral therapy as well as various types of group counseling. The prognosis is not too encouraging due to the lack of real experimental evidence.

Bulimia is an eating disorder common among teenage girls that involves binging and purging (eating huge amounts of food and then regurgitating), that is the result of extreme emotional discomfort. Many bulimics also resort to laxatives to empty the body.

Estimates of the incidence of bulimia range from 1 to 10 percent of adolescent girls and young women. The problems that result from bulimia include extensive tooth decay, gastric irritation, and hair loss.

A study by Humphrey (1986) lends some support to the Freudian explanation that bulimics turn to food out of psychological hunger for the affection and support that they did not get at home. Many bulimics reported in treatment that they felt unloved, abused and neglected. There is a possibility that this could be a regression to the oral stage of development with its Trust vs Mistrust Issues.

Drug Abuse

Drugs have been used for as long as history itself to relieve physical pain. The use of drugs today, however, has to do more with the relief of emotional pain. This use of drugs most often can lead to drug abuse. Although the use of drugs is less prevalent than in the 1960's, there is still a major drug problem in America as well as in other parts of the world. Drugs that are abused most are alcohol, nicotine, marijuana, LSD, amphetamines, heroin, barbiturates, and cocaine (the most addictive and dangerous form being crack cocaine. According to many experts, this results in addiction after the first use).

Each of the different street drugs produces a slightly different effect. Some of the drugs are used to create a feeling of euphoria or a "high," others are intended to create a sedated effect. It is assumed that the drug of choice in abusers has to do with the particular emotional dysfunction that they are attempting to avoid or escape. Each form of drug also represents its own particular harm. Adolescents who have chosen to drink alcohol instead of smoking marijuana (pot) feel that it is not as dangerous. However, the statistics of automobile accidents resulting in death because of drunk driving should convince even the most adamant skeptic that alcohol is every bit as dangerous as pot.

Ages 12-18

Sexually Transmitted Diseases

Another serious health hazard among teenagers is the problem of sexually transmitted disease (STDs). Coupling the increased sexual drive with the use of drugs in the inexperienced teen can easily lead to involvement in casual or illicit sex acts. The most common of the STDs include chlamydia, gonorrhea, and syphilis and in recent years the most dangerous of all, AIDS. Health agencies, parents and educators are frantically trying to find ways to protect adolescents from the ravages of AIDS.

The other STDs can be treated in most cases. Unfortunately, many of the young people who become infected are from lower socio-economic sectors and do not have access to the medical treatment necessary. The introduction of AIDS as a venereal disease has brought many campaigns to promote "safe sex" through the use of condoms. Schools are now teaching concepts of safe sex and are making condoms available to the students and encouraging the careful choice of sex partners.

The Christian community insists that the only "safe sex" is abstinence.

There was a time when AIDS was thought to be a disease limited to the homosexual community. This has long been disproven in that the disease can also be spread through blood transfusions and heterosexual contact. Literally hundreds of thousands have died from AIDS, and science does not seem to be close to the discovery of a cure.

Death in Adolescence

The high incidence of death in teenagers is attributable to their particular lifestyle. The main causes of death in this age group are accidents, homicide, and suicide. A great many adolescents experiment with alcohol and drugs, and because of their inexperience with the severity of the effects, they will often place themselves in extremely dangerous situations. Drunk driving is only one example. Teens are not fully aware of the consequences of certain "dare devil" behavior such as driving at high speeds while under the influence of alcohol or drugs. They are not aware of the fact that their reaction time is much slower when intoxicated or high on drugs. Automobile accidents claim the lives of many teens each year.

Some of the really abnormal and tragic behavior of adolescence is the result of certain drugs and mental illness. At the top of the list of tragic teenage behavior is that of teenage suicide. In many cases, the family and friends were completely taken by surprise. The young person was seen as intelligent, friendly, and well behaved. Suddenly he or she is dead as a result of self-inflicted injury or an intentional overdose of drugs. Mental health officials around the world have launched every effort imaginable to educate parents of the signs of suicidal depression and to seek to determine the real cause of the catastrophic epidemic in recent years. There is yet another area of real concern for teens.

Teenagers are dealing with the new and powerful surge of new sexual energy. They are not prepared for the force of the feelings that occur without warning at times. In modern Western culture and in many other cultures as well, the relatively new appearance of a new subculture has created some serious problems. This is the matter of homosexuality.

Simply defined, homosexuality is an erotic attraction toward persons of the same gender. At the root of homosexuality is a psycho-logical/emotional orientation.

Recent research has suggested that homosexual orientation may be caused by an abnormality in the brain structure of the gay individual. However, most theorists still believe that it is a natural occurrence that originally stems from certain psychological conflicts that begin during the highly sexual stage of adolescence. One of the issues of this stage is that of gender orientation and sexual behavior. It is crucial to distinguish between these two. Actual sexual behavior is determined more by social expectations, personal values, and morals than gender orientation. Actual sexual experience significantly influences psy-chological orientation.

There are a number of types of homosexual behavior and although this text deals primarily with human development, it seems proper to include a section on this very important topic. The main point to be made here is that homosexuality is not merely one stereotyped behavior pattern. Many people think of the homosexual as the "limp wristed pansy who speaks with a slight lisp and exhibits many feminine characteristics (for the female homosexual the stereotype is that of a woman with many masculine characteristics). People are often shocked to discover that an individual who appeared to be every bit a "he man" comes out of the "closet" to reveal that he is indeed a homosexual.

The Baker Encyclopedia of Psychology provides an excellent brief overview of the types of homosexuality (1985. pp. 519-521).

Experimental Homosexuality usually refers to adolescent experimentation with degrees of sexual interaction with both genders. At a minimal level many adolescents engage in same-gender sexual activity. Among males this is commonly mutual urination or masturbation contests. Among females the activity usually takes the form of breast and genital hair comparisons. Strictly speaking this is "homoerotic" activity rather than homosexual activity. There is sexual arousal association with the same gender, but the ultimate aim is heterosexual. In the extreme, there is sexual intercourse with both genders, but this experimentation usually leads to heterosexual resolution.

This is not to say that all adolescents who engage in sexual experimentation with someone of the same gender are going to eventually turn to heterosexual preference. Kinsey et. al. (1948) did report that 15% of youthful exclusive homosexuals became exclusive heterosexuals by the age 30.

Situational homosexuality involves homosexual behavior when heterosexual relations are not available.

This frequently occurs in prison, isolated military bases, and isolated work areas (military and boarding schools that are exclusively one gender and one very old study suggests that many submariners were latent homosexuals). Homosexual experience is primary for sexual release without affection or relationship. It appears that more immature personality structures may be necessary to participate in such situational sexuality.

Defensive homosexuality refers to a situational variant, often seen in prison, where aggressive homosexual behavior is used to demonstrate that one is not homosexual, i.e., the passive victim.

Reactive homosexuality represents fear of heterosexual encounters as dangerous (often castration anxiety). Although heterosexual behavior may be preferred, homosexual behavior is chosen because it is less dangerous.

Social role homosexuality involves the adoption of homosexual behavior as part of a required social role. Throughout history some societies have reared persons to enter special roles, such as actor, warrior, or priest, in which homosexuality is required as part of that role. The clearest example of socially required homosexuality is a recent anthropological study of a New Guinea tribe in which all males from 8-16 are required to play a passive homosexual role and from 16-22 an active homosexual role. Then they are required to marry and remain heterosexual thereafter. Over 95% of the tribal males successfully follow these socially prescribed sexual role behaviors. Of great theoretical import is the fact that sexual orientation and behavior can be so strongly socially determined.

Obligatory homosexuality refers to the sense of sexual orientation which a person comes to experience as an internal necessity. The person experiences no heterosexual response, but instead experiences homosexual arousal. This is usually a source of considerable anxiety and conflict because society's expectation of all males (or females) to be heterosexual. Although these individuals have good social relationships with persons of the opposite gender, they just do not experience any sexual arousal with them.

Preferential homosexuality occurs in those with bisexual arousal. Many homosexual persons experience heterosexual impulses and arousal, and may well perform heterosexual acts with some satisfaction. However, they find that they experience much more sexual gratification from a homosexual experience. Some of these individuals marry, but the marriage can only last if the person is allowed to experience homosexual relationships.

Homosexual panic is a phenomenon often seen in young adults (and teens). The adolescent will experience a sense of arousal in the showers at schools. He fears that this may indicate some homosexual tendency, but the fact may well be that the arousal is simply a reaction to the mass of naked bodies.

Generic sexual arousal describes the almost universal phenomenon of small degrees of fantasized sexual interest or response to many persons of both sexes. Personal interest, involvement, attraction, and intimacy are the psychological bases for any close relationship. Individuals usually learn to repress such feelings because of the social taboos against such feelings being expressed.

Women can be more demonstrative in relationships without being suspected of a homosexual relationship. Men must remain more distant.

Neurotic regressive homosexuality appears in persons as a retreat from personal conflict in a heterosexual relationship. In this case, the person has a heterosexual orientation, but regresses to homosexual levels of identity development.

There are a number of other sexual variants that will not be discussed at any length in this text, because they more properly belong in a text on sexual deviations. These variations, including transsexualism, transvestism, fetishes or paraphilias, may or may not have roots in the adolescence period. It is possible that they represent individuals who because of some abnormal neurosis, regress to some earlier stage of development in an unconscious effort to resolve some earlier conflicts.

An area that causes some concern for teenagers is the subject of **masturbation**. Masturbation is the act of self-stimulation with or without sexual climax and is usually the teenager's first sexual experience. Because of the social (especially for the Christian) stigma traditionally attached to the practice, many teenagers would not admit to masturbating, making reliable research difficult. The research that has been done indicates that more boys masturbate now than in 1960. This increase may be due to the fact that more are willing to admit it. One recent survey indicated that by the age of 18 well over half of boys, but only a minority of girls, say that they have masturbated. Even though more young people are willing to admit to the practice, most of them still feel that it is shameful. Less than 1/3 said that they feel no guilt when they masturbate.

The Christian church (as well as Judaism) has always had taboos against the practice. In years past, boys were told by their parents and teachers that the practice would cause blindness, insanity, and least frightening of all it would cause hair to grow on the palms of the hands. The latter warning was apparently intended to cause boys to abstain, knowing that they would be caught when the parents saw the hair growing on the palms of their hands.

Most of the problems that teenagers have with sexual problems can be attributed to the problem teens have communicating with parents about their concerns. Parents also have considerable difficulty dealing with the subject of sex with their teens. In recent years, the trend is toward a more open and liberal relationship that is promising. Schools are offering classes in sex education, but there is always some reserve in dealing with the real issues because of parental objections.

Teenage Pregnancy is a serious problem in America. Teenage pregnancy in America is the highest in the world.

The problem that the pregnant teenage girls face is what to do about the baby. There is raging in America an all-out-war over Abortions vs Right to Life. The Church for the most part is totally against abortion, which means that the girls who may be only 15 years old must carry the infant to term. The choice in this situation is what happens to the baby after birth. Do the girls, who are not really ready for the responsibilities of motherhood, try to raise the child, or is the child given up for adoption? Either scenario represents many problems, both for the mother and the infant. Often the infant is cared for by grandparents who, loving as they may be, are not always able to take on such a responsibility.

Abortion is not even an option to the "right to life" forces. But many of the girls who become pregnant feel that they have no other choice but to abort the fetus. There has been considerable research to indicate that girls who have aborted a child suffer for many years emotionally over the decision. The total story of the impact of either teenage abortion or of giving birth is yet to be researched and told.

Cognition

Many adolescents attain Piaget's stage of formal operations, which is characterized by the ability to think abstractly. People in this stage of formal operations can engage in hypothetical-deductive reasoning. They can think in terms of possibilities, deal flexibly with problems, and test hypotheses.

Since experience plays a more important part in the attainment of this cognitive stage than in that of previous Piagetian stages, not all people become capable of formal operations.

Most adolescents are at Kohlberg's conventional level (stages 3 and 4) of moral development. However, some young people in adolescence are at Piaget's pre-conventional state. Although the adolescent is not egocentric, in the sense that a younger child is, adolescents show egocentric tendencies. These include finding fault with authority figures, argumentativeness, self-consciousness, self-centeredness, indecisiveness, and apparent hypocrisy.

The search for identity is closely linked to vocational choice, which is influenced by several factors, including gender and parents' attitudes. A greater number of adolescents are working today than at any time in the past 30 years. However, work seems to have little benefit for the teenager's educational, social, or occupational development.

Personal Reflections

I personally see the developmental period of adolescence to be one of the most important stages in life. It is almost as if human existence can be divided into two periods: the childhood period and the adult period. The major changes that take place in a person's life at puberty have such a dramatic impact on the rest of his or her life that one can only assume that this is how God meant to separate the child from the adult. There are many questions that I have not been able to resolve in my mind about this stage, and neither has anyone else been able to give me any reasonable answers. I shall pose the questions with the hope that the reader will not be too critical of my beliefs and motives.

1. Why did God create man in such a way that he would suddenly come into a period of such forceful sexual feelings without providing a satisfactory way to express those feelings. Teenagers are sexually active long before they are able to find any acceptable outlet for the sexual energy that almost dominates their thought and their life. They are forbidden from heterosexual experiences by most of society, but especially by the church. They are told that it is wrong and even sinful, to masturbate, and horror of horrors the very thought of homosexual activities are a total abomination. I know what the Bible teaches about sexual relations with individuals of the same gender. I know what some Christians say the Bible says about masturbation, which I might add may be stretching things a little. What I can't seem to figure out is what is the teen to do? Is total celibacy the only answer? Science tells us that the male is at his sexual peak at eighteen, but most Americans would say that an 18 year old is not ready for the responsibilities of marriage. "Take a cold shower" and think about other things may be the only answer.

2. Why doesn't Christianity have a more defined rite of passage for adolescents? Although many may feel that the Jewish custom of Bar and Bat Mitzvah does not really serve as a rite of passage, at least it has to be better than nothing. Do some of the primitive cultures have some insights that we who are so civilized have overlooked? In fact, we are so civilized that we will hardly ever talk to our own children about the topic of sex. It is a standard joke that is repeated over and over in the entertainment field. A father is totally embarrassed when confronted by one of his children asking a question about sex. He usually turns the responsibility of answering the question over to his wife.

3. I am a pro-lifer. I do not believe in abortion, but I have to struggle with the old argument involving pregnancy that is the result of a rape. I also have problems with pregnancies that are without doubt going to result in the birth of a totally deformed infant. Nor do I know the answer to the age-old question of who lives, the baby or the mother, when there must be a choice.

4. I do not know all of the answers about what can be done to make the time of adolescence a little less stressful and turbulent, but certainly there must be something more than what is being done in Western culture. The time of adolescence could be such a wonderful time if we could only find ways of corralling some of the personality strength of this stage. For some reason, we do not seem to feel that teenagers are responsible enough to take any real responsibility. We want them to act grown up, but we are

so restrictive of their activities that they have little chance of exhibiting adult behavior. Some of the personality strengths of adolescence are listed by Papalia and Olds (1989. pp. 402-404).

Adolescents have considerable energy, or drive, and vitality. They are idealistic and have a real concern for their country and the world.

They frequently exercise their ability to question contemporary values, philosophies, theologies and institutions.

They have a heightened sensory awareness and perceptivity.

They are courageous, able to take risks themselves or stick their necks out for others.

The have a considerable feelings of independence.

They possess a strong sense of fairness and dislike intolerance.

More often than not, they are responsible and can be relied upon.

They are flexible and adapt to change readily.

They are usually very open, frank, and honest.

They have an above-average sense of loyalty to organizations and causes.

The have a sense of humor, which they often express.

More often than not, they have an optimistic and positive outlook on life.

They often think seriously and deeply.

They have great sensitivity to, and awareness of, other people's feelings.

They are engaged in a sincere and ongoing search for identity.

There were times in history when by the time a boy was a teenager he was already a general in the army. The question is, "Are we expecting too little out of teens?" With all of their energy, sexual and otherwise, is it possible that part of their frustration comes from the reluctance of adults, especially parents, to acknowledge their ability to perform?

Even as this chapter was being written, there came a news break on the radio telling of a 19 year old boy killing four people and then turning the shotgun on himself at a nearby health club. What could cause an otherwise intelligent, well liked teenager to result to such a heinous act? There is a need for much more research into the dynamics of development at this stage to see if somehow we have allowed a society to develop that has so restricted the free development of the adolescent that we have actually created a monster.

Juvenile delinquency is on the increase. Violent juvenile crimes are abounding in even the higher socio-economic areas. Teenage gangs are proliferating in cities all over the country and the authorities seem helpless to stem the tide.

A Time For Healing

Take time to do some real soul searching about your own adolescence. Was it a happy time? Did you have problems with your family? Did you have a struggle with the issue of sexual drive and societal or church taboos?

You may find it difficult talking to someone about your teenage experiences, but if you write them out, you will be able to analyze them in the light of what you have just finished reading. Also, with the help of the Holy Spirit, you can open up to God in honesty and confess those things that long have made you feel guilty and ashamed.

Many marriages struggle because one or both of the people involved did things during their teens that they would not want their mates to know. I am not suggesting that it is necessary to confess those wrong doing to your mate, but you must confess them to the Lord and then leave them to be buried in the deepest sea, never to be remembered against you again.

Because you confess your sins (at the time you were a teen you may not have even been aware of the sinfulness of what you were doing) does not mean that the devil is going to forget. He will continue to bring those dark secrets to your mind and tell you that someone is going to find out about your past. You must remember, however, that the devil is a liar without any power to do what he threatens to do. Call him a liar, and in the Name of Jesus, who bruised his head at the cross, tell Satan to leave you along. Resist the devil, and he will flee from you.

As long as you are in Jesus, there is no power in heaven or earth that can bring you to shame. Once you have confessed your past sins to the Lord, He removes them as far as the East is from the West, never to remember them against you again.

As a Christian counselor, I have often had to counsel with people who were guilty of the same type of sin that I had practiced before I became a Christian. There are times that I know that Satan would love to bring condemnation on me for those past sins, but I find great pleasure in telling Satan where to go with his accusation. I am a child of the King, and He has given me the authority and the power to resist the devil.

Ages 12-18

Review of Chapter 8

- The central issues of this age are Identity vs Role Confusion.
- Freud called this age the age of Puberty and adolescence.
- Anna Freud did more work in this stage than did her father.
- This stage can best be described as a roller coaster ride because of the many and rapid changes physically and emotionally.
- Puberty signals the passage from child to adult.
- Western culture has not had a realistic rite of passage for individuals going through this change.
- Some more primitive cultures have elaborate ceremonies to assist the youngster to pass from child to adult.
- The Jewish culture has the Bar Mitzvah, at 13 years of age for boys and the Bat Mitzvah, at 12 years of age for girls, as a rite of passage.
- Puberty in both boys and girls is evidenced by a number of physical changes that in turn can cause some emotional disturbances.
- The time and duration of pubescence varies greatly among cultures and within a particular culture.
- Freud referred to this stage as Puberty or the Genital Stage.
- He said that the oedipal feelings that had been repressed are now back in full force, and the child is big enough to do something about them in reality instead of in fantasy.
- Freud said that a part of the struggle of adolescence is the young person's effort to separate himself/herself from the parents. The male looks to find a wife of his own, and the female looks to find a husband of her own.
- Both Sigmund and Anna felt that a part of the reason for the resentment felt by most teenagers toward their parents had to do with the struggle they have with the oedipal complex.
- Teens find many ways to break the tie with parents, and Anna Freud mentions several of those ways.
- Anna Freud did not feel that the struggles that teens have with parents, etc., are indicative of a need for therapy.
- The psychosocial issue that Erikson says in this stage was Identity vs Role Confusion.

Review of Chapter 8

- Although Erikson agreed with the Freuds in much of what they said about this stage, he felt that a large part of the problem was that adolescents become overwhelmed and confused with new social conflicts and demands.

- The adolescent must deal with many changes in life: physical changes, emotional changes, social changes and so on.

- Erikson felt that humans form their sense of identity through a process he called identifications.

- Problems occur when teenagers try to identify too quickly with any group that seems to offer a resolution to their confusion.

- Teens will often take on an identity that is in direct conflict with their parents.

- These same teens often return, at least in part, to the ideals of their parents as they mature in life.

- Nutrition is very important at this stage, as it is at other stages. However the teen is more likely to eat too many fats and sweets.

- There are three main eating disorders, especially among teenaged girls: anorexia nervosa, bulimia and obesity.

- Although the misuse or abuse of drugs is on a slight decline in the past decade, drugs still present a major problem among teens.

- Evidence seems to indicate that more teens are returning to tobacco.

- The worst abuse of drugs in still in the urban areas.

- Sexually transmitted diseases are on the increase even with the sex education programs in school and the availability of free condoms.

- AIDS remains the most frequent disease among teens, however the problem is that other sexually transmitted diseases are not considered as bad as AIDS, and they often go untreated.

- The high incidence of death in teenagers is attributable to their lifestyle.

- The main causes of death in teens are accidents, homicide, and suicide.

- Teenagers must deal with the powerful sex urges that at times may lead them to undesirable sexual activity such as homosexuality.

- There are a number of different types of homosexual behavior.

Ages 12-18

- Teens usually fit into the experimental homosexuality type and most likely will prefer heterosexual relationships as they mature in life.
- Masturbation is not thought of as being as serious a problem as it once was.
- Kohlberg felt that most teens are at the conventional level of moral development.

Glossary for Chapter 8

Glossary of Terms

Adolescence — That period of life characterized by the passage from childhood to adulthood.

Adolescent Rebellion — The stress and storm of adolescence that results in rebellious behavior against adults in general.

Anorexia Nervosa — An eating disorder characterized by self-starvation.

Asceticism — Defense mechanism typical of adolescence, described by Anna Freud, which is characterized by self-denial as a defense against adolescents' fear of loss of control over their impulses.

Bar Mitzvah — In the Jewish religion it is the rite of passage for the male from a boy at the age of 13 to an adult member of the congregation.

Bat Mitzvah — In the Jewish religion it is the rite of passage for the female from a girl at the age of 12 to an adult member of the congregation

Bulimia — An eating disorder characterized by binging and purging.

Defensive Homosexuality — Often in institutions such as prisons, it is necessary for an individual to participate (passively) in homosexuality to prove he is not homosexual.

Experimental Homosexuality — It is thought that many teenagers experiment at least once in a homosexual activity.

Formal Operation — According to Piaget, the final stage of cognitive development, reached by some adolescents, which is characterized by the ability to think abstractly.

Gender Differences — Differences between males and females that may not be based on biological differences.

Heterosexuality — Sexual activity between two persons of different gender.

Homosexual Panic — The panic one may experience because of being aroused in the shower with other members of the same sex.

Homosexuality — Sexual activity between two persons of the same gender.

Identity vs Identity Confusion. — According to Eriksonian theory, the fifth critical alternative of psychosocial development, in which an adolescent must determine his or her own sense of self (identity), including the role he or she is to play in society.

Imaginary Audience — Observer who exists only in an adolescent's mind and is as concerned with the adolescent's thoughts and actions as is the adolescent himself or herself.

Intellectualization — A defense approach by adolescents in which they transfer aggression and sex into an abstract intellectual plane.

Male Climacteric — Period of physiological, emotional, and psychological reproductive system and other body systems changes.

Masturbation — Sexual self-stimulation.

163

Menarche — The beginning of the girl's first menstrual period.

Neurotic Regressive Homosexuality — Appears in person as a retreat from personal conflict.

Nubility — The time when a child is able to make a baby.

Obesity — Obesity is defined as being 20% over normal weight. Morbid obesity identifies a condition of obesity that is considered to be life threatening.

Obligatory Homosexuality — In certain cultures, young boys are required as a part of the rites of passage, to spend the first half of their adolescence in a passive homosexual situation.

Preferential Homosexuality — This refers to the individual who may be bisexual, but experiences more arousal from a homosexual relationship.

Primary Sex Characteristics — Characteristics directly related to reproduction; specifically, the male and female sex organs. These enlarge and mature during adolescence.

Prostate Gland — One of the glands of the male reproductive system.

Puberty — Time at which a person attains sexual maturity and is able to reproduce.

Pubescence — Period of development preceding puberty and characterized by rapid physiological growth, maturation of reproductive functioning, enlargement of the sex organs, and appearance of the secondary sex characteristics.

Reactive Homosexuality — Represents fear of heterosexual relations.

Rites of Passage — A term used to describe the various rituals held in various cultures to usher the child into an adult standing.

STDs — Disease that is transmitted by sexual contact.

Secondary Sex Characteristics — Physiological characteristics of the sexes which develop during adolescence (and do not involve the sex organs), including breasts in females, broadened shoulders in males, growth of body hair in both sexes, and adult voices in men and women.

Seminal Fluid — The fluid that carries the sperm in reproduction.

Seminal Vesicle — A pouch on either side of the male reproductive tract that is connected with the seminal tract and serves for temporary storage of semen.

Sexual Orientation — Sexual interest either in the other sex (heterosexual orientation) or in the same sex (homosexual orientation) usually expressed during adolescence; also called sexual preference.

Social Role Homosexuality — In certain cultures, males were destined to live and perform in roles, actors, singers, etc., that lead to homosexuality.

Spermarche — The first spontaneous ejaculation of seminal fluid.

Storm and Stress — In Hall's terminology, the idea that adolescence is necessarily a time of intense, fluctuating emotions; see adolescent rebellion.

"Marriage is our last, best chance to grow up."
—Joseph Barth

Chapter 9

Ages 19-35
Young Adulthood

Marriage and parenthood have been traditionally considered the norm in the developmental process of young adults. Until recent years, marriage was thought to be the normal step into adulthood. With the advent of women entering the professional workforce, marriage is often entered into at a later age than in past history.

There are many reasons for entering into marriage other than the obvious Judeo-Christian view having to do with procreation and replenishing of the earth.

In the beginning, God created woman to fill an emptiness or incompleteness in Adam.

> "Then the LORD God said, 'It is not good for the man to be alone; I will make him a helper suitable for him.'"
> —Genesis 2:18 (NAS)

> "So the LORD God caused a deep sleep to fall upon the man, and he slept; then He took one of his ribs and closed up the flesh at that place. The LORD God fashioned into a woman the rib which He had taken from the man, and brought her to the man. The man said, "This is now bone of my bones, And flesh of my flesh; She shall be called Woman, Because she was taken out of Man." For this reason a man shall leave his father and his mother, and be joined to his wife; and they shall become one flesh. And the man and his wife were both naked and were not ashamed."
> —Genesis 2:21-25 (NAS)

In Corinthians Paul covers more than one point:

> "Now concerning the things about which you wrote, it is good for a man not to touch a woman. But because of immoralities, each man is to have his own wife, and each woman is to have her own husband. The husband must fulfill his duty to his wife, and likewise also the wife to her husband. The wife does not have authority over her own body, but the husband does; and likewise also the husband does not have authority over his own body, but the wife does. Stop depriving one another, except by agreement for a time, so that you may devote yourselves to prayer, and come together again so that Satan will not tempt you because of your lack of self-control. But this I say by way of concession, not of command. Yet I wish that all men were even as I myself am. However, each man has his own gift from God, one in this manner, and another in that."
> —I Corinthians 7:1-7 (NAS)

In Hebrews, the sanctity of marriage is noted along with the apparent prohibition of whoremongering (seeking sexual satisfaction through prostitutes) and adultery.

> "Marriage is to be held in honor among all, and the marriage bed is to be undefiled; for fornicators and adulterers God will judge." —Hebrews 13:4 (NAS)

Many other scriptures support the value of marriage. In the following example finding a wife is not only a good thing, but is pleasing to God.

> "He who finds a wife finds a good thing And obtains favor from the LORD." —Proverbs 18:22 (NAS)

Although the Bible seems to teach the concept of monogamy (having only one wife) and suggests divorce is not acceptable except in certain situations, the incidence of divorce is increasing even in the Christian church. Even though divorce is apparently possible under certain conditions, such as adultery, there is a very strong prohibition of remarriage.

In the last 25 years the rate of divorce has more than doubled in the United States. Even in the Church, where divorce was very rarely found, there is a steady increase of divorces and remarriages among people who profess to be strong believers in the teachings of the Bible.

This book is not intended to be an examination of the biblical position on marriage, nor is it intended to pass any kind of judgment. The discussion presented above is intended only to note the change in social and religious practices not only in the church, but in society in general.

It seems apparent that if marriage and parenting is the goal (or at least the major goal) of this stage of development, there must be an ever increasing number of very unhappy, dysfunctional, emotionally distressed individuals in modern day society.

Erikson considered the main issues of this age group as **Intimacy vs Isolation**. Erikson was the first Freudian, and one of the first developmentalists to suggest separate stages for the adult years. There was little written about the adult years and Erikson was indeed charting new territory.

Erikson's stages of adult development describe steps by which people widen and deepen their capacity to love and care for others (Crain, 1985, p. 170).

If the increasing breakup of marriages is any indicator of the failure of people to successfully "love and care," then there is reason to believe that either people are entering young adulthood totally unprepared for the role of husband and wife, or the pressures of life in the modern world are so demanding that young people can no longer make the kind of commitments that seem necessary for full and healthy development at this stage of their lives.

Erikson realized the adolescent was self-absorbed, but as he moved into the stage of young adulthood he had to begin thinking about such things as love as a commitment and marriage as a life-long adventure. Adolescents fall in love with others, but much of the time the relationships are temporary (what some call "puppy love"). The adolescent was just too preoccupied about who he was to take up the real task of young adulthood.

Two important perspectives on adulthood are the **normative-crisis model** and the **timing-of-events model**.

The normative-crisis model is seen in the works of Erikson, Valliant, and Levinson. They proposed that there is a build-in plan for human development and that during each part of the life span, people must deal with a particular crisis or task.

Another way of describing what is meant by normative crisis model is that in childhood and adolescence internal maturational events signal the transition from one developmental stage to another. A baby says the first word, takes the first step, and loses the first baby tooth. A youngster's body changes signal the entry into pubescence (Papilia1989).

In adulthood, people move from "a biological to a social clocking of adult development" (Danish & D'Augelli, 1980). Physiological and intellectual maturation are now less important to growth than are the effects of such external events as marriage, parenthood, divorce, remarriage, widowhood, and retirement (Papilia, (1989).

Erikson suggested that the main crisis of the young adult was to be able to be intimate with another person. To be intimate with someone else means that some of one's egocentricity must be left behind. The issue at this stage is to be intimate or to end up being isolated and self-absorbed. The young adult must be able to abandon himself freely and tenderly with his sex partner. This kind of intimacy is difficult for the individual who has up until now thought only of gratifying his own sexual urges.

The sense of identity developed during adolescence enables young adults to fuse their identity with that of others. Young adults resolve conflicting demands of intimacy, competitiveness, and distance and develop an ethical sense. They are ready to enter into a loving heterosexual relationship with the ultimate aim of providing a nurturing environment for children.

Others have built on the original theories of men like Erikson. One of those men was George Vaillant, who conducted his research among 268 undergraduate, young university men at Harvard. His study was to become known as the Grant Study. Vaillant identified four types of **ego defense mechanisms**, or characteristic ways in which people adapt to life situations:

Mature mechanisms. The use of humor or helping others.

Immature mechanisms. Developing aches and pains with no physical basis. Vaillant (1977) said that immature mechanisms are those that were appropriate up until the age of 15, but in the adult they are no longer adequate. In discussing the use of the immature mechanism of **passive-aggressive behavior**, Vaillant gives the following example from the Grant Study, "an inquiry into the kinds of people who are well and do well, conducted in 1937 through a grant by William T. Grant, a philanthropist: "One man in the Grant Study (1937) had a chronic history of lateness and procrastination; when something annoyed him, he simply put it off. He was separated from his wife for many years, but he never divorced her and would not admit overt conflict. He dealt with his hostility passively, by not doing anything" (Hassett and White, 1989).

In contrast, **suppression** serves as a mature defense mechanism. Suppression involves a conscious decision to postpone attention to sources of conflict. For example, in World War II one subject in the Grant study became so angry at his superior officer that he wanted to hit him. He forced himself to think of other things and later discuss his anger with another officer (Hassett and White, p. 393.)

Psychotic mechanisms in which people distort reality. This type of mechanism could be demonstrated by the man (or woman) who develops a paranoia about his or her mate having an affair with someone else when there is really no evidence to indicate that such an affair is actually going on.

Neurotic mechanisms. Repressing anxiety, intellectualizing, or developing irrational fears. The mechanism can best be seen in the woman in the later part of the young adult stage, who becomes obsessed with her looks and fears she is no longer attractive to her husband. This is only neurotic in the case where the woman is not indeed losing her attraction; her fear is irrational.

The term **ego defense mechanisms** needs a little review before proceeding.

Anna Freud carried her father's work on ego psychology even farther than he did. She was primarily interested in the way people master their conflicts by means of ego defense mechanisms such as **rationalization, repression**, and **denial**. She believed that instead of viewing these defenses as being hindrances to treatment, they should be seen as a means of getting to the unconscious by giving a clue to the analyst that there was an unconscious conflict emerging (Benner, 1985, p. 344). The mechanisms used by Vaillant, though given different names, are similar to those suggested by A. Freud.

The men who used the mature mechanisms were the happiest and successful in every way (Vaillant, 1977).

Career consolidation and stages of development. Between the ages of 25-35, the men worked at consolidating their careers. Vaillant believed that career consolidation happened somewhere between ages twenty and forty and was true for both men and women. At this time the young adult becomes preoccupied with the strengthening of his or her own career.

During this same period the young people were also busy strengthening their marriage.

Daniel Levinson developed a theory know as **Life Structures** (Levinson, 1978). Levinson and his colleagues at Yale University used the interview method of research to question 40 young men who had first been given a personality test. He defined his theory of life structure as "the underlying pattern or design of a person's life at a given time" (1986, p.6).

Levinson classified people in four developmental stages:

1. Pre-adulthood (age 0 to age 22), the formative years from conception to the end of adolescence.

2. Early adulthood (age 17 to age 45), in which people make significant life choices and exhibit the greatest energy but also experience the most stress.

3. Middle adulthood (age 40 to age 65), when most people have somewhat reduced biological capacities but greater social responsibilities.

4. Late adulthood (age 60 on), the final phase of life.

A view of the crisis periods according to Levinson recorded in a table in Papalia and Olds (1989), lists the following:

Novice phase of early adulthood (17-33): building a provisional life structure; learning its limitations.

1. Early adult transition (age 17-22) — Moving out of parents' home: becoming more independent.

2. Entry life structure for early adulthood (ages 22-28) — Building a first life structure; choosing an occupation; marrying; establishing a home and a family; joining civic and social groups; following a dream of the future and finding an older mentor to help find ways to achieve that dream.

3. Age 30 transition (age 28-33) — Reassessing work and family patterns; creating the basis for the next life structure.

4. Culminating phases of early adulthood (ages 33-45) — Bringing to fruition the efforts of early adulthood.

5. Culmination life structure for early adulthood (age 33-40)

    a. "Settling Down" — Building life in a second adult structure; making deeper commitments to work, home, family; setting timetables for specific goals; establishing a niche in society; realizing youthful aspirations.

    b. "Becoming One's Own Man" — Getting out from under other people's power and authority; seeking independence and respect; discarding the mentor.

6. Mid-life transition (age 40-45) — Ending early adulthood; beginning middle adulthood.

Gender Differences and Identity

Various studies indicate that men and women arrive at their different gender identity by different paths. Men have traditionally defined themselves in terms of separation and autonomy. Females, however, seem to achieve identity through relationships and attachment.

Levinson (1986) states that in the early adult transition (ages 17 to 22) men (and also women) need to move out of pre-adulthood and move into adulthood. This may mean moving out of their parents' home and becoming more independent. Young people who enter college or the military actually enter a mid-stage between pre-adulthood and adulthood. It is during the novice stage of transition that an individual builds the entry life structure for adulthood.

This phase is a time of increased relationships with the other sex, less and less time spent with the family of origin, and becoming involved in work which may eventually lead to a choice of vocational goals. There is also some involvement in civic and social groups.

It is at the entry life structure that the concepts "dream" and "mentor" come into play. The dream refers to the forming of an ideal career. The vision of becoming an actor or a writer and achieving great honors is an important phase of this age group. It is also at this stage that the young adult begins looking to a mentor, an older person (teacher, minister) who takes an interest in guiding the younger person's career.

When men reach the age of 30, they will often take a second look at their lives and wonder whether the commitments they have made earlier (the previous decade) have been premature, or they make strong commitments for the first time. This phase, called Age 30 Transition by Levinson, can be very crucial with regard to the stress of passage. Some men pass through rather easily, while others may find that their job, marriages or their life situation as a whole is intolerable.

There is a peaking of the divorce rate during this phase. Many young adults at this phase enter psychotherapy in order to get help for the clarification of their goals. If the choices made now are solid, a strong foundation will be established for the next phase.

Marriage and Family

There was a time in the early 1970's when the marriage rate dropped, but marriage is still the major event in the lives of young adults. Most young people still marry, although evidence indicates that they are marrying later and later in life.

Predicting Success in Marriage

Although more and more people are opting for single parenting, marriage is still thought by the majority of people to be the best way to insure orderly raising of children and thus continuing the species.

It is thought that marriage meets a variety of fundamental needs in men and women. However, there is a trend to alternative lifestyles with regard to marital commitments. The old and reliable attitudes are being attacked by those who insist that such alternatives as homosexual marriages meet the same needs without some of the hazards of the traditional, heterosexual partnerships. The question remains, "does a heterosexual marriage stand a better chance of lasting than a homosexual one?" Or is there any validity to the assumption that children raised in a single parent home will fare as well as children raised in a typical heterosexual marriage?

Success in Marriage

What, then, is success in marriage? Is it to be measured by how long a couple stays together? Skeptics would point out that some marriages that have "lasted" for many years had actually died for all intents and purposes since almost the beginning of the relationship.

Can marriages be judged on the basis of how husbands and wives rate themselves and their marriage? Experience has shown that this criterion is flawed greatly, because often husbands and/or wives will not or cannot admit in a questionnaire that theirs isn't a good marriage

A few things seem to be fairly reliable predictors of success in marriage. One of those things is the age at which the couples marry. Young people who marry in their adolescence are among the most frequent causalities. Early marriages may affect career or educational aspirations, frustrating young people in their need to grow. People who wait until their late twenties or early thirties seem to have a better chance of success in marriage.

Marriages have a better chance of succeeding if the woman is not pregnant at the time of marriage. All too often the pregnancy is the "honorable" excuse for marrying rather than love and mature commitment.

It has been shown that black people, people who have not completed their education, and people whose parents were not happily married (or divorced) are more likely to fail in their marriages.

The success of a marriage depends to a large degree on the ability of the partners to learn to communicate and to deal with problem solving, decision making and resolution of conflicts. These people tend to stay married longer and derive greater happiness from their marriage during the middle adult years than others. (For more on marriage and parenting, see *Marriage and Family Life: A Christian Perspective* and *Parenting On Purpose*, both by Dr. DeKoven).

Violence between Spouses

Family violence and especially spousal abuse has become a growing concern for family counselors (See DeKoven, 2011, second edition). Evidence indicates that children born into a family that has experienced a considerable amount of violence such as spousal and child abuse will in turn become abusers themselves. A part of the pre-marriage counseling should always include an investigation into the kind of family from which each partner comes.

At times women will stay with the abusing husband because of their own personal emotional problems that tend to make them feel they deserve the mistreatment they are receiving. Some women stay in an abusive marriage because of a strong need to mother (and hopefully reform the abusing husband) and protect the children. Some women stay just because they are too afraid to leave.

In recent years more and more shelters are making their way onto the scene, and more and more education concerning the rights of battered women, men and abused children is resulting in some changes in the statistics.

Parenthood and Non-parenthood

At one time in the history of the United States (and the world in general) children were considered an economic necessity. When more people lived on farms, children were an inexpensive source of labor. Parents saw children as a real asset. As lifestyles began to shift from rural to urban, children no longer were an asset but became more a liability. As more and more women pursue careers or simply go to work to supplement the husband's income, married couples tend to lean more to either no children or only one child.

There can be no doubt that a child born into a family requires many changes, changes that young adults intent on making enough money to keep up with their friends and neighbors, are not readily willing to make. Families in America have been getting smaller and smaller during the past decade or two. The average number of children per marriage is slightly on the increase, but only by very small percentage points.

Parenthood can and does provide a new source of bond between people. In times of affluence, there is usually an increase in births. Among the lower socio-economic population there has always been a trend to unrestrained childbirth. The sociology and psychology of this segment of society is another matter altogether.

To Have or Not to Have

Among middle and upper socio-economic segments of society, there is an increase in family planning. Children are considered only when they may fit into the social and economic framework of the individual family structure. Of course, sometimes God and nature make plans completely independent of mere mortals.

Although family size does not seem to be increasing at any appreciable rate, more and more couples are opting to have children. With the recent medical discoveries more couples are able to have children than in years past.

Advantages of Having Children Early

Although most researchers suggest that there are some real advantages to having children early in the marriage, there is a growing trend, at least since the early 1980's, to delay having children until as late in life as possible. The decision to have the child is usually a result of the wife becoming aware of her biological time clock, indicating that time is running out.

Having children early in the marriage may mean that during the middle adult stage the couple will have more time for each other and for some of the travel and leisure activities that were not possible earlier in life because of involvement in work, etc.

Parenting: Development of Different styles

The development of parenting styles is largely influenced by the kind of family the father and mother experienced as children.

Diana Baumrind identified three categories of child-rearing styles and described typical behavior patterns of the children raised according to each style (Baumrind, 1971; Baumrind, 1967).

Authoritarian parents value control and unquestioning obedience. They try to make their children conform to a set standard of conduct, and they punish children forcefully for acting contrary to that standard. They are more detached and less warm than other parents, and their children are more discontent, withdrawn, and distrustful (see the discussion of Millon's personality theory in chapter 3).

Permissive parents value self-expression and self-regulation. They make few demands, allowing their children to monitor their own activities as much as possible. They consider themselves resources, not standard-bearers or models. They explain to their children the reasons underlying the few family rules that do exist, consult with them about policy decisions, and hardly ever punish. They are non-controlling, non-demanding, and relatively warm. Their children as preschoolers are immature — the least self-controlled and the least exploratory.

Authoritative parents respect a child's individuality, but they also consider it important to instill social values. They direct their children's activities rationally, with attention to the issues rather than to the children's fear of punishment or loss of love. They exert firm control when necessary, but they explain the reasoning behind their stands and encourage verbal give-and-take. While they have confidence in their ability to guide their children, they respect the children's interests, opinions, and unique personalities. They are loving, consistent, demanding, and respectful of their children's independent decisions, but they are firm in maintaining standards and willing to impose limited punishment. They combine control with encouragement. Their children apparently feel secure in knowing that they are loved and knowing what is expected of them. As preschoolers, these children are most self-reliant, self-controlled, self-assertive, exploratory, and content.

There can be little doubt that the authoritative parent style offers the most to be desired. However, several points need to be made with respect to the three styles. First, it is very rare that both parents have the same training or background to prepare them to be the ideal parents. The fact remains that research has borne out that children tend to become parents with a parental style similar to the parental style of their parents. All behavior is learned. The authoritarian parent is usually the parent whose father and/or mother were authoritarian in their style of parenting.

The fact of the matter is that parenting styles tend to be self-perpetuating. Some exception to this rule of fact may occur as a result of teenagers taking parenting classes before marriage, but even then all of the intentions of young adults to become ideal parents can be lost as a result of the stresses of marriage.

In many families, parenting is left to one of the two parents. It may be that the father is too busy to be "bothered" with the details of child guidance and the entire responsibility is left to the mother. In other situations, the mother may be too emotionally weak to deal with the hassles of discipline and that task is left to "just wait until your father gets home". Then the father is forced to deal with a situation that he is totally unaware of with punishment that is deemed proper by the mother, who was unable to administer it.

Summary

Studies show that development continues through life.

The normative-crisis model of adulthood is exemplified by Erikson, Vaillant, and Levinson. It proposes that there is a built-in ground plan for human development and that during each part of the life span, people must deal with a particular crisis or task.

Erikson's sixth psychosocial stage crisis is **Intimacy vs Isolation**. Successful development, according the Erikson, involves young people fusing their identities in a close, intimate, heterosexual relationship that leads to procreation. Negative outcomes that may result during this period are self-absorption and isolation.

Vaillant found that men who used "mature defenses" were more successful in many ways than those who used less mature adaptive techniques. This period also shows a time of career consolidating that characterized men in their thirties.

Levinson believed that the goal of adults was to build a life structure. He found periods of transition and periods of stability alternating throughout adulthood.

Intimate Relationships and Personal Lifestyle have been in a process of change over the past decade or two.

The United States has the highest divorce rate in the world.

More people are choosing to remain single, which may indicate the inability of young people to become intimate.

The number of people cohabitating has risen higher than ever before. Again this trend leads one to wonder if the idea of intimacy is too threatening to more and more young people. It is much easier to get out of a relationship that is based on a loose commitment rather than a marriage which requires a divorce.

Having children makes a major difference in a married couple's life. Most of the time, the difference is for the better. Occasionally a marriage is not ready for the additional financial and emotional burden of a child.

Many couples today are choosing to have fewer or no children. These decisions are usually based on economic reasons. Many couples depend on two incomes to maintain the lifestyle that they both seem to enjoy. The prospects of one person not being able to continue working or the additional cost of child care would mean an end to their affluent style of living.

The use of artificial insemination has made it possible for many couples to have children who were not able to conceive.

There are many moral and spiritual questions that have yet to be adequately considered with respect to having children by this method. Some of the most devastating types of experiences have been through the courts, causing legal and ethical questions to which there just do not seem to be answers.

Personal Reflections

Although the summary above reflects some of my own personal opinions, I do not wish to leave the subject of this chapter without a few more comments.

As a minister and a counselor for many years, I have had to do a considerable amount of marriage and pre-marital counseling. It is amazing to discover how many people, both young and old, come in for counseling with the idea that marriage will be the answer to all of their problems. Even some of the couples who have been divorced and are now wanting to remarry seem to think that the second time will be some kind of magic charm.

Marriage is a very complex relationship. It implies a lifelong commitment to love, honor, and obey until death do us part. It is amazing to discover how many people have made that kind of commitment two or more times in their lives.

Even the church has become less adamant about its position on divorce and remarriage. I do not wish to imply that I am wholeheartedly in favor of the stand of some of the denominational groups concerning divorce and remarriage, but I do feel that there has been a gross lack of teaching in churches about the sanctity of the marriage and of the marriage vows. I also feel that the church as well as the educational community has been grossly negligent in preparing young people for their entrance into the adult world.

For example, we have consistently taught that one should save oneself sexually for the marriage, implying that the matter of sex and sexual problems will automatically be solved in marriage. A large percent of marriages are dissolved because of sexual incompatibility. Marriage doesn't solve problems. Marriage creates new problems that must be worked out by two intellectually well prepared individuals who desire the intimacy that marriage can bring rather than the isolation that is the alternative.

If more counselors and ministers would become better trained in the Scripture and in the entire area of human development and human behavior, we would be able to better prepare young people for the most mystical and marvelous experiences of their lives. The Scriptures suggest that our relation to Jesus Christ is like a marriage. Jesus is spoken of as the bridegroom and the church is called the bride.

I believe that if the biblical instructions for both man and woman were to be made the leading principle of married life, there would be less divorces and more happy marriages. Here are a few scriptures that serve as an example of my premise:

> "Husbands, love your wives, just as Christ also loved the church and gave Himself up for her"
> —Ephesians 5:25 (NAS)

> "Husbands, love your wives and do not be embittered against them." —Colossians 3:19 (NAS)

> "Wives, be subject to your own husbands, as to the Lord."
> —Ephesians 5:22 (NAS)

> "But as the church is subject to Christ, so also the wives ought to be to their husbands in everything. Husbands, love your wives, just as Christ also loved the church and gave Himself up for her" —Ephesians 5:24-25 (NAS)

> "So husbands ought also to love their own wives as their own bodies. He who loves his own wife loves himself"
> —Ephesians 5:28 (NAS)

A Time for Healing

After having read this chapter you may have discovered some things about marriage that you had not given much thought to before. If you are married, or have been married, write a short evaluation of your marriage in light of what you have learned in this chapter. If your marriage is fairly solid, talk over with your spouse what you have learned and get his/her response. If you find that there are some serious concerns about your marriage relationship, try to get your spouse to go with you to a good Christian counselor. Don't wait until it is too late. Your pastor should be able to recommend a counselor to you.

If it is already "too late" spend some real soul searching time trying to understand what went wrong. Remember a marriage break-up is seldom the fault of one person alone. Talk to a friend about what you have discovered. Remember, you can only change one person, yourself. The Lord can, and often does help the other part of the marriage, but you must allow the Lord the opportunity to work in His own way. If you are not yet married, write a short history of your family of origin. How well did your parents get along? What was your home life like? Was there love expressed openly, or were your parents rather cordial toward each other and also to you? How would you describe your parents? Were they authoritarian, permissive, or authoritative in their dealing with you and your siblings?

Did you have brothers or sisters? How did you get along with them? Were either you or your siblings abused as children? What effect has the abuse had on your life? How have you coped with the results of that abuse?

If there has been abuse in your past, be sure that you get into counseling with a good Christian counselor, and be certain that all of the issues of that abusive past have been resolved.

Remember that the key to healing in cases of abuse (either spousal or child abuse) is **forgiveness**. You cannot be completely forgiving without the help of the Lord. Let the Holy Spirit prepare your heart, and then ask Jesus to stand with you as you forgive from your heart those who have hurt you.

Review of Chapter 9

- The Eriksonian issue of this time of life is Intimacy vs Isolation.

- Unlike the "puppy love" relationship of adolescence the young adult is now looking for a meaningful, long-range relationship that includes the concept of intimacy.

- The sense of identity that adolescents developed enables them to now fuse their identity with that of others.

- George Valliant's study of young men resulted in several types of ego defense mechanisms:

  - Mature mechanisms
  - Immature mechanisms
  - Psychotic mechanisms
  - Neurotic mechanisms

- This is a time of career consolidation.

- Levinson introduced the idea of life structures: the underlying pattern or design of a person's life at any given time.

- Levinson suggested that in the early adult transition (17-22) men (and also women) need to move out of pre-adulthood and move into adulthood.

- It is at this time that many young adults select a mentor to assist them with their transition.

- People at this stage move from a biological clock to a social clock of adult development.

- Erikson said that the main crisis of the young adult was that of being able to be intimate.

- Of the various mechanisms, suppression serves as a mature defense mechanism.

- Levinson classified people into four developmental stages:

  - Pre-adulthood
  - Early Adulthood
  - Middle Adulthood
  - Late Adulthood

- There was a time in the 1970's when the marriage rate dropped.

- Marriage is still considered the most orderly way of raising children.

- Although it is thought that marriage meets a variety of needs in men and women, there is a trend toward alternative lifestyles. A discussion on how a marriage can be deemed to be a successful one.

- The younger a couple is at the time of marriage the less chance there is of the marriage being a lasting one.

- Marriages have a better change of enduring if the woman is not pregnant at the time of the marriage.

- Success in marriage depends to a large extend on the ability of the husband and wife being able to communicate and solve problems.

- Family violence and especially spousal abuse has become a growing concern for family counselors.

- Women sometimes stay with the abusing husband because of their own emotional problems.

- Shelters for the abused are becoming more popular.

- Some adults must decide on whether or not to have children because of their affluent lifestyle.

- Having children early in the marriage may permit the married couple to have more time for each other in middle and later life after the children are grown and moved out.

- There are different parenting styles:
    - Authoritarian parents
    - Permissive parents
    - Authoritative parents

- Authoritative parents are considered best because they respect the child's individuality but are still willing to guide and direct them into the correct choices.

- Parenting styles tend to be self-perpetuating.

- In many families, the responsibility of parenting is left to one or the other of the parents. It should be a shared responsibility.

Glossary for Chapter 9

Glossary of Terms

Denial — One defense mechanism for dealing with unpleasant or difficult problems. Used in this chapter with relation to intimate relationships.

Ego Defense Mechanisms — Various ways of dealing with life's difficulties.

Immature Mechanism — One of the defenses in which the person will develop aches and pains without any physical symptoms.

Life Structure Test — Levinson's test that shows the underlying pattern of design of a person's life at a given time.

Neurotic Mechanism — For example, repressing anxiety, intellectualizing, or developing irrational fears.

Non-Normative Life Events — Those events that people do not expect in life, such as traumatic accident, loss of job, etc.

Normative Crisis Model — A theory that there is a predictable sequence of age-related changes throughout adult life.

Normative Life Events — Events that people expect in life.

Timing of Events Model — Looking at events as indicators of development instead of physical changes.

"If one advances confidently in the direction of his dreams, and endeavors to live the life which he has imagined, he will meet with a success unexpected in common ways."
— Henry David Thoreau

Chapter 10

Ages 35-65

This stage is called **Middle Adulthood**. Erikson saw the main issues in this age period as **Generativity vs Stagnation**.

Physical Development

Some very significant physical changes take place during this stage of life; most of them are not for the better. Persons at this stage of life can expect some changes in their vision, hearing, taste, and smell. Although many people have vision problems early in life, and some spend most of their lives wearing glasses, during the middle adult stage a condition called **presbyopia** (farsightedness) develops, making the use of reading glasses necessary. Usually by this age, most people are wearing bifocal or even trifocal lenses. People at this stage also need more light to see to compensate for the loss of light reaching the retina (Belbin, 1967; Troll, 1985).

There is also a gradual loss of hearing in this stage, especially with regard to the upper frequencies. This condition is known as **Presbycusis**. After the age of 55, hearing loss is greater for men than for women. (Troll, 1985).

There is a decline of taste sensitivity during these years. Taste buds begin to decline after childhood and foods that seem to be tasteful to younger people may seem bland to middle adults. Middle adults are often critical of their children because their tastes differ considerably.

Sensitivity to smell is one of the last senses to decline, except when it is a result of some diseases.

If middle adults do not keep up a program of exercise, they will lose some of their strength, coordination, and reaction time. Usually the loss is not significant. Reaction time slows about 20% from age 20 to age 60.

A change in reproduction and sexual capacity is another development change that many adults do not enjoy. Men usually continue to talk about their ability to perform, long after this decline. It is at this time that the woman will go through **menopause**, a biological occurrence when a woman stops ovulating and menstruating and can no longer have children. The period of menopause may take from 2-5 years to complete all of the physiological changes. The **climacteric** is the time during which the changes are taking place.

During the climacteric, a woman's body reduces its production of the female hormone **estrogen**. After menopause, or in case the woman has a **hysterectomy** (surgical removal of all or most of the female reproductive organs) the woman may need to take estrogen to avoid some of the unpleasant side effects of menopause, such as heat flashes, urinary dysfunction, etc. The decrease in estrogen can also lead to osteoporosis, a condition in which the bones become thinner and more susceptible to fracture. **Osteoporosis** can also lead to a deformation of the posture with slumped shoulders as one of the evidences. Women can avoid osteoporosis by eating the right vegetables and taking a vitamin supplement with calcium.

The Male Climacteric — Men can continue to father children until quite late in life. Some middle adult men experience a decrease in fertility and frequency of orgasm and an increase in impotency.

The male climacteric is characterized by a period of physiological changes involving the male reproductive system and other body systems. It generally begins about ten years later than the woman's climacteric and the pattern of symptoms vary (Weg, 1987). Some of the symptoms may include mood changes, depression, fatigue, sexual inadequacy and other physical complaints (Henker, 1981).

Many of the health problems that occur in middle adulthood are the result of loss of **reserve capacity**, the body's organs' and systems' inability to provide extra effort in times of stress or dysfunction.

Middle Adults are subject to some chronic ailments noted especially in this stage. Some of the ailments include asthma, bronchitis, diabetes, arthritis and rheumatism, as well as some circulatory, digestive, and genitourinary systems.

One of the main health problems of middle adults is high blood pressure, known as **hypertension**. This can be a life threatening condition if not properly treated with medication and diet.

Among middle adults, the main causes of death are cancer, heart disease, and accidents for the first half of this stage. Adults, ages 35-54 also suffer more cancer and heart disease and now are more apt to die of stroke.

It has been shown that middle adult individuals do not have any decrease in intelligence or cognition. During the next stage, older adults encounter such debilitating conditions an **Alzheimer's disease** which is characterized by loss of memory.

Middle Adults are usually at the peak of their career or work situation or are on the brink of changing to a new career. Some individuals change their vocation because after years at the same work, they experience "burnout" and are simply no longer able to sustain enough interest in the work to be productive.

One of the most difficult problems of modern times is that of unemployment, particularly unemployment that comes to a middle or upper management person who is at the age when it will be very difficult to find another job in his or her field.

Erikson's psychosocial development

Now that the individuals have established a measure of intimacy, their interests begin to turn beyond just the two of them. They begin being concerned with raising a family. In Erikson's terms, they enter a stage of **productivity vs stagnation**.

Generativity (same as productivity) refers not only to the creation and care of children but the production of things and ideas through work. Erikson, however, has focused more on the former, the care of children.

Generativity means much more than just having children, they must be adequately fed, cared for and guided. At the same time people can have a sense of generativity without having children. Some people at this stage gain their sense of generativity by guiding the children of others in such professions as teachers, medical professionals, Boy Scout volunteers, ministers, etc.

Some individuals, however, do not develop at this stage. There can be several reasons according to Erikson (1959. p. 97).

Sometimes the parent's own childhood was so empty or frustrated that the parent cannot see how it is possible to do more for his or her children. In other cases, the difficulty seems more cultural. In the United States in particular, values tend to emphasize one's own independent achievements. This can affect them to such an extent that people can become too exclusively involved in themselves and their successes, and neglect the responsibility of caring for others. Erikson says that this can result in people becoming stagnant (inactive or lifeless).

Peck (1955) suggested four critical psychological developments related to successful adjustments to middle age. They are:

1. Valuing Wisdom vs Valuing Physical Powers — People realize that the knowledge they have gained through the years, enabling them to make their life choices wisely, more than makes up for their declining physical powers and youthful attractiveness.

2. Socializing vs Sexualizing — People learn to appreciate the unique personalities of others as they learn to value them as friends rather than as sex objects.

3. Emotional Flexibility vs Emotional Impoverishment — Deaths of parents and friends force breaks in meaningful relationships. People must develop the ability to shift their emotional investments from one person to another. Physical limitations can require a change in activities.

4. Mental Flexibility vs Mental Rigidity — Flexibility enables people to use their past experiences as provisional guides to the solution of new issues.

Peck says that none of these developments need wait until middle age; some may already have developed in early adulthood. However, if they do not develop by middle adulthood, Peck doubts if the person will be able to make a successful emotional adjustment.

A study done by Vaillant (1977) of Harvard University men indicated some interesting points about men in "midlife transition." Vaillant posited these points as:

1. Midlife is stressful, as adolescence is stressful, because of the demands of entrance into a new stage of life. Much of the pain comes from having the maturity to face pain that was suppressed for years. Many men reassessed their past, reordered their attitudes toward sexuality, and seized one more chance to find new solutions to old needs. The best adjusted men were the most generative and found these years (from 35-49) to be the happiest of their lives.

2. Tranquil fifties. Males become more nurturing and expressive. Sexual differentiation lessens. The fifties are generally a mellower time of life.

Levenson (1978, 1986) in his study of the stages of midlife development in men discovered the following:

1. Midlife transition (age 40 to age 45) — Questioning one's life — values, desires, talents, goals; looking back over past choices and priorities; deciding where to go now; coming to terms with youthful dreams; developing a realistic view of self.

2. Entry life structure for middle adulthood (age 45 to age 50) — Reappraisal leads to a new life structure involving new choices. Some men retreat into a constricted or well-organized, overly busy middle age.

3. Age-50 transition (age 50 to age 55) — This is offered as a projection: Men who have not gone through their midlife crisis earlier may do so now. Others may modify the life structures they have formed in their mid-forties.
Some people do not experience an actual crisis during their midlife transition. For men, midlife crisis may be connected to such physical factors as being overweight or having high blood pressure, but it is how an individual feels about health or virility that is particularly important. The psychological changes of menopause can cause problems for women, but most of the symptoms are likely to be less significant than the social and psychological problems of midlife transition. Women who have chosen a career over a family now hear

the "biological clock" ticking out their last childbearing years. The contrast between youth and middle age may be especially upsetting for men who matured earlier in adolescence and were sociable and athletic rather than intellectual (Block, 1971).

4. Culminating life structure for middle adulthood — a time of great fulfillment.

5. Late adulthood transition (age 60 to age 65) — Middle age ends, preparation for late adulthood begins.

The stages posited by Levinson listed above deal with the psychological changes that take place in men during middle adulthood. The question arises "Do women undergo Levinsonian changes?" A few researchers have applied Levinson's biological technique to women (ages 44 to 53). They found that for these women, the midlife transitions were not as clear-cut as with men. It was found that these women remained unstable after the transition, because the women had not yet come to the point in their careers where they could assess their achievements and make a definite change of direction (Droege's dissertation, 1982), analyzed by P. Roberts and Newton (1987).

Papalia and Olds (1989) raise a very important question in a "food for thought" section in their book, p. 510. "Does personality change in middle age?" They point out that many people seem to experience changes in their personality during adulthood, but the question of the permanence of the changes has been researched by a number of psychologists. It has been suggested as a result of some of the research that people in general tend to become introverted and introspective as they get older.

It was also noted that men tend to become more in touch with feelings and more interested in developing intimacy, while women tend to become more assertive, self-confident, and achievement oriented.

The reasons for the changes are at best speculative. Some feel that the changes are due to hormonal changes. Others speculate that environmental changes may be a factor, i.e., more women are climbing the corporate ladder to higher positions in almost every field of employment.

Carl Jung (1875-1961) was one of the first persons to develop a theory of development dealing with adult life. It is not too difficult to see that some or most of the theories that have been presented thus far in this chapter may have their roots in Jungian concepts.

Jung was psychoanalytical in his orientation, having been a follower of Freud early in his career. He broke with Freud because he could not accept Freud's contention that all unconscious events were somehow tied to sexual drives. Jung believed that the unconscious contains many kinds of strivings, including religious and spiritual ones. In 1912, he decided to develop his own ideas, and in 1913 he and Freud severed ties.

This text will not go into great detail regarding Jung's concepts and theories, although they are worth study for the serious student of psychological development, especially in the middle and older years.

Freud was one of the first to develop a theory (although his stage theory stopped at adolescence) regarding midlife crisis. He suggested that at about the age of 40 the psyche begins to undergo a transformation. He said that the individual begins to feel that the goals and ambitions of life which once seemed to be so important have lost their meaning. People at this stage quite often feel depressed, stagnant, and incomplete, as if something very important were missing. Jung noticed that this happens even among people who have been reasonably successful and have achieved reasonable social success. However, the cost of having reached such levels of achievement was a diminution of personality giving rise to a sense of disillusionment and despair (Jung, 1933).

Jung suggested that the psyche itself provides a way out of this crisis. It urges the person to "turn inward and examine the meaning of his or her life." He felt that at this stage man begins to realize that most of the repressed and unlived aspects of the self, have grown and clamor to be heard (Jung 1933, pp. 1-18, 62-63).

Jung believed that the unconscious speaks to man primarily through dreams. Individuals, according to Jung, can discover the cause of their depression and feeling of meaninglessness by paying attention to the content of the images of their dreams. Some therapists still use dream analysis to assist clients in discovering the basis for their psychological problems.

Jung referred to the road toward health and growth as **individuation** (Jung 1933). He felt that individuation involves not only achieving a measure of psychic balance but "separating ourselves from our ordinary conformity to the goals and values of the mass culture."

Individuation is a synthetic process of integrating the various components of personality to the point that the parts, especially the conscious and the unconscious, begin to complement rather than oppose one another. The result is a self that is superordinate even to the conscious ego.

Jung's concept of individuation should not be confused with Mahler's concept of separation-individuation, which refers to a much earlier developmental process occurring in the mother-child relationship mentioned in Chapter 4 (Benner, 1985).

Crain (1985) relates that an older colleague once told him, "As you get older you will find that achievement counts for less and friendship counts for far more. Women on the other hand, become more aggressive and independent."

Jung postulated that during the second half of life, the greatest failures come when adults cling to the goals and values of the first half of life (Jung, 1933). He cited as examples the middle-aged woman who endeavors desperately to maintain the physical attractiveness of her youth. Or the middle-aged man may talk incessantly about his past athletic glories. This represents a kind of regression that results in individuals missing out on further development, which can emerge only when the risk of the confrontation with the neglected parts of self is squarely faced.

What makes middle-aged couples split up or stay together?

This question has been asked many times over by many different researchers. Most researchers agree that how the marriage fares in middle-age depends largely on the quality of the marriage in the years leading up to middle-age. The marriage that has been good all along stands a better chance of lasting and becoming better than ever (Troll & Smith, 1976). The passionate love of newlyweds, with its emotional ups and downs, fades as day to day life together dispels the sense of mystery. But in a strong marriage, companionate love, loving friendship marked by affection, attachment, commitment, and security, deepens as a couple share joys and sorrows, trust and loyalty, and an intimate knowledge of each other (E. Walster & Walster, 1978).

In a marriage that is shaky from the start such things as the "empty nest" syndrome, the transition that takes place when the last child leaves home, may be a personal and marital crisis. The crisis is greatest in the home where a mother has found her sense of identity in the raising of the children. When the children are all gone, she no longer seems to feel any true sense of worth. It is at this time that such a woman will begin to think about whether or not she really wants to spend the rest of her life with her husband, who it seems has contributed little to her needs as a woman.

Personal Reflections

"'Vanity of vanities,' says the Preacher, 'Vanity of vanities! All is vanity.'" —Ecclesiastes 1:2 (NAS)

"I have seen all the works which have been done under the sun, and behold, all is vanity and striving after wind."
—Ecclesiastes 1:14 (NAS)

"I said to myself, "Come now, I will test you with pleasure. So enjoy yourself." And behold, it too was futility."
—Ecclesiastes 2:1 (NAS)

"Thus I considered all my activities which my hands had done and the labor which I had exerted, and behold all was vanity and striving after wind and there was no profit under the sun." —Ecclesiastes 2:11 (NAS)

> "Then I said to myself, 'As is the fate of the fool, it will also befall me. Why then have I been extremely wise?' So I said to myself, 'This too is vanity.'"   —Ecclesiastes 2:15 (NAS)

> "So I hated life, for the work which had been done under the sun was grievous to me; because everything is futility and striving after wind."   —Ecclesiastes 2:17 (NAS)

> "And who knows whether he will be a wise man or a fool? Yet he will have control over all the fruit of my labor for which I have labored by acting wisely under the sun. This too is vanity."
>   —Ecclesiastes 2:19 (NAS)

> "When there is a man who has labored with wisdom, knowledge and skill, then he gives his legacy to one who has not labored with them. This too is vanity and a great evil."
>   —Ecclesiastes 2:21 (NAS)

> "Because all his days his task is painful and grievous; even at night his mind does not rest. This too is vanity."
>   —Ecclesiastes 2:23 (NAS)

I have included the above few verses from Ecclesiastes as an example of the kind of despair that many feel at the time of middle adulthood when their lives have not been particularly productive or generative.

As a minister and a marriage counselor, I have come to believe that this stage of development can be the most traumatic in many ways. This is the time when marriages that seemed to be solid suddenly come apart. It is the time when people often make decisions with the hope that that particular decision will be the solution to all of their problems.

Research seems to bear out that married people who work at staying together for a longer period of time can look forward to 20 or more years of married life after the last child has left the home. There was a time when the Christian church could contend that Christian marriages last longer than non-Christian marriages. It was the belief of the church that the Bible strongly prohibited divorce and especially remarriage. So people in the Christian church tended to stay married because they believed that God forbade divorce and even if there was a reasonable reason to get divorced, the Christian was not to remarry, at least while the first spouse was still living. There are still many denominational groups that support these teachings. However, the incidents of divorce and remarriage among Christians are on the rise. One can only guess that part of the reason for the increase in divorce and remarriage among Christians is that, although the teaching against such practices is still held, the level of stigma is not as high. Many Christians have become convinced that a "loving God would not hold them accountable in seeking to find the happiness that they are convinced can only be found if they can make a change in their marital situation."

The problem is that so many of the individuals who get divorced and remarried to someone else find that their problems are not solved. I do not wish to engage in a discourse on the rightness or wrongness of divorce and remarriage in this book. There are many very fine books that deal with the matter in detail. I only wish to share that from my experience as a minister and counselor, many of "second time around" marriages end up dealing with the same problems as were experienced in the first marriage. In fact, so many divorce, remarry, and divorce and remarry, and on and on, many times without ever finding a marriage partner who can "solve all of the problems of the individuals in the relationship." In most cases, it is not the marriage that needs fixing; it is the individuals themselves that need healing.

There are many things that can put a strain on the marriage during this stage. With the children gone from the home the husband and wife become dependent on one another to keep the marriage alive and growing. While the children were living at home, they provided diversion or activities or served as a scapegoat for the conflicts between the parents (Litz, 1968). The couple now has more time together, and they may find themselves becoming bored since they have forgotten how to enjoy each other's company without the children.

In many cases, the parents endure a less than enjoyable marriage relationship because of the children. Those marriages that last until the children are all gone from the house may quickly dissolve after they are gone. I have often counseled couples with this type of family situation, and it is very difficult to convince them that their divorce will be just as hard on the children, even though they have moved out on their own.

At times, the male in a marriage, in his desperate attempts to keep from losing the image of masculinity, will divorce his wife of many years and marry a younger woman. I counseled a minister several years ago who fit into this category. I was called by his wife to come to their home in a city some 365 miles from our home. She didn't share the whole story with me at the time, but only said that her husband was in the hospital and was very ill. When I arrived at the hospital, I was surprised to hear the minister, whom I had known for many years, relate to me that he had been having an affair with a younger woman in his church. I reasoned with him for some time, pointing out how difficult this whole affair would be on his wife and young son. His defense was, "I know that it is wrong, and that many people will be hurt, but if I had it to do over again, I would do it in a second. She was the best (sexual experience) I have ever had." He added that the woman's husband was looking for him with a gun, but that seemed to be of little consequence.

In what I would now admit was a very poor example of good counseling, I said to him, "Good Lord, Dan (not his real name), can't you see that this woman is only making love to her father, and you are only a substitute for her father?"

Very often men will divorce and remarry a younger woman thinking that her attraction to him was his sexual virility, when, in fact, the younger woman is seeking to satisfy her own unmet needs for loving and taking care of a father that was a disappointment to her.

The death of one spouse or the other also presents some problems for the middle adulthood stage. When the husband dies, often the woman will not remarry, especially to a younger man. When the wife dies the widower, because he is less capable of taking care of himself and a home, may seek a new wife as soon as possible.

Other problems that plague marriages at this stage are:

1. Vocational problems — Remember: Men tend to become more introverted and feelings oriented during this period, and women, in turn, become more aggressive, demanding more and more physically and materially from the marriage.

2. Poor health — This is the age span when many illnesses such as hypertension, ulcers, diabetes, and especially heart disease become more and more a part of life. The reasons for the increased health problems are many, including job stress, family stress, changes in body metabolism, etc. The issue here is that it was easier to deal with illness when it involved the children, but now that the marriage is threatened by some life threatening illness, the stress becomes much greater.

At times one spouse or the other will use illness to escape the responsibilities of marriage, even though a physician may say that there is no reason for the couple to curtail any of the normal activities (such as sex) because of the illness.

Another problem that may cause considerable disturbance in marriages during the middle adulthood stage has to do with children who do not leave the nest but continue to demand emotional and/or financial support long after they should have been on their own. In most situations, the woman is much more sympathetic toward the child or children, while the father considers the situation as a constant source of irritation. Often these situations will result in dissolution of the marriage when the ultimatum is made, "Either the kids go or I go."

In all of the situations mentioned in these reflections, counseling by a good marriage, family and child therapist can often help resolve the conflicts and save the marriage. However, a preventative program of marriage seminars, family retreats, etc., sponsored by local churches can be effective in heading off problems before they become so monumental that little can be done to save the marriage, and incidentally, the individual lives involved.

On a more positive note, grandchildren can bring a new glimmer of hope and happiness into an otherwise lackluster marriage. That is, of course, if the grandparents are able and allowed to enjoy the grandchildren.

> "Grandchildren are the crown of old men, And the glory of sons is their fathers." —Proverbs 17:6 (NAS)

> "A righteous man who walks in his integrity — How blessed are his sons after him." —Proverbs 20:7 (NAS)

> "Her children rise up and bless her; Her husband also, and he praises her, saying..." —Proverbs 31:28 (NAS)

A Time for Healing

Middle adulthood is the time in life when many people will seek out a counselor. As the author has indicated, there are many problems that begin to surface at this time of life.

The Christian counselor must prepare for the counseling sessions well in advance. It may be wise to begin now. As you go through other courses in marriage and family counseling, you will learn many techniques. None of those techniques will work as well as the healing Word of God.

The author has listed a number of scriptures in the text, but there are many more that you should look-up for yourself. A very good method of gathering scriptures for use in counseling is to type them out on a 3 X 5 index card and keep them sorted by topic. There is no reason why a counselor couldn't simply read the scriptures from the Bible or from the cards themselves, but it is far more effective to commit many of the main scriptures to memory.

When counseling a middle-aged couple, it is not too wise to ask them to look up scriptures at home together. They may be hardly speaking to each other and are not likely they will follow up on the Bible reading. After they have been in counseling for a period of time, it is possible that they might each look up a few scriptures on their own and share them at the next counseling session.

Do not be afraid to ask each of the individuals in a marriage counseling situation to comment on what they think the Bible scripture means.

When counseling people of this age group, there may be children involved. Minor children should be included in counseling sessions. They are a part of the family and may well be a part of the problem.

Prayer is a powerful weapon for use in the counseling session. Always pray before the session, at the beginning of the session, and after the session. The Holy Spirit can do wonders in the hearts of people when the counselor is able to recognize that without His help our efforts will most likely fail.

Ages 35-65

Review of Chapter 10

- This is the period of Middle Adulthood.
- Some very significant changes take place physically for the adult at this stage.
- Presbyopia and presbycusis are two common physical problems of this stage.
- This is also the time of the climacteric, the female menopause.
- The male may also go through a climacteric, but it is not as noticeable.
- Middle adults are subject to a number of other diseases such as asthma, bronchitis, diabetes, arthritis, and rheumatism.
- Hypertension is one of the main physical conditions that plague people at this age.
- Intelligence does not seem to decrease for people at this stage.
- Unemployment is a real problem for this age group.
- Erikson said that the psychosocial issue of this stage is Productivity vs Stagnation.
- Generativity has to do with being able to produce something of value, not just children.
- Peck suggested four critical psychological developments related to successful adjustment in middle age:
    - Valuing Wisdom vs Valuing Physical Powers
    - Socializing vs Sexualizing
    - Emotional Flexibility vs Emotional Impoverishment
    - Mental Flexibility vs Mental Rigidity
- Middle life is stressful just as was adolescence.
- Males become more nurturing and expressive.
- Personality seems to change in middle life.
- Freud said that at about age 40 the psyche begins to undergo a transformation.
- Jung suggested that the psyche itself provides a way out of this crisis.
- Jung believed that the unconscious speaks to man primarily through dreams.

- Jung referred to the road toward health and growth as individuation.

- Individuation is a synthetic process of integrating the various components of personality.

- Jung postulated that during the second half of life, the greatest failure comes when adults cling to the goals and values of the first half of life.

- Middle aged couples tend to split up for a number of reasons, one of which is the empty nest syndrome.

Ages 35-65

Glossary for Chapter 10

Glossary of Terms

Alzheimer's Disease — A mental disease characterized by the loss of memory.

Climacteric — The time when menopause takes place.

Estrogen — A female hormone. After menopause or a hysterectomy, a woman may need to take a manufactured estrogen.

Generativity — Eriksonian term which refers to not only the creation of and care of children but the production of things and ideas through work.

Hysterectomy — The surgical removal of all or most of the female reproductive organs.

Individuation — A Jungian concept that denotes the process by which a person becomes a psychological individual, i.e., an indivisible unity or whole.

Male Climacteric — The time during a man's life when he is going through the change of life.

Menopause — A biological occurrence when a woman stops ovulating and menstruating and can no longer bear children

Midlife Transition — Sometimes referred to as midlife crisis. It is the change of life from young adulthood to middle adulthood.

Osteoporosis — A condition in women caused by the lack of calcium resulting in the thinning of the bones.

Presbycusis — Loss of hearing common in middle adulthood.

Presbyopia — Farsightedness usually begins in middle adulthood.

Productivity — The same as generativity in Eriksonian terminology.

Reserve Capacity — The lack of reserve capacity results in the body not being able to recover quickly from stress or dysfunction.

"Old age is a time of humiliations, the most disagreeable of which for me, is that I cannot work long at sustaining high pressure with no leaks in concentration."   —Igor Stravinsky

Chapter 11

Over 65

Maturity is the term that is most often used to classify this age group. Erikson felt the major issues of the mature adult had to do with **Ego Integrity vs Despair**. He also referred to this group as Old Age.

The psychological literature on old age, which is still sparse, typically views this period as one of decline. This is the end of life, the goal which every human being born must reach. The elderly must cope with a series of physical and social losses. They lose their physical strength; they lose their jobs and much of their income through retirement. In America, they also lose much of their status because they are elderly and often thought to be "useless." In addition to the losses of so much of the material things of life, they often suffer the ultimate loss of their mates. It may be that some or all of their children have also preceded them in death. In the final analysis, the way to cope with old age is to somehow adjust to the physical and social setbacks.

Erikson was aware that the elderly had many adjustments to make and that they cannot be as active as they once were. His emphasis was not on external adjustment but on internal adjustment. He felt that in spite of all of the setbacks, the elderly could experience growth and even wisdom. He called the struggle **Ego Integrity vs Despair**. Butler (1963) says that as older people face death, they engage in what he called life review. They look back on their lives and wonder whether or not they were worthwhile. In this process, they face the ultimate despair of feeling that life was not all that it should have been. The song that was popular a few years ago says, "Is That All There Is?" The lyrics state that after looking at various things in life, one is forced to wonder if that is indeed all there is to life.

Erikson says (1976) that the crisis of old age is most admirably illustrated by Ingamar Bergman's film, *Wild Strawberries*. The film, in Erikson's words:

> "records an old Swedish doctor's journey by car from his place of retirement to the city of Lund. There, in the ancient

cathedral, Dr. Isak Bork is to receive the highest honor of his profession, a Jubilee Doctorate marking fifty years of meritorious service. But this journey by car on marked roads through familiar territory also becomes a symbolic pilgrimage back into childhood and deep into his unknown self"
— Erikson (1976, p.1)

The film begins with Borg writing in his diary and then plunges into a terrifying dream symbolizing his fear of death. Upon awakening, Borg decides to travel to Lund by car instead of airplane, and to take along his daughter-in-law, Marianne. She is in the midst of a marital crisis with which Borg has so far refused to help. As soon as they are in the car, they begin to quarrel, and Marianne tells him that "even though everyone depicts you as a great humanitarian you are an old egotist, Father (Bergman, 1957, p.32). Along the journey, Borg engages in other encounters with Marianne and others, and he is visited by vivid dreams and memories about the past. These dreams and memories are extremely humiliating to him. He comes to realize that throughout his life he has been an isolated onlooker, moralistically aloof, and in many ways incapable of love. We see, then, that Borg's initial sense of integrity was superficial; as he imagines death and reviews his life, he confronts many failures.

In the end, however, Borg's insights do not lead to a final despair but to a new kind of wisdom and an acceptance of the past. While he is receiving his Jubilee Doctorate, which by now has become a rather trivial event, he begins to see "a remarkable causality" in the events of his life — an insight which sounds remarkably similar to Erikson's statement that ego integrity includes a sense of the inevitable order of the past. Even more impressive, though, is a change in character. At the end of the film, Borg expresses his love for Marianne and offers to help her and his son (recorded in Crain, (1985. pp. 172-173).

The ultimate question that the elderly must ask is, "Was my life, as I face death, a meaningful one?" What indeed makes a life meaningful?

Medicine has made it possible for people to live longer, but the question must be asked, is just living longer a goal in and of itself without any particular thought to the quality of life? A long life that is not productive, or worse filled with physical and emotional pain, cannot be considered a "good life."

Robert Peck (1955) expanded Erikson's theory of stage 8 by emphasizing three major psychological crises that older people must resolve for healthy psychological functioning. The three crises are:

1. **Broader Self-Definition vs Occupation Work Role** — Peck sees this, *Ego Differentiation vs Work Role Preoccupation*, as being able to differentiate the person from the work he or she does. Many older people feel that their life no longer has real meaning if they are no longer able to work or perform at a certain job or profession. The

question becomes, "Who are you?" more than "What do you do?" (Peck, 1955 cited in Newgarten, 1968, p. 90).

2. **Transcendence of the Body vs Preoccupation with the Body** — Here the issue is being able to overcome concerns about one's physical condition and to find other compensating satisfactions. Peck calls this *Body Transcendence vs Body Preoccupation*. This issue refers to those individuals who have all of their lives thought of their healthy physical condition as a basis for a happy life. As people get older and the body begins to manifest itself in aches and pains, the older person must learn to focus on relationships with people and on absorbing activities that do not depend on perfect health. This orientation away from preoccupation with the body should be developed in early adulthood, before the aches, pains, and other physical crises begin to be manifest.

3. **Transcendence of the Ego vs Preoccupation with the Ego** — Peck described this crisis as *Ego Transcendence vs Ego Preoccupation*. This is probably the most difficult task for older people because it means to become less concerned with the need to continue living in the here and now and to become more accepting of their own inevitable death (Peck, 1955, cited in Neugarten, 1986, p. 91).

There are two major theories dealing with aging successfully: the **disengagement theory**, and the **activity theory**.

The disengagement theory is characterized by a mutual withdrawal by an individual from social and political activities. As the individuals begin to contemplate their death, they may begin to drop relationships and become more and more secluded in their personal life.

The Activity Theory holds that the more active older people remain, the more successfully they age. People in this model remain more and more like middle-age persons continuing to work at their vocation or finding a substitute for that work.

Neugarten (1973) suggested four major personality types, subdivided into the eight patterns of aging based on a study of 59 people 70 to 79-years-old. These include:

1. **Integrated** (17 of the 59 people) — These people were functioning well and had complex inner lives, competent egos, intact cognitive abilities, and high levels of life satisfaction. They fell into three life patterns:

    a. Reorganizers were highly active; they had reorganized their lives, substituting new interests for old, and they engaged in a wide variety of activities.

    b. Focused people showed medium levels of activity; they had become selective, devoting energy to and gaining satisfaction from one or two roles (like the retired man now preoccupied with his role as homemaker, parent, and husband).

    c. Disengaged people showed low levels of activity; by personal preference. They had withdrawn into self-contained lives and were content.

2. **Armor-defended** (15 of the 59 people) — These people were achievement-oriented, striving, and tightly controlled.

    a. People in a holding-on pattern retained the lifestyle of middle age as long as possible. They engaged in high or medium levels of activity and were high in life satisfaction.

    b. Constricted people tried hard to defend themselves against aging by limiting expenditure of energy, social interaction, and experience. They achieved high or medium life satisfaction while showing either low or medium activity.

3. **Passive-dependent** (11 of the 59 people) — These people fell into one of two life patterns, succorance-seeking or apathetic.

    a. Succorance-seeking people needed to be dependent on others; as long as they could lean on one or two people, they could maintain high or medium life satisfaction. They engaged in high or medium levels of activity.

    b. Apathetic people seemed to have been passive all their lives; they did little, and they achieved medium or low life satisfaction.

4. **Unintegrated** (7 out of the 59 people) — These people showed a disorganized pattern of aging; they had gross defects in psychological functioning, poor control over their emotions, and deterioration in thought processes. They managed to stay in the community but with low activity and low life satisfaction.

Physical Changes in Old Age

There is a decline in sensory and psychomotor functioning in this stage. There is a great deal of individual variation in the amount and speed of the decline.

    Vision is one of the senses that decline during this stage. Most people become affected by farsightedness before the age of 65, and the condition does not seem to get worse with time. However, stage 8 adults do suffer from some very serious visual problems. Cataracts are a condition in which a cloudy or opaque film forms over an area of the lens of the eye allowing less and less light to pass through. This is common among the elderly. Modern medical research has developed some very successful procedures to remove the cataracts, however, there are some dangers to the procedures and at times the condition is not helped.

Glaucoma is another frequent cause of blindness in the elderly. The loss of sight is caused by a build-up of fluid that damages the eye internally. If this disease is detected early enough it may be treated and controlled with medication, eye drops, laser treatments, or surgery.

There are other causes of the loss of sight in the elderly. One major cause is diabetes.

Hearing is another of the senses that tends to decline in later years. Hearing loss is very common in old age, affecting about 3 out of 10 people between the ages of 65 and 74. More than 10 million people in the United States are hearing-impaired.

Hearing loss among the elderly affects the higher frequency sounds. They will need to use a higher level of sound on the radio and the television than most people. While older models of hearing aids had background sound problems, the newer models all but eliminate these difficulties.

Older people gradually lose their sense of taste, or at least the sense of taste is greatly changed. This loss is caused partly by the loss of the sense of smell. Taste depends to a large degree on the ability to smell.

Older people also suffer a decline in strength, coordination, and reaction time. Birren et al., (1980) and Salthouse, (1985) said it most clearly when they said, "Older people can do most of the things younger people can do, from reeling in a fish to shingling a house. But older people take longer to do things because their reflex response and information processing are slowed."

A very common physical change, especially among women, is shrinking in size, which is the result of disks between their vertebrae beginning to atrophy. Also the bone condition called osteoporosis, a thinning of the bone due to a lack of calcium, results in many women developing the "widow's hump" at the back of the neck.

Other minor changes include the graying (and often thinning) of the hair, high susceptibility to certain diseases of the internal organs, especially the heart, liver, and kidneys, and a problem with the digestive system in general.

In recent years, there has been a general improvement in the health of the elderly, partly due to the decrease in smoking and certain carcinogenics in foods. Medical science has succeeded in extending life expectancy, but only the aged can improve the quality of their life through proper diet and exercise.

Death and Dying: A Many sided Occurrence

Facing death is a universal matter that everyone must face. Not only does one face his or her own mortality, which presents its own problems, but most individuals must from time to time in their life face the death of someone close to them. The effect death and dying has on different individuals depends in part on the way that they handle the reality of the situation.

Elizabeth Kubler-Ross has been a pioneer in the area of death and dying. As a psychiatrist, she has done much to influence the medical community and the public at large about the importance of talking about themselves and their feelings about their impending death. She has also done much to help the family and friends of those who have died to process the grief in a healthy, productive way. Kubler-Ross suggested that there are five stages in the coming event of death: 1) denial (refusal to accept the reality of what is happening); 2) anger; 3) bargaining for extra time; 4) depression; and 5) ultimate acceptance (Kubler-Ross, 1970).

Kubler-Ross's stages are not the same as the stages in a true stage theory in that not everyone goes through all five stages, and people may go through the stages in a different sequence. The following discussion of the five stages of dying is taken from her books (1969, 1970).

Stage 1: Denial — Most people respond with shock to the knowledge that they are about to die. Their first thought is, "Oh, no, this can't be happening to me." When people are young, the patients also deny reality. They have no one to talk to and, as a result, feel deserted and isolated. When allowed some hope along with the first announcement and given the assurance that they will not be deserted no matter what happens, people can drop the initial shock and denial rather quickly.

As an example, Kubler-Ross tells of Mrs. K., age 28 and a mother of two young children who was hospitalized with a terminal liver disease. After visiting a faith healer, she told the hospital chaplain, "It was wonderful, I have been healed. I am going to show the doctors that God will heal me. I am all well now" (1970, p. 43). Eventually she showed that she was no longer denying her illness, when, holding the doctor's hand, she said, "You have such warm hands. I hope you are going to be with me when I get colder and colder" (1970, p. 45).

Stage 2: Anger — After realizing that they are dying, people become angry. They ask, "Why me?" They become envious of those around them who are young and healthy. They are really angry not at these people, but at the youth and the health that they themselves do not have. They need to express their rage to get rid of it.

The example given by Kubler-Ross is a Mr. O., a successful businessman, who had been a dominant, controlling person all his life. He became enraged as the Hodgkin's disease took away his control of his life. His anger dissipated somewhat after his wife and the hospital nurses gave him back a measure of control by consulting him on the time and length of family visits and times for various hospital procedures.

Stage 3: Bargaining — The next thought may be, "Yes, it's happening to me — but." The "*but*" is an attempt to bargain for time. People may pray to God, "If you just let me live to see my daughter graduate, or my grandchild born then I'll be a better person. I won't ask for anything more or I'll accept my lot in life." These bargains represent the acknowledgment that time is limited and life is finite. When people drop the "*but*", they are able to say, "Yes, me."

A woman in great pain was very sad at the thought that she would not be able to attend the wedding of her oldest and favorite child. With the aid of self-hypnosis, she controlled her pain; and during the period before the wedding she promised that she would ask no more if she could live only long enough to be there. She did attend, a radiant mother of the groom, and when she returned to the hospital, despite her fatigue she told her doctor, "Now don't forget, I have another son" (1970, p. 83).

Stage 4: Depression — In this stage people need to cry, to grieve for the loss of their own life. By expressing the depths of their anguish, they can overcome depression much more quickly than if they feel pressured to hide their sorrow.

Mr. H., who had enjoyed singing in the choir, teaching Sunday School, and doing other church and community work, was no longer able to carry out these activities, because of his illness. He said, "The one thing that makes life worthless right now is the fact that I looked upon myself ... as not ever being able to go back to these things" (1970, p. 103). Other elements in his depression were his feeling that his wife did not appreciate his involvement in those non-paying activities that he considered valuable, and the fact that he had never completed the mourning process for his parents and a daughter who had died. After he reviewed his feelings with the doctor and the chaplain and his wife reassured him that she did appreciate him, his depression lifted.

Stage 5: Acceptance — Finally, people can acknowledge, "My time is very close now, and it's all right." This is not necessarily a happy time, but people who have worked through their anxieties and anger about death and have resolved their unfinished business end up with a feeling of peace with themselves and the world.

Mrs. W., aged 58, was facing the pain and the knowledge of abdominal cancer with courage and dignity, until her husband begged the surgeons to do an operation that could prolong her life. She changed radically, becoming restless and anxious, asking often for pain relief, and screaming and hallucinating in the operating room so that the surgery did not take place. After husband and wife spoke separately with the doctor, it became clear that Mrs. W. was ready to die but felt that she could not until her husband was able to accept her illness and let her go.

When he finally said that his need to keep her alive conflicted with her need to detach herself from the world (including him) and die, both partners were able to share their feelings and accept her death.

It is not just the person who is about to die that is affected by the finale of life, but those who are left behind will go through the same stages of death and dying that were suggested by Kubler-Ross. Those who are the survivors of the death of a loved one or a close friend will experience the further emotional feelings that have been referred to as **bereavement**, **mourning**, and **grief**.

Bereavement is the objective fact of loss, such as in the change from a wife to a widow or a child to an orphan.

Mourning refers to the behavior that the bereaved and the community engage in after a death. It has been suggested that the Irish all-night wake is an accurate example of mourning. The Irish traditionally mourn by gathering friends and relatives to keep vigil and toast the memory of the dead person. The Jews keep a week-long *shiva*, when the family remains to receive friends and relatives. It is customary to fly the flag at half-mast in neighborhoods when a tragedy claims the lives of one or more individuals in the city or neighborhood.

Grief is the emotional response of the bereaved, which can be expressed in many ways, from rage to a feeling of emptiness.

Many examples of the emotional process of grief can be found in the Bible, often characterized by the rending of clothing, applying of ashes to the body, and weeping or even wailing and gnashing of teeth.

> "Now Reuben returned to the pit, and behold, Joseph was not in the pit; so he tore his garments."
> —Genesis 37:29 (NAS)

> "Then he examined it and said, "It is my son's tunic. A wild beast has devoured him; Joseph has surely been torn to pieces!" So Jacob tore his clothes, and put sackcloth on his loins and mourned for his son many days."   —Genesis 37:33-34 (NAS)

> "Then David took hold of his clothes and tore them, and so also did all the men who were with him."
> —2 Samuel 1:11 (NAS)

In the book of Esther when the king is persuaded to kill all of the Jews, Mordecai begins mourning their death even before the slaughter is carried out. This is a form of **anticipatory grief** which may begin before the death occurs.

> "When Mordecai learned all that had been done, he tore his clothes, put on sackcloth and ashes, and went out into the midst of the city and wailed loudly and bitterly. He went as far as the king's gate, for no one was to enter the king's gate clothed in sackcloth. In each and every province where the command and decree of the king came, there was great mourning among the Jews, with fasting, weeping and wailing; and many lay on sackcloth and ashes. Then Esther's maidens and her eunuchs came and told her, and the queen writhed in great anguish. And

she sent garments to clothe Mordecai that he might remove his sackcloth from him, but he did not accept them."

—Esther 4:1-4 (NAS)

Normal grief follows a fairly predictable pattern. Brown and Stoudemire (1983) and Shultz (1978) suggested three phases of normal grief:

1. The initial phase, which may last for several weeks (especially after a sudden or an unexpected death), is shock and disbelief, which may protect the bereaved from intense reactions. Survivors often feel lost, dazed, and confused. They may suffer from physical symptoms such as shortness of breath. They may also experience an initial sense of numbness that gives way to overwhelming feelings of sadness usually accompanied by frequent crying.

2. The second phase, which lasts 6 months or longer, is preoccupation with the memory of the deceased. During this phase there is frequent insomnia, crying and a constant going over of every detail of the life of the dead person, especially if that person was a spouse. The physical symptoms in phase two can often result in severe medical problems.

3. The final phase, resolution, has arrived when the bereaved person resumes interest in everyday activities. It is at this phase that memories of the departed one brings fond feelings instead of deep sadness.

There are some researchers who feel that there is a need for some type of education to help people deal with death and dying. Leviton (1977) especially felt that death education was very important in helping both children and older people alike deal with death and dying in a much healthier manner. He suggested that the following are some of the reasons for death education:

- To help children grow up with as few death-related anxieties as possible.

- To help people develop their own individual belief systems about death and dying.

- To help people see death as a natural end to life.

- To help people prepare for their own death and the death of those close to them.

- To help people feel comfortable around those who are dying and treat them humanely and intelligently for as long as they live.

- To help both laypeople and health-care professionals, such as doctors and nurses, get a realistic view of the professional and his or her obligation to the dying and their families.

- To understand the dynamics of grief and the ways in which people of different ages typically react to loss.

- To understand and be able to help a suicidal person.

- To help consumers decide what kind of funeral services they want for themselves and their families and to show them how to purchase them wisely.

- To make dying as positive an experience as possible by emphasizing the importance of minimizing pain, offering warm personal care, involving the family and close friends in the care of the dying person, and being sensitive to that person's wishes and needs.

For more information on grief and the treatment of grief, see *Grief Relief* by Dr. Stan DeKoven, Vision Publishing.

Some other problems older people must face.

Financial hardship, living arrangements, and vulnerability to crime.

The income of older people is usually much lower than it was when they were gainfully employed or actively engaged in business. In the case where social security is the only source of income, the elderly must live at a much lower standard than they may have enjoyed in earlier years. The lower income forces many older people to live in much smaller living quarters and often in less desirable neighborhoods.

As age progresses, there may develop a disabling disease that forces the person or persons to live in a convalescent home or a retirement home. In these living arrangements, although the basic needs of the individuals may be met in an adequate way; there is a certain level of isolation that does nothing to encourage the elderly. At one time, in rural America, older people continued to live in the home in which they raised their family. The children then cared for the farm, and took over the responsibility of caring for the family business and the family.

The vulnerability of the elderly to crime, especially in the large metropolitan areas, has become an increasing problem for the authorities and for the families of the victims. These older people make an easy target for the drug users who need to have large sums of money to support their habits but most of the time are not able to burglarize or rob in a more sophisticated fashion because of the problems caused by the need of a new fix. These young criminals find the elderly an easy mark.

Some other problems older people must face.

Elder Abuse

One of the saddest problems of the aged is the problem of elder abuse. Society is enraged when they hear of a small child being shackled to a bed in a dark apartment for several hours on Christmas day because he had opened one of his presents too soon. The horrific stories of child abuse and neglect can rally all of the social services of a city in a moment. However, the stories of the increasing number of elder abuse cases are not adequately mentioned in the media, though thankfully, this is beginning to change.

There are many rationalizations given for the neglect and abuse of the elderly. It becomes almost impossible for some middle and lower income families to care for their elderly. There are still many elderly who receive no income in their old age. If they do receive Social Security, it is so little that they are, simply put, a burden to their families and subsequently to society as a whole.

The neglect of the elderly is bad enough, but there is an increasing number of actual abuse cases being reported each year. One can only surmise that people abuse their elderly out of sheer frustration. Old people can be a problem. They tend to become hard of hearing, poor of sight, and often very demanding and obstinate.

Older people often feel that they are still in command of the family and find it difficult, if not impossible, to be ordered around by their children (or any younger person for that matter).

As people get older, they tend to become more accident and sickness prone. This can put a great strain on a family trying to raise their own children while at the same time trying to cope with the idiosyncrasies of the aged.

Many older people enjoy good health late into old age. Most of them have taken care of themselves and are reaping the benefits. In some cases when one of the partners in a marriage dies, the other will not continue to be as concerned about his or her health.

The elderly often become frustrated because of the loss of what is referred to in the literature as **reserve energy**. This simply means that unlike their younger years, their bodies do not regenerate or regain energy lost in work or sickness. Many elderly people still have the desire to work or at least enjoy an active leisure life but find that the energy is just not there anymore.

Health Care

Of course, health care for the emerging Baby Boomers is in the news almost daily in the United States. The elderly often find that when they retire from the work force, they are without the protection of paid health care. Those fortunate enough to be eligible for social security benefits are often able to afford a co-payment plan such as an HMO. That part of the elderly population that was fortunate enough to have accumulated a sizable amount of retirement funds often finds that one major sickness can all but completely deplete even a sizable bank account.

As people get older, they often find themselves unable to come and go as much as they did before because of the increase in crime against them. The incidence of violent crimes against older people is on the increase. They are often prime prey to the con artists who convince them to hand over all of their savings in some elaborate con game. For some reason older people tend to become more like trusting little children in their old age.

Intellectual development

There is no research evidence that as people get older they cease to continue to develop intellectually. There are mental problems that the elderly may encounter such as temporary loss of memory, or the more tragic version, Alzheimer's disease. Medical science has not as yet been able to find a complete cure for this ailment in which the patient loses most of their memory. For the student interested in knowing more about this curse of old age, D. S. Brown has written a sensitive and practical book on the subject from the viewpoint of the author whose mother was a victim. There are other books on the market as well. The person who wishes to be a family counselor needs to know as much as possible about this disease in order to help families who may be struggling with a parent who is a victim.

Lifelong learning

Many older people find that there is much pleasure to be gained through continuing to learn through adult education classes and courses offered at various senior citizen centers located in most cities. The old adage, "You can't teach an old dog new tricks," is simply not true.

History presents many examples of individuals who started writing, painting, doing creative needlepoint, creative gardening, etc., in their golden years often with monetary or at least public acclaim.

More and more seniors are finding great fulfillment in volunteering to tutor children in schools in the inner-city. The need is so great, and the work is so rewarding. Most cities of any size offer a service to place volunteers in different community services where they can be a real blessing to others in need.

Personal Reflections

Most of this chapter has been written from personal experience, although I found that many of the books that included a section on old age as a stage of development dealt with the same basic issues that I have covered.

As a conclusion for this chapter and, for that matter, a conclusion of the cycle of life, I wish to remind my readers that as sure as we are born, so shall we surely die one day. It would seem that life is a journey from the cradle to the grave. It is only what man does with his life that matters for that short span we call a lifetime.

Man cannot really learn to live until he is able to come to grips with the reality of death. One day I shall no longer be on this earth. The world will go on. My family will mourn for a season, but then they will go on with their lives. I can only pray that I have contributed something meaningful to their lives and to the lives of others I have touched.

The Apostle Paul expressed so beautifully how a Christian should feel about the end of life here on earth when he said in Philippians 1:21 "For to me, to live is Christ and to die is gain." Paul was not afraid of dying because his life had meaning. Listen to his words again as he says in 2 Timothy 4:7-8 "I have fought the good fight, I have finished the course, I have kept the faith, in the future there is laid up for me the crown of righteousness, which the Lord, the righteous Judge, will award to me on that day; and not only to me, but also to all who have loved His appearing."

Many Christians have problems dealing with a lot of the psychoanalytical theories. They especially have problems with men like Freud and Carl Jung. I cannot say that I can accept all or even most of what Jung said, but I would like to close this chapter with a few quotes from Jung that might make one wonder if perhaps some of those men didn't have some truth mixed in with their theory. Jung believed that man cannot face death in a healthy way unless he has some image of the hereafter (Crain. 1985).

Listen to Jung as he says, "with increasing age, contemplation, and reflection, the inner images naturally play an ever greater part in man's life" (1961. p. 320). "In old age one begins to let memories unroll before the mind's eye..." (1912. p. 320). He said that the old person tries to understand the nature of life in the face of death. If "I live in a house which I know will fall about my head within the next two weeks, all my vital functions will be impaired by this thought; but if on the contrary I feel myself to be safe, I can dwell there in a normal and comfortable way" (1931. p. 112). Jung believed that man must entertain thoughts of an afterlife, and he wasn't just prescribing some artificial tranquilizer.

In Jung's view, "life after death is a continuation of life itself" (Crain. 1985. p. 205).

The last chapter of this text will present some suggestions for further research based on the material in the book. Nothing can make life more meaningful than to have left something of value for the next generation to use in their search for meaning and especially the meaning of life itself.

Finally, I wish to remind the reader of the position of God's Word with regard to how the church, especially the younger Christians, should relate to the elderly members of the body.

Read what the Apostle Paul says to young Timothy:

Over 65

"Do not sharply rebuke an older man, but rather appeal to him as a father, to the younger men as brothers, the older women as mothers, and the younger women as sisters, in all purity. Honor widows who are widows indeed; but if any widow has children or grandchildren, they must first learn to practice piety in regard to their own family and to make some return to their parents; for this is acceptable in the sight of God. The elders who rule well are to be considered worthy of double honor, especially those who work hard at preaching and teaching."
—I Timothy 5:1-4, 17

Review of Chapter 11

- Maturity is a term that is most often used to classify this age group.
- Psychological literature is rather sparse on the developmental change that takes place during this time.
- Erikson's psychosocial issue for this group is Ego Integrity vs Discuss or Despair.
- This is the stage at which people ask in all seriousness, "What is the meaning of Life (and Death)."
- Robert Peck expanded on Erikson's concepts by suggesting three crises:
    1. Ego Differentiation vs Work Role Preoccupation
    2. Body Transcendence vs Body Preoccupation
    3. Ego transcendence vs Ego Preoccupation
- These are the declining years physically.
- Vision and hearing may tend to decline considerably.
- The elderly also begin to lose their sense of taste and smell.
- Death and dying are major issues at this stage.
- Elizabeth Kubler-Ross said that there were five stages of dying:
    1. Denial
    2. Anger
    3. Bargaining
    4. Depression
    5. Acceptance
- Grief is the emotional response of the bereaved which can be expressed in many ways, from rage to a feeling of emptiness.
- Normal grief follows the following three stages:
    1. Initial Phase
    2. The Second Phase
    3. The Final Stage or Resolution
- There is a need for children to learn how to deal with death and dying.
- Other problems that older people face are:

Over 65

1. Loss of income
2. Disease
3. Vulnerability to violent crime
4. Elder abuse

- Health care for the elderly can be a problem as they can no longer afford regular medical insurance.

- Mobility also becomes a problem to the elderly.

- There is no research evidence that intelligence decreases with age. Memory may be a problem with some, especially in the case of Alzheimer's disease.

Glossary for Chapter 11

Glossary of Terms

Ageism — Prejudice or discrimination against a person (most commonly an older person) based on age.

Anticipatory Grief — Grief that begins before an expected death and helps family and friends to prepare for bereavement.

Bereavement — Loss due to death, which leads to a change in the survivor's status (for example, from wife to widow).

Compassionate Love — Loving friendship marked by affection, attachment, commitment, and security. This kind of love tends to deepen with the passage of time.

Death Education — Programs to educate people about dying and grief to help them deal with these issues in their personal and professional lives.

Dementia — Apparent intellectual and personality deterioration sometimes associated with old age and caused by a variety of irreversible physiological conditions: sometimes called senility.

Disengagement Theory — Theory of aging that holds that successful aging is characterized by mutual withdrawal between the older person and society.

Elder Abuse — Neglect or physical or psychological abuse of dependent older persons, often by their children as a result of the stress of caring for the parents.

Gerontologists — Persons engaged in the study of aging and the aged.

Integrity vs Despair — According to Erikson, the eighth and final critical alternative of psychosocial development.

Living Will — A document specifying the type of care wanted by the maker in the event of terminal illness.

Normal Grief — Grief that follows a death, usually in a fairly predictable pattern consisting of three phases: initial shock and disbelief, preoccupation with the memory of the dead, and resolution.

Passive Euthanasia — Deliberate withholding of life-prolonging treatment from a terminally ill person in order to minimize suffering or carry out the wishes of the patient.

Reserve Capacity — Ability of body organs and systems to put forth 4 to 10 times as much effort as usual in times of stress or dysfunction; also called organ reserve.

Selective Optimization with Compensation — In the dual-process model of Baltes, the ability of older people to maintain or enhance their intellectual functioning through the use of special abilities to compensate for losses in other areas.

Senescence — Period of the life span during which people experience a decrease in bodily functioning associated with aging.

Thanatology — The study of death and dying

"By wisdom a house is built, And by understanding it is established; And by knowledge the rooms are filled With all precious and pleasant riches." —Proverbs 24:3-4 (NAS)

Chapter 12

Review, Conclusions, and Implications for further study

All of the knowledge and understanding that has been presented in this book is of little value unless there are some significant implications for use in the field of the caregiver professional, or at least in the interpersonal relationship of individuals trying to understand themselves and others.

The search for knowledge without gaining an understanding of what that knowledge means would be a total waste of time and energy. Knowledge must be understood before it can be considered truth or before it can be applied to the everyday business of living.

The third important element that also must enter into the pursuit of knowledge is wisdom. Wisdom permits a man or woman to apply the knowledge that they have learned and have been able to understand to the situations of life as they live it.

Solomon was considered the wisest man in the Old Testament. He struggled with the facts of the meaning of life until he was finally at a point of despair. However, after much soul searching and some help from the Lord, Solomon was finally able to formulate a meaning of life by which he could live.

> "The conclusion, when all has been heard, is: fear God and keep His commandments, because this applies to every person. For God will bring every act to judgment, everything which is hidden, whether it is good or evil."
> —Ecclesiastes 12:13-14 (NAS)

This final chapter will be devoted to a review of the main points of the first 11 chapters. At the end of the chapter there will be a few suggestions

Review, Conclusions, and Implications for further study

for themes for a master's thesis and also a few suggestions for research projects for a doctoral dissertation.

Appendix A
Prenatal Development

STAGE	TIME	CHARACTERISTICS[1]
Germinal		Sperm penetrates the egg
	12 hours	Division of the fertilized egg begins
	72 hours	The zygote reaches the uterus
Embryonic	2 weeks	The zygote/embryo is implanted in the uterine wall and is drawing nutrition.
	4 weeks	The embryo is approximately one-fifth inch in length. A primitive heart is beating. The head and tail are established. The mouth, liver, and intestines begin to take shape.
Fetal	8 weeks	The embryo/fetus is now about one inch in length. For the first time it begins to resemble a human being. Facial features, limbs, hands, feet, fingers. and toes become apparent. The nervous system is responsive, and many of the internal organs begin to function.
	12 weeks	The fetus is now three inches long and weighs almost one ounce. The muscles begin to develop and sex organs are formed. Eyelids, fingernails, and toenails are being formed. Spontaneous movements of the trunk can occasionally be seen.
	16 weeks	The fetus is now approximately five inches long. Blinking, grasping, and mouth motions can be observed. Hair appears on the head and body.

Appendix A: Prenatal Development

	20 weeks	The fetus now weighs about one half pound and is approximately ten inches long. Sweat glands develop and the external skin is no longer transparent.
	24 weeks	The fetus is able to inhale or exhale and could make a crying sound. The eyes are completed and taste buds have developed on the tongue.
	28 weeks	The fetus is usually capable by this time of living outside the womb, but would be considered immature at birth.
	38 weeks	The end of the normal gestation period. The fetus is now prepared to live in the outside world.

---

[1]Source: *Marriage and the Family: A Christian Perspective*, Stephen A. Grunlan, Grand Rapids, Zondervan Publishing House, 1984, p 226.

Appendix B
Time Table for Development

From Rosenbilth, Page 22

STAGE	TIME	EVENTS
Initial Development		
Zygote	0-40 hours	Cleavage divisions
Morula	40 hours to 4 days	Reaches uterus. embryonic cell masses develop
Blastocyst	4-8 days	Development of 2 layered (bilaminar) disk; implementation begins, embryonic membranes start to develop
Embryo-Early	12-13 days	Implantation complete
	14 days	Mature placenta begins to develop
	15-20 days	Development of three layered (Trilaminar) disk, neural tube begins to form; disk becomes attached to uterine wall by short, thick umbilical cord; placenta develops rapidly
	21-28	days Eyes begin to form; heart starts beating; crown-rump length 5mm (less than .25 inches); growth rate about 1 mm per day; neural tube closes (otherwise spina bifida); vascular system develops (blood vessels); placental maternal-embryonic circulation begins to function.
Embryo-late	5 weeks	Arm and leg buds form
	7 weeks	Facial structures fuse (otherwise facial defects, e.g., cleft palate).

Appendix B: Time Table for Development

	8 weeks	Crown-rump length 3 cm (slightly over 1 in.); weight 1 gm. (about .03 oz.); major development of organs completed, most external features recognizable at birth present.
Fetal Development		
Fetus	8-12 weeks	Movements of arms and legs; startle and sucking reflexes. facial expressions and external sex organs appear; fingerprints develop; respiratory and excretory systems develop, but are not functional, lanugo develops.
	End of First Trimester	Length 7.6 cm 9 about 3 in.); weight 14 gr (about .5 oz.); simple abortion by curettage no longer possible[2].
	13-16 weeks	Skin and true hair develop.
	17-20 weeks	Length 20 cm (about 8 in.); weight 450 gr (less than one pound); movements become obvious to mother; (quickening"); heartbeat can be heard through a stethoscope; old cells discarded and replaced by new (hence cells in amniotic fluid).
	25-28 weeks	Begins to develop subcutaneous fat; terminals of lung and associated blood vessels develop.
	End second Trimester	Good chance of survival if born prematurely
	By 38 weeks	Fetus becomes plump; lanugo usually shed; testes of male usually descend

---

[2] The author of this present text is in no way in favor of any kind of abortion at any time during the pregnancy!

Appendix C
Who's Who in the Study of Human Development

Albert Bandura — Albert Bandura was born in 1925 in the province of Alberta, Canada. He grew up in the small town of Mundare. Bandura attended the University of British Columbia as an undergraduate and the University of Iowa as a graduate student in psychology. At the University of Iowa, he studied with Robert Sears, one of the pioneers in social learning. He joined the faculty at Stanford University in 1953 where he continues to teach. In 1974 he served as president of the American Psychological Association. His main point of view was that, in social situations people often learn much more rapidly simply by observing the behavior of others. He is known for his development of a social theory (or as it is sometimes referred to modeling), of personality and abnormal behavior.

Bruno Bettelheim (1903-1994) — Bruno Bettelheim was born in 1903 in Vienna where he grew up and began his work as a psychoanalyst. Early in his career he became interested in a disorder called "autism" a condition in which children are totally unresponsive to people. He cared for an autistic girl in his own home but the treatment was disrupted when Hitler invaded the country. He spent 1938-1939 in the concentration camps of Dachau and Buchenwald. He has written extensively and in 1944 he came to the United States and took over the directorship of the Orthogenic School in Chicago. It was his experiences in the concentration camps that gave him hope to create environments that can foster rebirth in the autistic individual. In 1967, he wrote his well published book entitled, "The Empty Fortress." Autism (often referred to as infantile autism), has been one of the most difficult disorders for researchers. A "cure" has not been found although Bettelheim contributed greatly to an understanding of the condition and has made some important contributions as to the cause or causes.

John Bowlby (1907-1990) — John Bowlby was born in 1907 in London. He received training in medicine and in psychoanalytic therapy. In

Appendix C: Who's Who in the Study of Human Development

1936, he became interested in the disturbances of children raised in institutions. He found that children raised in institutions or orphanages often showed various emotional problems, including the inability to form close and intimate relationships. He posited that the problems evident in these children were the result of their not having had the opportunity of forming a solid attachment to a mother-figure. Much of the modern emphasis on the importance of attachment, or bonding for infants can be credited to Bowlby.

Noam Chompsky — Noam Chompsky was born in 1928 in the city of Philadelphia. His interest in linguistics came from his father who was a respected Hebrew scholar. Chomsky studies linguistics at the University of Pennsylvania. He soon became bored with his studies and was ready to drop out of college when he met Zellig Harris. He became totally absorbed in Harris's work which may have been the impetus that caused him to go on and receive his Ph.D. from the University of Pennsylvania and then to go on to do post-graduate work at Harvard. He is known for his innovations in linguistics.

Charles Darwin (1809-1882) — Charles Darwin, was the son of a dis-tinguished English family. His family held little hope for Charles ever achieving anything of value. He studied medicine for a time and then theology at Cambridge, but his accomplishments were not outstanding in the least. One of his professors recommended that he take a position as a naturalist on the world-wide voyage of the *H. M. S. Beagle*. It was on this voyage that Darwin made the observations that led to his theory of evolution. Darwin's theory of natural selection, although not readily accepted by the Christian community (and all creationists) was nevertheless a basis for much of the ethological theories that would follow through such men as Lorenz, Tinbergen, and Bowlby.

Erik Erikson (1902-1990) — Born of Danish parents in the year 1902 in Frankfurt, Germany, Erikson was raised by his mother until he was three years old. His father separated from Erikson's mother shortly before he was born. His mother married a local pediatrician, Dr. Homburger, and although his mother and stepfather were Jewish, Erik looked different being tall, blond and blue eyed. He was tormented as a child, often being called a "goy" by other children.

Erikson married in 1930, but he and his wife, the former Joan Serson, fled Europe in 1933 because of the rise of Hitler. They settled in Boston, where Erikson became the city's first child psychoanalyst. Although he never had an earned degree, he was given a professorship at Harvard in 1960. He was later awarded many honorary degrees and wrote a classic on the topic of human development entitled "Childhood and Society" in which he presented his eight step stage theory of human development. Although he was primarily a Freudian in practice, he disagreed with Freud as far as the emphasis that Freud placed on the sexual pleasure principle. Erikson believed that human development was more a matter of psychosocial issues rather than psychosexual.

Anna Freud (1985-1982) — Anna Freud was the daughter of Sigmund Freud and is credited with carrying her father's work one step further, in that she developed a more thorough theory of the development of adolescence. She contended that a child experiences a dangerous resurgence of oedipal feelings at an age when the young person has the size and strength to act on these sexual conflicts of the oedipal complex.

Sigmund Freud (1856-1939) — Sigmund Freud was born in 1856 in Freiberg, Moravia (later to become a part of Czechoslovakia). He was a blended child in that he was the first son of his 20 year old mother, and the third child of his 40 year old father, although the two sons of the father were grown by the time Sigmund was born.

In 1859, his family moved to Leipzig and then a year later to Vienna where Freud attended medical school. Because he was such a bright child, and his parents always encouraged him in his studies, Freud possessed a broad liberal education. While in medical school he decided he wanted to do physiological research rather than practice medicine. He journeyed to Paris and there was influenced by the eminent neurologist Charcot. It was there that he was introduced to the fascinating world of hysteria and hypnosis. From 1889 to 1895 he gradually shifted his attention from hypnosis to a concept called free association as a means of therapy. In the area of human development, he is best remembered for his four stages of development which are called psychosexual development and focus on the Oral, Anal, Phallic, Latency and Puberty stages. For a concise and condensed summary of Freudian psychology the student is referred to the book by Calvin S. Hall, *A Primer of Freudian Psychology.*

Freud's theory of defense mechanisms is a very important part of modern therapy.

Arnold Gessel (1880-1961) — Gessel's major contribution to the study of human development was the introduction of the concept of biological maturation. Gessel grew up in a small town in Wisconsin. He described his youth as "idyllic." He wrote a book on child-rearing, advocating a child-centered approach. He was best known as the "baby doctor" in the early 1940's. Dr. Benjamin Spock was partly influenced by Gesell. His belief was that, "the child is a product of his or her environment, but that the child's development is more directly influenced from within, by the action of the genes."

Carl Jung (1875-1961) — Carl Jung was born in Kesswil, a village in northeastern Switzerland. He had a most unhappy childhood. His mother was earthy, his father spiritually removed. Eight of his uncles were clergymen and his father was a Lutheran pastor who struggled with his faith throughout his life. Jung experienced the tensions of his parents' marital difficulties and was usually quite lonely. He was bored with school and often suffered fainting spells presumably brought on by his boredom. He went to church because his father was a pastor, but be often had bitter religious arguments with him. He enjoyed exploring nature and reading books of his own choosing.

Jung studied at the University of Basel and the University of Zurich and in spite of his problems did manage to finish school and received a medical degree. He began practicing psychiatry in Zurich. Jung's work, including his invention of the word association test, suggested the importance of Freud's ideas. He disagreed with and finally disassociated himself from Freudian ideas because of Freud's attempt to reduce all unconscious events to sexual drives. Jung introduced, among many other concepts, the concept of the anima and animus, which concludes that all humans are bisexual in that there is some female and male characteristics in everyone.

One of Jung's contributions to the theory of human development was the theory about mid-life crisis. This suggests that at about the age of 40, the human psyche begins to undergo a transformation. The individual begins to believe that the ideals, goals and ambitions of life that were once thought to be eternal have lost their meaning. He also suggested that man could not face death in a healthy way without some belief and image of the hereafter. Many ministers, priests, and others who work with emotionally distressed people find that the work of Jung provides a valuable bridge between religious and psychiatric professions.

Lawrence Kohlberg (1927-1987) — Kohlberg was born in 1927 in Bronxville, New York. He attended Andover Academy in Massachusetts. He was a very bright student, but he did not go directly to college. Instead he served in the Israeli cause and served as an engineer on an old freighter. In 1948, he enrolled in the University of Chicago and only had to take a few courses to get his bachelor's degree. He continued at the University of Chicago for graduate work in psychology, being interested in the work of Piaget. It was there that he began interviewing children at Children's Hospital in Boston concerning moral issues.

His doctoral dissertation (1958) was the beginning of a new stage theory about moral judgment. He taught at the University of Chicago from 1962-1968, and then in 1968 he moved to Harvard University. His most important book, *The Philosophy of Moral Development*, is well worth studying.

John Locke (1632-1704) — Locke was an English philosopher who proposed that children are neither innately good of innately bad. They are born innately nothing at all. Locke introduced the theory that suggested initially the child's mind as a *tabula rasa*, a blank slate, and that whatever the child becomes is a result of learning environment. His theory is rightly called "environmentalism."

Locke was born in the small village of Somerset, England, and because his ideas came about in the time of the Enlightenment, they were very well accepted. He was the son of a strict father and a loving and pious mother. He believed in democracy and also wrote on government. He was educated at Oxford, where he stayed on to teach Greek. He also studied medicine.

Locke admitted that individuals have differing temperaments, but on the whole it is the environment that forms the mind. He used words like *association, repetition, limitation and rewards and punishments* as ways that the mind is formed by the environment.

Konrad Lorenz (1903-1989) — Lorenz is thought of as the father of modern ethology (the science and study of animal behavior). He was born in 1903 in Austria. He earned a Ph.D. in Zoology at the University of Vienna. He began his studies of ethology in the early 1930s. Ethologists believe that animal behavior and development can only be understood if the animals are studied in their own environment. It is also the belief of many that humans, too, can only be understood if studied in their own environment. It was Lorenz, along with others such as Tinbergen and Bowlby, who introduced the concept of imprinting, which has in turn been a basis for the work in bonding.

Abraham Maslow (1908-1970) — Abraham Maslow was born in Brooklyn, New York. He was the son of poor Russian immigrant parents. He liked high school, but found it difficult to adjust to college. He finally earned a B.A. from the University of Wisconsin where he stayed to continue in graduate work in psychology. His early work and training was under such men as E. L. Thorndike and Harry Harlow and focused on abnormal psychology. Very early in his career he was sold on behaviorism and believed that people are subject to conditioning from the external environment. He was annoyed, however at the one-sided proposition of the behaviorist that ignored the fact that people also had an inner life and potential for growth, creativity, and a free choice.

Maslow finally arrived at a belief that certain people were self-actualizers. His key finding was that self-actualizers, compared to most people, have maintained a certain independence from their society. They are primarily motivated by, their own inner growth, the devel-opment of their potential and their mission in life (1954, pp. 223-28). Others joined Maslow in what has become known as humanistic psychology. Other names associated with this movement are: Carl Rogers, Gordon Allport, and others.

Maria Montessori (1870-1952) — Montessori was born in the province of Ancona, Italy. Her father had the traditional ideas of women's place in society, while her mother hoped that Maria would go as far as she could in life. Maria became the first woman physician in Italy at the age of 26. Montessori's first interest was in the area of mental retardation. As a result of being inspired by several people working with retarded children, she began developing materials of her own. She argued that it is wrong to assume that children are whatever we make them, for children also learn on their own, from their own maturational prompting (Montessori, 1936b. p. 17, 223). Her success in teaching children, who lived in a tenement in the slums of San Lorenzo, a section of Rome, brought her great acclaim. The Montessori Method, often with some modern modifications, is still a very popular approach to the education of young children. Her main contribution to the entire field of education is that children learn best when they are developmentally ready and able to learn.

Jean Piaget (1896-1980) — Piaget is best remembered for his most comprehensive and compelling theory of intellectual development. Piaget was born in a small town in Switzerland where his father was a medieval historian at the University. He was a very precocious and intelligent young man, who at the age of 15 experienced an intellectual crisis when he realized that his religious and philosophical ideas lacked a scientific foundation. At the age of 23 he began his research studies in child psychology, studying the development of the mind. He posited that children did not think in the same way the adults think. Their thought processes were entirely different.

Piaget's earliest work was the result of observing his own children, and many of his most important ideas came from those early observations. At first many researchers objected to his methodology, but his theories remained. His major works include: *The Origin of Intelligence* (1936), *The Psychology of Intelligence* (1947), *Six Psychological Studies* (1964), and *Genetic Epistemology* (1970).

Carl Ransom Rogers (1902-1987) — Carl Rogers was the founder of the person centered (client centered) or non-directive, therapy. He was born in Chicago, the middle child of a family of six. His family was fundamentally Protestants where the work ethic was revered. His family was loving but non-communicative. He was a lonely youth. Early in his life he turned from Christianity to liberal humanism.

He was influenced considerably by John Dewey, an influence that led him away from his early training as a Freudian to a more eclectic approach to psychotherapy.

His later years indicated some change in his early convictions. In 1970, he became a fellow at the Center for the Study of the Person. It was here that he became very interested and involved in group therapy. His best books include: *On Becoming a Person* (1961), *Freedom to Learn* (1969),*Carl Rogers On Encounter Groups* (1970), and *A Way of Being* (1980)

Jean Jacques Rousseau (1712-1778) — Rousseau agreed with Locke that children are different than adults, but he did not trust the powers of the environment, especially the social environment, to form "healthy individuals." He believed that the environment needed to be structured in order to produce the desirable affect. His revolt against society grew out of his own life experiences which were far from perfect. Rousseau wrote books and essays about the social system of the day. His most important works were *The Social Contract* (1662b.) and *Emile* (1762b). The latter work was a work of fiction in which he takes on the raising and education of a young boy, Emile. His methods of teaching were almost completely based on Emile's interests and readiness to learn. There is much of the influence of Rousseau to be found in the later work of Maria Montessori.

A major point that was made by Rousseau was that "the wisest writers devote themselves to what a man ought to know, without asking themselves what a child is capable of learning. They are always looking for the man in the child, without considering what he is before he becomes a man" (Rousseau, 1762b. p. 1).

Ivan Petrovich Pavlov (1849-1936) — Pavlov was born in Ryazan, Russia. He was the son of a village priest and planned to enter the priesthood himself, until at the age of 12 he decided that it was more interesting and exciting to pursue a career in science. When Pavlov was 50 years old, he began his work on conditioned reflexes.

He developed the classical conditioning paradigm, in which he experimented with dogs. He developed the terms: *unconditioned stimulus*;*conditioned stimulus*; *unconditioned reflexes*; and *conditioned reflexes*. This whole system was called classical conditioning. His work is interesting because it later led men like John B. Watson and B. F. Skinner to conduct research and experimentation that formed the school of a learning theory of conditioning as a means of learning. All of these men are known as behaviorists, and their ideas may be summarized in a statement made by Watson in 1924:

> "Give me a dozen healthy infants, well-formed, and my own specific world to bring them up in and I'll guarantee to take any one at random and train him to become any type of specialist I might select, doctor, lawyer, artist, merchant, chief, and yes, even beggar-man and thief, regardless of his talents, penchants, tendencies, abilities, vocations, and race of his ancestors"
>
> —Watson, 1924, p. 104

One interesting observation of the theories of these men is that the concept of "Programmed Instruction" developed as a result of their work.

Ernest Schachtel (1903-1975) — Schachtel was born and grew up in Berlin, Germany. In 1933 he was imprisoned by the Nazis and sent to a concentration camp. After his release from concentration camp, he studied in England and Switzerland. He came to New York in 1935 where he received training in psychoanalytic therapy. Schachtel was most interested in the problem of *infantile amnesia*, our inability to remember most of the events of our first five or six years of life. He disagreed with Freud that this amnesia was a product of repression of early sexual and aggressive feelings. His thesis was that infantile amnesia was the result of *perceptual modes of experience*. In other words, we did not have the perceptual ability at that age to truly understand the things that were happening to us.

Schachtel introduced the terms, *autocentric*, sensations that are felt inside the body, and *allocentric*, sensations that come from without the body.

His ideas have special importance for child-rearing and education as he wanted to preserve and encourage the young child's bold and natural curiosity.

Heinz Werner (1890-1964) — Werner was born and grew up in Vienna, Austria. At first he entered the University hoping to become a composer, but soon broadened his interests to include philosophy and psychology. This change came about because of listening to a lecture on the philosophy of Emmanuel Kant.

In 1917 he joined the Psychological Institute in Hamburg, which later became a part of the University. At about that time a new theoretical movement was being discussed in Hamburg. It was called Gestalt psychology. Gestalt psychologists argued that we perceive things from forms, *gestalt*, and that these forms cannot be analyzed into separate parts. In 1933, Werner was dismissed form Hamburg by the Nazis, and he moved to the United States where he took a number of positions at Wayne County Training School in Detroit, Michigan, later to become Wayne State University. Among his number of positions, he served as a research psychologist.

Werner believed that development involves a change in structure, which may be defined according to the *Orthogenic principle*: "Whenever development occurs, it proceeds from a state of relative lack of differentiation to a state of increasing differentiation and hierarchic integration" (Werner and Kaplan. 1956, p. 866). For example, the embryo begins as a global unit, which separates into different organs (brain, liver, etc.). As the organism develops it comes under the control of higher regulating centers.

All of his thinking led to the idea that psychological processes should, as far as possible, be studied as they occur with the whole, acting, feeling, striving organism.

Although Werner wrote very little on the practical application of his many theories for child rearing and education, many other important practitioners have incorporated his ideas into their work.

Closing Note

The names and biographical information produced in this section, a veritable Who's Who in Human Development, does not in any way reflect all of the individuals who have made significant contributions to the study of the how humans develop. I hesitated including this section because it would be impossible to mention, even briefly, all of the re-searchers who have contributed to current knowledge of the marvels of the human being. Many of the people included in this section worked from a non-Christian position but were still able to give to the science some important insights.

Very few Christians would agree with even a part of Freud's basic premises, but as it has been said, "Freud was a giant upon whose shoulder others have been able to get a better perspective of man".

As Christians interested in working in the field of counseling or some other care ministry, we need to be able to sift through the teachings of all of these great men and women of science and take that which is truth and apply that to our bank of knowledge. All truth is God's truth. Simply because some person who was not a "born again Christian" was able to discover some important truth about man is no reason for Christians to dismiss that truth as not acceptable.

I had the privilege of studying under a marvelous woman, Dr. Marie Rasey, at Wayne State University during my undergraduate years. I started my college career intending to become a teacher, which I eventually did become; however the life and teachings of this woman inspired me to continue to pursue my search for the great truths about man. In the inspired words of the Apostle Paul,

> "Finally, brethren, whatever is **true**, whatever is **honorable**, whatever is **right**, whatever is **pure**, whatever is **lovely**, whatever is of **good repute**, if there is any **excellence** and if anything **worthy of praise**, dwell on these things."
> — Philippians 4:8 (NAS)

Dr. Joseph Bohac

Bibliography

Abraham, K. (1924a). A Short Study of the Development of the Libido Viewed in Light of Mental Disorders. *Selected papers of Karl Abraham.* New York: Basic Books, 1927.

Abraham, K. (1924b). The Influence of Oral Eroticism on Character Formation. *Select papers of Karl Abraham.* New York: Basic Books, 1927.

Ainsworth, M.D.S. (1979). *Infant-Mother Attachment. American Psychologist,* 34 (10), 932-937.

Ainsworth, M.D.S. (1982). Attachment: Retrospect and Prospect. In C. M. Parkes & J. Sevenson-Hinde (eds.). *The place of attachment in human behavior.* New York: Basic Books.

Abrams, Jeremiah. (1990). *Reclaiming the inner child.* Los Angeles: Tarcher, Inc.

Bem, S.L. (1983). Gender schema theory and its implications for child development: Raising gender-aschematic children in a gender-schematic society. *Signs,* 8, 598-616.

Bem, S.L. (1985). Androgyny and Gender Schema Theory: A Conceptual and Empirical Integration. In T.B. Sonderegger (ed.), *Nebraska Symposium on otivation, 1984. Psychology and gender.* Lincoln: University of Nebraska Press.

Benner, D. (ed.) (1985). *Baker Encyclopedia of Psychology.* Grand Rapids: Baker Book House.

Berk, L.A. (1989). *Child Development.* Boston: Allyn and Bacon.

Bettelheim, B. (1967). *The Empty Fortress: Infantile Autism and the Birth of Self.* New York: Free Press.

Bilbin, R.M. (1967). Middle Age: What Happens to Ability? In R. Owen (Ed.) *Middle Age.* London: BBC.

Birrin, J., Woods, A., & Williams, M. (1980). Behavioral Slowing With Age: Causes, Organization, and Consequence. In L.W. Poon (Ed.) *Aging in the 1980's.* Washington: American Psychological Association.

Brand, Paul & Yancey, Phillip. (1980). *Fearfully and Wonderfully Made; A Surgeon Looks at the Human & Spiritual Body.* Grand Rapids: Zondervan Publishing House.

Bowlby, J. (1960). *Separation Anxiety.* International Journal of Psychoanalysis. 41, 89-113.

Brown, J. & Stoudemire, A. (1983). *Normal and Pathological Grief.* Journal of the American Medical Association. 250, 378-382.

Butler, R.N. (1963). The Life Review: An Interpretation of Reminiscence in the Aged. Psychiatry, 26, 65-76. Reprinted in B.L. Neugarten (Ed.) *Middle Age and Aging.* Chicago: University of Chicago Press, 1968.

Chomsky, N. (1957). *Syntactic Structures.* The Hague: Moulton.

Clouse, Bonnidell. (1985). *Moral Development: Perspectives in Psychology and Christian Belief.* Grand Rapids: Baker Book House.

Crain, William C. (1985). *Theories of Development: Concepts and Applications.* Englewood Cliffs: Prentice Hall.

Cratty, B.J. (1970). *Perceptual and Motor Development in Infants and Children.* New York: Macmillan.

Dreyer, P.H. (1982). Sexuality During Adolescence. In B.B. Wolman (ed.). *Handbook of Developmental Psychology.* Englewood, NJ: Prentice Hall.

Erikson, Erik. (1950). *Childhood and Society.* New York: Norton.

Erikson, E.H. (1976). Reflections on Dr. Borg's Life Cycle. *Daedalus,* 105, 1-28.

Espenschade, A. (1960). Motor Development. In W.R. Johnson (ed.)., *Science and Medicine of Exercise and Sports.* New York: Harper & Row.

Freedman, D. G. (1971). An Evolutional Approach of Research on the Life Cycle. *Human Development,* 14, 87-89.

Freud, A. (1936). *The Ego and the Mechanisms of Defense.* New York: International Universities Press. 1946.

Freud, S. (1905). Three contributions to the Theory of Sex. *The Basic Writings of Sigmund Freud* (A.A. Brill, trans.) New York: The Modern Library.

Gavotos, L.A. (1959). Relationships and Age Differences in Growth Measures and Motor Skills. *Child Development,* 30, 333-340.

Gessell, A. (1945). *The Embryology of Behavior.* New York: Harper & Row.

Haswell, K., Hock, e. & Webar, C. (1981). Oppositional Behavior of Preschool Children: Theory and Prevention. *Family Relations,* 30, 440-446.

Harlow, H.F., & Zimmerman, R.R. (1959). Affectional Responses in the Infant Monkey. *Science.* 130, 421-432.

Heneker, F.O. (1981). Male Climacteric. In J.G. Howells (Ed.) *Modern Perspectives in the Psychiatry of Middle Age.* New York: Brunner/Mazel.

Jung, C. (1933). *Modern Man in Search of a Soul* (W.S. Dell and C.F. Baynes, Trans.). New York: Harvest Books.

Jung, C. (1961). *Memories, Dreams, Reflections* (A. Jaffe, Ed., R. & C. Windston, trans.). New York: Vintage Books.

Kessler, J.W. (1966). *Psychopathology of Childhood.* Englewood Cliffs, N.J.: Prentice Hall.

Kamii, C. (1972). A Sketch of the Piaget-Devised Preschool Curriculum Developed by the Ypsilanti Early Education Program. In S.J. Braun

& E. Edwards (eds.). *History and Theory of Early Childhood Education.* Worthington, Ohio: Charles A. Jones.

Kohlberg, L. (1958a). *The Development of Modes of Thinking and choice in the Years 10 to 16.* Unpublished Doctoral Dissertation. The University of Chicago.

Lefrancois, Guy R. (1989). *Of Children: An Introduction to Child Development.* Belmont: Wadsworth Publishing Company.

Levinton, D. (1977). Death Education. In H. Feitel (ed.). *New Meanings of Death.* McGraw-Hill.

Linn, Matthew, Linn, Dennis, & Fabricant, Sheila. (1988). *Healing the Eight Stages of Life.* New York: Paulist Press.

Litz, T. (1968). *The Person: His Development Throughout the Life Cycle.* New York: Basic Books, Inc.

Lorenz, K. (1935). Companions As Factors in the Bird's Environment. In Lorez, K. *Studies in Animal and Human Behavior* (Vol. I) (R. Marin, trans.). Cambridge, Mass.: Harvard Press, 1971).

Mead, M. (1928). *Coming of Age in Somoa.* New York: Morrow.

Mead, M. (1935). *Sex and Temperament in three Primitive Societies.* New York: Morrow.

Meier, Paul D., Minirth, Frank B., Wickhern, Frank B., & Ratcliff, Donald. (1991). *Introduction to Psychology and Counseling. Second Edition.* Grand Rapids: Baker Book House.

Millon, T. (1981). *Disorders of Personality: DSMIII: Axis III.* New York: John Wiley & Sons.

Mindel, C.H. (1983). The Elderly in Minority Families. In T.H. Brubaker (ed.). *Family Relationships in Later Life.* Beverly Hills, CA: Sage.

Missildine, W. Hugh. (1963). *Your Inner Child of the Past.* New York: Pocket Books.

Montessori, Maria. *The Absorbent Mind.* Holt, Rinehart & Winston. 1967.

Munroe, R. (1955). *Schools of Psychoanalytic Thought.* New York: Henry Holt and Co., Inc.

Neugarten, B. (1968). Adult Personality: Toward a Psychology of the Life Cycle. In B. Neugarten (ed.) *Middle Age and Aging.* Chicago: University of Chicago Press.

Papalia, Diane E. & Olds, Sally Wendkos. (1989). *Human Development. Fourth Edition.* New York: McGraw-Hill Book Company.

Pearce, J.C. (1977). *Magical Child: Rediscovering Nature's Plan for Our Children.* New York: Bantam Books.

Piaget, J. (1923). *The Language and Thought of the Child.* London: Routledge and Kegan Paul, Ltd.

Rosenblith, J.F. (1992). *In the Beginning: Development from Conception to Age Two.* (2nd ed.). Newbury Park: Sage Publications.

Schachtel, E.G. (1959). *Metamorphosis.* New York: Basic Books.

Schultz, R. (1978). *The Psychology of Death, Dying, and Bereavement.* Reading, MA: Addison Wesley.

Sostek, A.J. & Wyatt, R.J. (1981). The Chemistry of Crankiness. *Psychology Today.* 15 (10), 120.

Troll, L.E. (1985). *Early and Middle Adulthood (2nd ed.).* Monterey, CA: Brooks-Cole.

Weg, R. (1987). Menopause: Biomedical Aspects. In G.L. Maddox (ed.). *The Encyclopedia of Aging.* (pp. 433-437).

Glossary

Accommodation — Piagetian term for a change in an existing cognitive structure to cope with new information.

Achieving Stage — Second of Schale's five cognitive stages, in which young adults use knowledge to gain independence and competence and do best on tasks relevant to life goals they have established for themselves.

Acquired Adaptations — In Piagetian terminology, reorganized schemes for particular behavior earned by accommodation.

Active Proximity Seeking — According to the attachment theory, stage three is characterized by the infant now being able to seek out the primary care-taker and avoid separation anxiety.

Adaptation — Piagetian term for effective integration with the en-vironment (problem solving) through the complementary processes of assimilation and accommodation.

Adolescence — That period of life characterized by the passage from childhood to adulthood.

Adolescent Rebellion — The stress and storm of adolescence that results in rebellious behavior against adults in general.

Ageism — Prejudice or discrimination against a person (most commonly an older person) based on age.

Aggressive Behavior — Hostile actions intended to hurt somebody or to establish dominance.

Allocentric Senses — Hearing, and especially sight; coming from outside the body.

Alzheimer's Disease — A mental disease characterized by the loss of memory.

Ambivalent Attachment — Pattern of attachment in which an infant becomes anxious before the primary caregiver leaves, is extremely upset during his or her absence, and both seeks and resists contact upon his or her return; also called resistant attachment.

Ambivalent Passive — One of Millon's eight personality patterns.

Ambivalent-Active — One of Millon's eight basic personalities.

Amniocentesis — An intrusive prenatal procedure where a sample of the amino fluid is extracted and analyzed to determine whether any of certain genetic defects are present

Anal Compulsive — A Freudian concept that describes

those individuals that have developed compulsive behavior as a result or problems during the anal stage of development. These are very neat and clean individuals.

Anal Expulsive — These are the same as the compulsives except that they develop a pattern of messiness during the anal stage.

Anal Stage — According to Freudian theory, the psychosexual stage of toddler hood (12-18 months to 3 years), in which the chief source of sensual gratification is moving the bowels; toilet training forces the child to delay this gratification.

Androgynous — Personality type integrating positive characteristics typically thought of as masculine with positive characteristics typically thought of as feminine.

Animism — Attribution of life to inanimate objects; according to Piaget, characteristic of Preoperational thought.

Anorexia Nervosa — An eating disorder characterized by self-starvation.

Anoxia — Lack of oxygen, which may cause brain damage.

Anticipatory Grief — Grief that begins before an expected death and helps family and friends to prepare for bereavement.

Apgar Scale — Standard measurement of a newborn's condition; it assesses appearance, pulse, grimace, activity, and respiration.

Arteries — Any blood vessels which carry blood away from the heart to the rest of the body.

Asceticism — Defense mechanism typical of adolescence, described by Anna Freud, which is characterized by self-denial as a defense against adolescents' fear of loss of control over their impulses.

Assimilation — Piaget's term for the incorporation of new information into an existing cognitive structure.

Attachment — Active affectionate reciprocal relationship specifically be-tween two persons (usually infant and parent), in which interaction reinforces and strengthens the link.

Authoritarian Parents — Baumrind's terminology - parents whose child-rearing style emphasizes the values of control and obedience and who use forceful punishment to make children conform to a set of standards of conduct. Compare with authoritative parents

Authoritative Parents — Parents, whose method of child-rearing blends respect for a child's individuality with an effort to instill social values in the child.

Autocentric Senses — According to Schachtel, these are senses felt in the body, such as taste or smell.

Autoerotic — Freudian term that suggests that certain areas such as the mouth, anus or genitals are highly sensitive to pleasurable sensations.

Autonomy — Independent self-determination.

Autonomy vs Shame and Doubt — According to Erikson, the second critical pair of alternatives in psychosocial development (from 12-18 months to 3 years), in which toddlers develop a balance of autonomous control (independence, self-determination) over shame and doubt.

Avoidant Attachment — Pattern of attachment in which an infant rarely cries when separated from the primary caregiver and avoids contact upon his or her return.

Bacteria — Microscopic one-celled organisms found everywhere - even in our bodies. Most are harmless, some are essential, such as those in the intestines, a few cause disease.

Bar Mitzvah — In the Jewish religion it is the rite of passage for the male from a boy at the age of 13 to an adult member of the congregation.

Basic Trust vs Basic Mistrust — Erikson's theory that the first critical balancing of alternatives in psychosocial development (from birth to 12-18 months), in which the infant develops a sense of whether or not the world can be trusted; the quality of interaction with mother in feeding is a primary determinant of the outcome of this stage.

Bat Mitzvah — In the Jewish religion it is the rite of passage for the female from a girl at the age of 12 to an adult member of the congregation

Bayley Scale of Infant Development — Standardized test for measuring the intellectual development of infants; the test consists of a mental scale and a motor scale. Each of these yields a development quotient (DQ) computed by comparing what a particular baby can do at a certain age with the performance of a large number of previously observed babies at the same age.

Behavior Modification — Changing undesirable behavior by rewarding desirable behavior. Based loosely on the theories of Pavlov and B.F. Skinner.

Bereavement — Loss due to death, which leads to a change in the survivor's status (for example, from wife to widow).

Bile — Greenish liquid produced by the liver and stored in the gall bladder. It helps to digest fat in the small intestine.

Birth Trauma — Birth-related brain injury caused by oxygen deprivation, mechanical injury, or infection or disease at birth. The term is also used to describe the physical trauma of the birthing process itself.

Blended Children — Children in a marriage to which one or both parents bring children from a previous marriage, and then may have children of the new marriage.

Blood Vessel — Any of the many tubes arteries, veins and capillaries that carry blood around the body.

Brazelton Neonatal Behavioral Assessment Scale — Neurological and behavioral test to measure neonates' response to the environment; it assesses interactive behaviors, motor behaviors, physiological control, and response to stress.

Bronchus — One of the branches of the windpipe, leading to the lungs.

Bulimia — An eating disorder characterized by binging and purging.

Capillaries — The smallest type of blood vessel.

Cardiac — Referring to the heart.

Cartilage — Soft, elastic tissue, often called gristle.

Castration Complex — Phenomenon described by Freud in which a male child, seeing that girls do not have a penis and overwhelmed by guilt about his Oedipal feelings and fear of his father's power, becomes fearful that he will be castrated by his father.

Cells — The basic living units of the body, sometimes called the "building blocks" of life. Every part of the body is made up of cells - one trillion of them in an average man.

Central Nervous System — The brain and spinal cord.

Cephalcodal — Refers to the theory that the fetus develops from the head to the lower extremities (head to tail).

Cephalocaudal Principle — A principle that development proceeds in a head-to-toe direction, i.e., the upper parts of the body develop before the lower parts.

Cesarean Section — Most commonly called a C Section. It is the surgical removal of a fetus from the uterus when the mother is not able to deliver normally or vaginally.

Childhood Depression — Affective disorder characterized by a child's inability to form and maintain friendships, have fun, concentrate, and display normal emotional reactions.

Chorionic Villus Sampling (CVS) — Prenatal diagnostic procedure in which tissue from villi (hairlike projections of the membrane surrounding the embryo) is analyzed for birth defects.

Chromosomal Aberrations — A defect in one or more of the chromosomes from either the mother or father that will result is some type of abnormality, i.e., Down's syndrome.

Chromosome — One of the 46 structures found in the nucleus of every human cell. Chromosomes carry the genes which determine inherited characteristics, such as sex, hair color, and height (among others).

Cleavage — The process of cell division that begins almost immediately after fertilization.

Climacteric — The time when menopause takes place.

Clinical Method — Study done in a controlled situation instead of simple observation in natural surroundings.

Cognitive Development — Changes in thought processes that result in a growing ability to acquire and use knowledge.

Cognitive Play — Forms of play that are real and that enhance children's cognitive development.

Colon — Lower part of the large intestine.

Compassionate Love — Loving friendship marked by affection, attachment, commitment, and security. This kind of love tends to deepen with the passage of time.

Compensation — The Piagetian term meaning that a child has learned to reason that one change cancels out another.

Concrete Operations — Third stage of Piagetian cognitive development (about age 5-7 to age 11), during which children develop logical but not abstract thinking.

Conservation — A Piagetian concept in which a child is required to respond to two or more dimensions of a stimulus simultaneously.

Coronary — Referring to the blood vessels that supply the heart. Coronary arteries over the surface of the heart provide oxygen to its cells.

Critical Period — The period of development starting at 2 weeks because of certain critical growth necessary at that time.

DNA (Deoxyribonucleic Acid) — Complicated chemical that makes up genes and chromosomes.

Death Education — Programs to educate people about dying and grief to help them deal with these issues in their personal and professional lives.

Deaver's Developmental Screening Test — Test given to children 1 month to 6 years old to determine whether or not they are developing normally; it assesses gross motor skills, fine motor skills, language development, and personal and social development.

Decenter — In Piagetian terminology to consider all significant aspects of a situation simultaneously. Decentration is characteristic of operational thought.

Defense Mechanisms — According to Freudian theory, way in which people unconsciously combat anxiety by distorting reality.

Defensive Homosexuality — Often in institutions such as prisons, it is necessary for an individual to participate (passively) in homosexuality to prove he is not homosexual.

Deferred Imitation — In Piagetian terminology, reproduction of an observed behavior after the passage of time by calling up a stored symbol of it.

Dementia — Apparent intellectual and personality deterioration sometimes associated with old age and caused by a variety of irreversible physiological conditions: sometimes called senility.

Denial — One defense mechanism for dealing with unpleasant or difficult problems. Used in this chapter with relation to intimate relationships.

Dependent-Active — One of Millon's basic personalities.

Dependent-Passive — One of Millon's basic personalities.

Detached Active — According to Million's theory a personality type resulting from a parental style of reject. Detached passive – In Million's theory a personality style that is the result of a parental style of neglect.

Diaphragm — Flat muscle which separates the chest from the abdomen.

Disengagement Theory — Theory of aging that holds that successful aging is characterized by mutual withdrawal between the older person and society.

Distractibility — One of the nine components of temperament suggested by the New York Longitudinal Study that describes how easily an individual can be distracted.

Dizygotic — Fraternal twin that is the result of two eggs being fertilized.

Donor Eggs — Method of conception in which an ovum of a fertile woman is implanted in the uterus of a woman who cannot produce normal ova.

247

Ectopic Fertilization — An ovum in some area other that the fallopian tube.

Ego — In Freudian theory, an aspect of personality that develops during infancy and operates on the reality principle, seeking acceptable means of gratification in dealing with the real world.

Ego Defense Mechanisms — Various ways of dealing with life's difficulties.

Elder Abuse — Neglect or physical or psychological abuse of dependent older persons, often by their children as a result of the stress of caring for the parents.

Electra Complex — According to Freudian theory, the female counterpart of the Oedipus complex, in which the young girl in the phallic stage feels sexual attraction for her father and rivalry toward her mother.

Electronic Fetal Monitoring — Monitoring of fetal heartbeat by machine in labor and delivery, enabling delivery personnel to determine if the fetus is in distress

Embryo — The name given to the new life during the early stage of gestation.

Embryology — The science given to the study of nature and development of embryos.

Embryonic Stage — Second stage of gestation (2 to 8-12 weeks), characterized by rapid growth and development of major body systems and organs.

Encephalitis — An inflammation of the brain.

Environmental Influences — Non-genetic influences on development attributable to experiences with the outside world.

Enzymes — Chemical substances that speed up chemical reactions within the body and control processes such as digestion.

Epiglottis — Small flap at the back of the tongue which blocks the windpipe when you swallow and so prevents food "going down the wrong way."

Esophagus — Gullet or food pipe leading from the throat to the stomach.

Estrogen — Female hormone; its decrease during the climacteric may result in hot flashes, thinning of the vaginal lining, and urinal dysfunction.

Etiology — A division of medical science dealing with the systematic study of the causes of mental and physical diseases.

Experimental Homosexuality — It is thought that many teenagers experiment at least once in a homosexual activity.

Failure to Thrive — An apparently healthy, well-fed baby's failure to grow, often as a result of emotional neglect.

Fertility Drugs — Drugs that are given to women who are having a problem conceiving.

Fertilization — The penetration of a male sperm into a female egg resulting in the egg becoming fertile, and it begins the development process.

Fetal Alcohol Syndrome — (FAS). Mental, motor, and developmental abnormalities (including stunted growth, facial and bodily malformations, and disorders of the central nervous system) affecting the offspring of some women who drink heavily during pregnancy.

Fetal Alcohol Syndrome (FAS) — Mental, motor, and developmental abnormalities which may include stunted growth, facial and bodily malformation and disorders of the central nervous system. These effect the offspring of some women who drink heavily during pregnancy.

Fetal Stage — Final stage of gestation (8-12 weeks to birth), characterized by increased detail of body parts and greatly elongated body size.

Fetal Tobacco Syndrome — Growth retardation of offspring of some women who smoke heavily during pregnancy. Some believe that the same affect could be caused by the continuous breathing in of second-hand smoke in the workplace.

Fetoscopy — An intrusive procedure in which a small tube is inserted into the womb, and through which a fiber optical lens is passed to observe the inside of the womb.

Fetus — What the embryo is called after the first 8 weeks.

Fixation — In Freudian theory, an arrest in development that occurs be-cause a child has been gratified too much or too little during a particular psychosexual stage.

Follicle — Small pocket in the skin from which a single hair grows.

Formal Operation — According to Piaget, the final stage of cognitive development, reached by some adolescents, which is characterized by the ability to think abstractly.

Gall Bladder — Small sac, about 3-4 inches long, which stores bile.

Gamete — Sex cell (sperm or ovum) gene basic functional unit of heredity, which determines an inherited characteristic.

Gender — Significance of being male or female.

Gender Conservation — Realization that one's sex will always stay the same.

Gender Differences — Difference between males and females that may or may not be based on biological differences.

Gender Identification — The concept of identity popularized by Erickson in which the individual learns gender identity through relationships in family and society.

Gender Identity — Awareness developed in early childhood, that one is male or female.

Gender Roles — Behaviors, interests, attitudes, and skills that a culture considers appropriate for males and females and expects them to fulfill.

Gender Stereotypes — Exaggerated generalizations about male or female role behavior.

Gender Typing — Socialization process by which a child, at an early age, learns the appropriate gender role.

Generativity — Eriksonian term which refers to not only the creation of and care of children but the production of things and ideas through work.

Generativity vs Stagnation — According to Erikson, the seventh critical alternative of psychosocial development in which mature adults develop concern with establishing and guiding the next generation or else experience stagnation (a sense of inactivity or lifelessness).

Genes — Combinations of DNA which make up the chromosomes in each cell.

Genetic Counseling — Clinical service that advises couples of their probable risk of having children with particular hereditary defects.

Genetics — Study of hereditary factors affecting development.

Germinal Stage — First 2 weeks of prenatal development, characterized by rapid cell division and increased complexity; the stage ends when the conceptus attaches itself to the wall of the uterus.

Gerontologists — Persons engaged in gerontology, the study of the aged and the process of dying.

Glands Organs — in the body, such as the salivary glands, the kidneys, and liver, which produce or work on chemical substances.

Heredity — Inborn influences on development, carried in the genes inherited from the parents.

Heteronomous Morality — Piaget's concept that children tend to view morality from a egocentric point of view.

Heterosexuality — Sexual activity between two persons of different gender.

Homosexual Panic — The panic one may experience because of being aroused in the shower with other members of the same sex.

Homosexuality — Sexual activity between two persons of the same gender.

Hormones — Sometimes called the body's chemical messengers, produced in certain glands and released into the blood. They control many body processes, such as growth, the amount of sugar in the blood.

Hospitalism — Decline in a child's intellectual and psychological functioning resulting from long institutionalization.

Humanistic Perspective — View of humanity that sees people as having the ability to foster their own positive, healthy development through the distinctively human capacities for choice, creativity, and self-realization.

Hysterectomy — The surgical removal of all or most of the female reproductive organs.

Id — In Freudian theory, the instinctual aspect of personality (present at birth) that operates on the pleasure principle, seeking immediate gratification.

Identification — Process by which a person acquires characteristics, beliefs, attitudes, values, and behavior of another person or of a group; an important personality development of early childhood.

Identity vs Identity Confusion — According to Eriksonian theory, the fifth critical alternative of psychosocial development, in which an adolescent must determine his or her own sense of self (identity), including the role he or she is to play in society.

Identity vs Identity Confusion. — According to Eriksonian theory, the fifth critical alternative of psychosocial development, in which an adolescent must determine his or her own sense of self (identity), including the role he or she is to play in society.

Imaginary Audience — Observer who exists only in an adolescent's mind and is as concerned with the adolescent's thoughts and actions as is the adolescent himself or herself.

Immature Mechanism — One of the defenses in which the person will develop aches and pains without any physical symptoms.

Immune System — The body's own defenses against infection.

Imprinting — Instinctive form of learning in which, after a single encounter, an animal recognizes and trusts one particular individual.

In Vitro Fertilization — Fertilization of an ovum outside the mother's body.

Independent-Active — One of Millon's basic personalities.

Independent-Passive — One of Millon's basic personalities

Individuation — A Jungian concept that denotes the process by which a person becomes a psychological individual, i.e., an indivisible unity or whole.

Industry vs Inferiority — Erikson's fourth critical alternative of psychosocial development, occurring during middle childhood, in which children must learn the productive skills their culture requires or else face feelings of inferiority.

Infant Mortality — Death during the first year of life. The most common is SIDS: Sudden Infant Death Syndrome.

Infantile Amnesia — According to Schachtel's theory, our inability to remember most of the events of our first five years. Freud's explanation was that it was a product of repression.

Infantile Autism — Developmental disorder that begins within the first 2 1/2 years of life and is characterized by lack of responsiveness to other people. Bruno Bettelheim referred to these children as "empty fortresses."

Initiative vs Guilt — In Eriksonian theory this is the third psychosocial stage of development occurring between the ages of 3 and 6, in which children must balance the urge to form and carry out goals with their moral judgment about what they want to do. Children develop initiative when they try out new things and are not overwhelmed by failure.

Integrity vs Despair — Erikson's eighth and final critical psychosocial alternative is development in which people in late adulthood either accept their lives as a whole and thus accept death, or yield to despair because their lives cannot be relived.

Intellectualization — A defense approach by adolescents in which they transfer aggression and sex into an abstract intellectual plane.

Intestines — The long tube, beginning at the stomach and ending at the anus, in which food is digested.

Intimacy vs Isolation — Erikson's sixth critical alternative of psychosocial development, in which young adults either make commitments to others or face a possible sense of isolation and consequent self-absorption.

Glossary of Terms

Introjection — In the development of the superego, it is the process by which values are incorporated.

Invisible Imitation — Imitation with parts of one's body that one cannot see, e.g., the mouth.

Justification — Piagetian term to describe the action of a child in reasoning that if nothing has been taken away and nothing added, a substance is the same regardless of how it is reshaped.

Karyotype — Chart in which photomicrographs of a prospective parent's chromosomes are arranged to size and structure to reveal any chromosomal abnormalities.

Keratin — The hard substance found in hair, nails, and skin.

Kidneys — Two organs that filter waste from the blood and produce urine, which collects in the bladder. They are located on either side of the spine.

Language Acquisition Device — In Chomsky's theory, an inborn mental structure that enables children to build linguistic rules by analyzing the language they hear.

Lanugo — Fuzzy prenatal body hair, which drops off within a few days after birth.

Larynx — The voice box, located at the top of the trachea and containing the vocal chords.

Latency Period — Freudian term for the elementary grade child.

Life Structure Test — Levinson's test that shows the underlying pattern of design of a person's life at a given time.

Ligaments — Tough elastic bands of tissue which hold bone together at a joint.

Liver — The body's largest gland; it stores iron and some glucose. Processes amino acids and produces bile.

Living Will — A document specifying the type of care wanted by the maker in the event of terminal illness.

Low Birth-Weight Babies — Babies who weigh less than 5 1/2 pounds at birth because they are premature or small for date.

Lymph — Clear liquid which contains white blood cells. It flows through a set of vessels (tubes) called the lymphatic system.

Male Climacteric — Period of physiological, emotional, and psychological reproductive system and other body systems changes.

Malnutrition — Many mothers will not eat a well-balanced diet during pregnancy resulting in an undernourished fetus.

Marrow — Soft, jelly-like substance found in the center of bones. Blood cells are made in some bone marrow.

Masturbation — Sexual self-stimulation.

Maternal Blood Test — Prenatal diagnostic procedure to detect the presence of fetal abnormalities. This is used particularly when the fetus is at risk of defects in the central nervous system.

Maturation — Unfolding of a biologically determined, age-related sequence of behavior patterns programmed by the genes, including the readiness to master new abilities.

Menarche — The beginning of the girl's first menstrual period.

Meninges — Any of the three membranes that envelop the brain and the spinal cord.

Meningitis — Bacterial disease in which inflammation of meninges occurs.

Menopause — A biological occurrence when a woman stops ovulating and menstruating and can no longer bear children

Miconium — Fetal waste matter excreted during the first few days after birth. Medicated delivery – Childbirth in which the mother receives anesthesia.

Midlife Transition — Sometimes referred to as midlife crisis. It is the change of life from young adulthood to middle adulthood.

Monozygotic — Identical twins that result from one ovum dividing into two after fertilization.

Morality of Autonomous Moral Principles — In Kohlberg's system, the highest level of moral development, normally reached after the age of 12 (if it is ever reached at all), in which people follow internally held moral principles and make choices between conflicting moral standards.

Morality of Constraint — First of Piaget's two stages of moral development, characterized by rigid, simplistic judgments; also called heteronomous morality.

Morality of Conventional Role — One of Kohlberg's substages of morality development.

Morality of Conventional Role Conformity — Second of Kohlberg's three levels of moral reasoning, normally reached between the ages of 10-13, in which children have internalized the standards of authority figures and obey rules to please others or to maintain order.

Morphemes — The smallest element of speech that has meaning.

Mother-Infant Bond — A mother's feeling of a close, caring connection with her newborn.

Naturalistic Observation — Method of research in which people's behavior is studied in natural settings without the observer's intervention or manipulation.

Neonatal Period — First four weeks of life, a time of transition from intrauterine dependency to independent existence.

Neonate — A newborn baby.

Neurotic Mechanism — For example, repressing anxiety, intellectualizing, or developing irrational fears.

Neurotic Regressive Homosexuality — Appears in person as a retreat from personal conflict.

Non-Normative Life Events — Those events that people do not expect in life, such as traumatic accident, loss of job, etc.

Normal Grief — Grief that follows a death, usually in a fairly predictable pattern consisting of three phases: initial shock and disbelief, preoccupation with the memory of the dead, and resolution.

Normative Crisis Model — A theory that there is a predictable sequence of age-related changes throughout adult life.

Normative Life Events — Events that people expect in life.

Nubility — The time when a child is able to make a baby.

Obesity — Obesity is defined as being 20% over normal weight. Morbid obesity identifies a condition of obesity that is considered to be life threatening.

Obligatory Homosexuality — In certain cultures, young boys are required as a part of the rites of passage, to spend the first half of their adolescence in a passive homosexual situation.

Oedipus Complex — Phenomenon described by Freud in which the young boy in the phallic stage feels sexual attraction for his mother and rivalry toward his father.

Oral stage — In Freudian terms, the psychosexual stage of infancy (birth to 12-18 months) characterized by a sensual gratification in the oral region, chiefly through food (sucking).

Organ — Group of tissues which work together such as the heart or the liver.

Osteoporosis — A condition in women caused by the lack of calcium resulting in the thinning of the bones.

Ovulation — Expulsion of ovum from ovary, which occurs about every 28 days from puberty to menopause

Pancreas — Gland which produces the hormone insulin which controls the level of glucose in the blood.

Passive Euthanasia — Deliberate withholding of life-prolonging treatment from a terminally ill person in order to minimize suffering or carry out the wishes of the patient.

Penis Envy — Phenomenon, described by Freud, in which a girl envies the male's penis and wants one of her own.

Permissive Parents — parents whose child-rearing style emphasizes the cause of self-expression and self-regulation. Compare with authoritarian parents and authoritative parents.

Personality — A person's collective pattern of character, behavioral, temperamental, emotional, and mental traits.

Phallic Stage — According to Freudian theory, the stage of psychosexual development between the ages of 3 and 6 in which the child receives gratification chiefly in the genital area.

Phenyketonuria (PKU) — A congenital metabolic disorder resulting from the inability of the body to convert phenylalanine, an essential amino acid.

Phobias — Irrational, involuntary fears inappropriate to the real situation. Pre-conventional morality : According to Kohlberg, the first level of moral development, in which children aged approximately 4 to 10 years obey the rules or standards set by others, in order to gain rewards or avoid punishment.

Phocomelia — The malformation of a fetus caused by the use of the drug thalidomide during pregnancy. The word means "seal limbs".

Piagetian Approach — Study of intellectual development by describing qualitative stages, or typical changes, in children's and adolescent's cognitive functioning; proposed by Piaget.

Plasma — Liquid part of the blood.

Preconvention Morality — According to Kohlberg, the first level of moral development, in which children aged approximately 4 to 10 years obey rules or standards set by others, in order to gain rewards or avoid punishment.

Preferential Homosexuality — This refers to the individual who may be bisexual, but experiences more arousal from a homosexual relationship.

Preformationism — A belief that lasted from about the fifth century until the second half of the eighteenth century, that a fully formed little adult existed in either the male sperm or the female ovum.

Prelinguistic Speech — Sounds that young children make that resemble speech that they have learned by imitation, accidental or deliberate.

Prenatal — That time in the development of a human being from conception until birth, normally nine months.

Preoperational Stage — In Piagetian theory, the second major period of intellectual development (approximately from age 2 to 7), in which children can think about things not physically present by using mental representation but are limited by their use of logic.

Presbycusis — Loss of hearing common in middle adulthood.

Presbyopia — Farsightedness usually begins in middle adulthood.

Pretend Play — Play involving imaginary situations; also called fantasy play, dramatic play, or imaginative play.

Preterm Babies — Babies born before the thirty-seventh week of gestation, dated from the mother's last menstrual period; also called premature babies (preemies).

Primary Sex Characteristics — Characteristics directly related to reproduction; specifically, the male and female sex organs. These enlarge and mature during adolescence.

Private Speech — Talking aloud to oneself with no intent to communicate, common in early and middle childhood.

Productivity — The same as generativity in Eriksonian terminology.

Programmed-aging Theory — Theory that bodies age in accordance with a normal development pattern built into every organism of a particular species; compare with wear-and-tear theory of aging.

Project Head Start — Compensatory preschool education program begun in the United States in 1965.

Prosocial Behavior — Behavior intended to help others without external reward.

Prostate Gland — One of the glands of the male reproductive system.

Proteins — Bodybuilding chemicals, made of amino acids.

Proximodistal Law — Principle that development proceeds from within to without, i.e., that parts of the body near the center develop before the extremities.

Psychosexual Development — In Freudian theory, an unvarying sequence of stages of personality development during childhood and adolescence, in which gratification shifts from mouth to the anus and then to the genitals.

Psychosocial-Development Theory — Theory of Erik Erikson that societal and cultural influences play a major part in healthy personality development. According to this theory, development occurs in eight maturational predetermined stages throughout the life span, each revolving around a particular crisis or turning point in which the person is faced with achieving a healthy balance between alternatives of positive and negative traits.

Puberty — Time at which a person attains sexual maturity and is able to reproduce.

Pubescence — Period of development preceding puberty and characterized by rapid physiological growth, maturation of reproductive functioning, enlargement of the sex organs, and appearance of the secondary sex characteristics.

Pulse — The rhythmic throbbing which can be felt in the arteries as the heart beats.

Pus — The whitish-yellow liquid produced in certain infections made up mostly of dead white blood cells.

Reaction Formation — In Freudian theory, a defense mechanism characterized by replacement of an anxiety-producing feeling by the expression of its opposite.

Reactive Homosexuality — Represents fear of heterosexual relations.

Recessive Inheritance — Expression of a recessive (non-dominant) trait, which, according to Mendel, occurs only if the offspring receives the same recessive gene from each parent.

Reflex Behaviors — Automatic responses to external stimulation. Reflexes, by their presence or disappearance, are early signs of an infant's neurological growth.

Regressive — Having to do with going back psychologically to an earlier stage of emotional development.

Reintegrate Stage — Fifth of Schale's cognitive stages, in which older people choose to focus energy on tasks that have meaning for them.

Reserve Capacity — The lack of reserve capacity results in the body not being able to recover quickly from stress or dysfunction.

Resilient Children — Children who in spite of severe difficulties in the developmental process are able to overcome and do more than simply survive.

Responsible State — Third of Schale's five cognitive stages, in which middle aged people are concerned with long range goals and practical problems often related to their responsibility for others.

Reversibility — A Piagetian term used to describe a child's ability to reverse a cognitive observation in the Object Permanence stage of cognitive development.

Rites of Passage — A term used to describe the various rituals held in various cultures to usher the child into an adult standing.

Rubella — Maternal rubella is a disease that the mother contracted while infected with German measles.

STDs — Disease that is transmitted by sexual contact.

Saliva — Liquid released by three pairs of glands in the mouth. It starts the process of digestion.

Schema — According to Sandra Bem (1983, 1985) it is a mentally organized pattern of behavior that helps a child sort out perceived information.

Scheme — In Piagetian terminology, a basic cognitive structure that the infant uses to interact with the environment; an organized pattern of thought and behavior.

Schizoid — A personality disorder characterized by withdrawal, reservation, and reclusiveness.

Sebaceous Gland — Oil-producing gland in the skin.

Secondary Sex Characteristics — Physiological characteristics of the sexes which develop during adolescence (and do not involve the sex organs), including breasts in females, broadened shoulders in males, growth of body hair in both sexes, and adult voices in men and women.

Selective Optimization with Compensation — In the dual-process model of Baltes, the ability of older people to maintain or enhance their intellectual functioning through the use of special abilities to compensate for losses in other areas.

Self-Awareness — Realization, beginning in infancy, of separateness from other people and things, allowing reflection on one's own actions in relation to social standards.

Self-Recognition — Children's ability to recognize their own physical image; occurs at about 18 months.

Self-esteem — Person's self-evaluation or self-image.

Seminal Fluid — The fluid that carries the sperm in reproduction.

Seminal Vesicle — A pouch on either side of the male reproductive tract that is connected with the seminal tract and serves for temporary storage of semen.

Senescence — Period of the life span during which people experience a decrease in bodily functioning associated with aging.

Sensorimotor Stage — First of Piaget's stages of cognitive development, when infants (from birth to 2 years) learn through their developing senses and motor activities.

Separation Anxiety — Distress shown by an infant, usually beginning in the second half of the first year, when a familiar caregiver leaves; it is commonly a sign that attachment has occurred.

Sex Chromosomes — Pair of chromosomes that determine sex: XX in the normal female, XY in the normal male.

Sex-linked Inheritance — Pattern of inheritance in which certain characteristics carried on the sex chromosomes (usually the X chromosome) are transmitted differently to males and females.

Sexual Orientation — Sexual interest either in the other sex (heterosexual orientation) or in the same sex (homosexual orientation) usually expressed during adolescence; also called sexual preference.

Sexually Transmitted Disease (STDs) — Disease transmitted by sexual contact; also called venereal disease.

Sinuses — Four sets of cavities in the skull, where air that is breathed is warmed.

Social Role Homosexuality — In certain cultures, males were destined to live and perform in roles,

Glossary of Terms

actors, singers, etc., that lead to homosexuality.

Social-Learning Theory — Theory, proposed chiefly by Bandura, that behaviors are learned by observing and imitating models and are maintained through reinforcement.

Spermarche — The first spontaneous ejaculation of seminal fluid.

Spina Bifida — A birth defect characterized by an incomplete closure of the spine.

Spinal Cord — The thick cord of nerves which begins at the base of the brain and extends to the bottom of the back.

Spleen — An organ that is part of the lymphatic system and helps to fight infection.

Spontaneous Abortion — Natural expulsion from the uterus of a conceptus that cannot survive outside the womb; also called miscarriage.

Storm and Stress — In Hall's terminology, the idea that adolescence is necessarily a time of intense, fluctuating emotions; see adolescent rebellion.

Stranger Anxiety — Phenomenon that often occurs during the second half of the child's first year (in conjunction with separation anxiety), when the infant becomes wary of strange people and places; commonly a sign that attachment has occurred.

Stress — The organism's physiological and psychological reaction to demands made on it.

Superego — According to Freudian theory, the aspect of personality representing values that parents and other agents of society communicate to a child. It develops around the age of 5 or 6 as a result of resolution of the Oedipus or Electra complex.

Symbolic Function — In Piaget's terminology, ability to learn by using mental representations (symbols or signs) to which a child has attached meaning; this ability characteristic is shown in deferred imitation, symbolic play and language.

Symbolic Play — In Piaget's terminology, play in which a child makes an object stand for something else.

Systematic Desensitization — An experiment involving gradual exposure to the feared object in phobias.

Temperament — Person's characteristic style of approaching and reacting to people and situations. Considered to be an innate character, genetic predisposition.

Tendons — Very strong bands of tissue which connect muscles to bones.

Teratogenic — Capable of causing birth defects.

Tertiary Circular Reaction — A baby's purposeful variations of behavior to test novel ways of producing desired results; characteristic of the fifth sub-stage described by Piaget.

Thanatology — The study of death and dying

Thymus — Gland in the neck which helps the immune system.

Thyroid — Gland in the neck that produces a hormone, thyroxin, which controls growth rate and the speed of chemical processes.

Timing of Events Model — Looking at events as indicators of development instead of physical changes.

Tissues — Groups of similar cells which form various parts of the body, such as nerve or muscle.

Trachea — Windpipe, leading from the larynx to the lungs.

Tumor — Swelling caused by abnormal growth of cells. It may be benign or cancerous.

Ulcer — Open sore on the skin, or on a membrane inside the body.

Ultrasound — Prenatal medical procedure using high-frequency sound waves to detect fetus, judge gestational age, detect multiple pregnancies, detect abnormalities or death of the fetus, and determine whether the pregnancy is progressing normally.

Ureters — Tubes which carry urine from the kidneys to the bladder.

Urethra — Tube which carries urine from the bladder to the outside of the body.

Veins — Blood vessels which carry used blood back to the heart.

Vernix Caseosa — Oily substance on a neonate that protects against infection. It dries within a few days after birth.

Viruses — Microorganisms that cause disease if they invade the body.

Vitamins — Group of about 15 substances found in foods. They are needed for good health.

Vocal Cords — Two ligaments stretched across the larynx. They vibrate as air passes over them enabling speech.

Zygote — One-celled organism resulting from the union of sperm and ovum.

www.ingramcontent.com/pod-product-compliance
Lightning Source LLC
Chambersburg PA
CBHW071701160426
43195CB00012B/1543